THE GENTLE ARTS OF NATURAL MAGIC

Use the Symbols and Powers of Natural Magic to Expand Your Own Experience of Life, and to Benefit Everyone Around You

THE
GENTLE ARTS
OF NATURAL MAGIC

Magical techniques to help
you master the crafts of
the Wise.

MARIAN GREEN

THOTH PUBLICATIONS
Loughborough, Leicestershire

By the same author:

A WITCH ALONE
EVERYDAY MAGIC
WILD WITCHCRAFT
NATURAL WITCHCRAFT
PRACTICAL TECHNIQUES OF MODERN MAGIC
THE MODERN MAGICIAN'S COMPANION
THE MODERN MAGICIAN'S HANDBOOK
THE PATH THROUGH THE LABYRINTH
THE GRAIL SEEKER'S COMPANION
(with John Matthews)

First published 1987
Revised and Expanded 1997
Reprinted 2003, 2021

© 1987&1997 Marian Green

A CIP catalogue record for this book is available
from the British Library.

Cover design by Helen Surman

ISBN 978-1-913660-23-9

Published by Thoth Publications
64, Leopold Street, Loughborough, LE11 5DN

Web address: www.thoth.co.uk
email: enquiries@thoth.co.uk

DEDICATION

To all those who have proved that 'the Way through the Woods'
is not closed; from the Grove of Whitethorn to the Alder thicket.

CONTENTS

The Song of the Year

Now, in the sky, the bright stars are burning,
I sing you the song of the long year turning.
From the dark gate of Samhain, through Spring into Falling,
Hear how the voices of Nature are calling.
Gathered the flocks and the folk for All Hallows,
The summer sun's power has gone with the swallows.
Merry the feasting at the Great Assembly,
Look in the mirror for what is to be.
On move the stars in the sky's distant wheel,
The folk gather again at the season of Yule.
Quiet is the hall where the newborn one cries,
Lord over men, to be Lord of the Skies.
Long nights of winter pass, bitter winds rage,
Twelve magic years pass with each day of his age,
His Mother is honoured with the harbingers of spring,
New armed he goes forth, with the host following.
Now, when the first flowers are opening wide,
We welcome the Lady, his lover and bride.
He hunts in the forest as May buds appear,
To seek for the White One who runs with the deer.
They leap over the bonfires, this May Day so bright,
The balefires of Beltane illumine the night.
The grass it grows green and the leaves, they unfold,
The hot sun at midday turns swelling corn gold.
Soon folk at harvest will toil in the field,
Slaying the Corn King and hoarding his yield.
Weep for the Bright One, cut down in his prime,
Dance and be merry at this harvest time.
Gather the apples, the berries and nuts,
The puffballs and mushrooms that grow in the Butts,
Brown are the leaves autumn rains now are dulling,
Cattle and pigs are brought in for the culling.
Full are the storehouses, no one need fear,
When again the stars shine on the Gate of the Year.
Bright in the sky the winter moon's burning,
I sing you the song of the long year turning.

Marian Green 1975

INTRODUCTION

Many people believe magic is a very secret art and not for the likes of them. They fear its powers and distrust what they have heard or read about it, and yet like many another hidden subject, it has a strong and undeniable appeal. The aim of this book is to show that anyone who has an ounce of common sense can master at least some of the arts and skills of ancient magic, and use them to expand their own experience of life, and for the benefit of all the people around them.

Some people seek out the magical path because they imagine it will lead away from the everyday hassles and troubles of life, and take the seeker to a new and better world where everything will go exactly the way that they wish it to be. These people may feel that because they cannot cope with the world as it is, then magical powers will change it for their sole benefit. The very first lesson any student of magic, on any path or tradition, will learn is that this is *not so.* Magic is a collection of applied arts, which are the technologies of the trained mind, and they are just as real and deal with the apparent world, not with some other sphere of imagination. The skills of magic are concerned with change, recognising it, shaping it and learning to cope with it. A world which is free from change is dead, and within its fossilised remains no life will be found.

Everything which lives suffers change, either fast or slow depending on its nature. A simple animal may live out its entire lifespan in a few days and distant galaxies and star-spun patterns may take millions of years to change, yet all, at their own rate, are evolving and growing into a new design. To cling desperately to the old way, just because it is old, is not the way of thinking or acting along, which we, who live at the end of the twentieth century, should proceed. Indeed there is a case for preserving some of the old ways and restoring some that have been lost in the mists of time, but these should all be carefully examined in the light of our present, ever growing knowledge. Old ways of revering life, of using natural methods of healing and diet, or working in harmony with the earth beneath our feet, not greedily raping her for minerals, crops and firewood, will surely prove to be the only way we are able to continue our lives and evolution on this little planet circling the Sun.

To learn to accept the inevitability of change, and the need for it is the first step on the road to making use of it, through magical skills, so that it is beneficial and not destructive in its effects. Often the mere fact that we are willing to accept something new, and that we begin to take steps to overcome our basic state of inertia will result in magical-seeming effect upon our lives.

Modern magic draws on an enormous bank of inherited wisdom and practical knowledge, and by gently reshaping its ways to suit the contemporary minds and skills of new seekers, it reinterprets these ancient arts in ways that make them far more accessible to us now. We have new terms to call our arts and skills; we have whole new areas of study and expertise which did not exist in the time of the mages of the past - like psychology, computer science, advanced theories of subatomic particle physics and knowledge of animal behaviour. Widely differing subjects, you may say, yet all have a direct bearing on the many arts of magic, and all, too, are concerned with change and progress.

Slowly we are learning that science has not given us wisdom to apply all its arts for the benefit of the entire world. Pollution, over-use of resources, destruction of forests and their animal inhabitants, acid rain, chemical spillage, nuclear accidents, artificial farming methods, both arable and animal husbandry - all need careful rethinking and new planning before the fragile system of mankind and earth is destroyed forever. We have seen droughts, floods, earthquakes, volcanic eruptions and the terrible effects of ravaging forests for their timber, without a single thought for the future. Some of these disasters are beyond our knowledge to prevent, some have effects we cannot alleviate, but many are due to the declining relationship between people and their mother, the Earth. The Gentle Arts of magic try to rebalance that delicate system, for Nature is kind and bounteous, so we must take only what we need, and return thanks, both in the mind and by real acts of restitution. Our chance to learn these vital lessons is upon us, and we must not let it slip by without taking heed of past mistakes.

In the past, magic taught the science of Alchemy, the perpetual search for methods of refining base metal into pure and spiritual gold. Some of these methods gave rise to chemistry and later physics, some gave rise to the studies of the mind and soul and resulted in psychology and many forms of psychotherapy. By taking some raw ore and by patiently applying the arts of change, of dissolution, of combination, of chemical change wrought by heat and shown by varying colour, and of coagulation, that primeval substance was purified and ultimately emerged, phoenix-like, as the fine gold of the alchemists. We, too, have to master the art of spiritual or psychological alchemy, and working with care and determination upon the raw material of our untrained wills, eventually evolve them into the potent magical instrument that can change the world.

This book is about the Gentle Arts, for many new 'ologies' have sprung forth from the minds of 'world-improvers' which offer techniques for personal growth and renewal which in themselves are destructive. They have thought that by the use of brutal verbal and psychological methods the individual, cowering hopelessly in his invisible prison, could be set free, to grow spiritual wings and soar with the elite. Often this is not the case; the browbeaten trainee retreats further into his self-imposed cell, and any hope for growth and evolution is stifled. In the methods mentioned here you will be working on your own progress, no one will rush you, or push you. If you were training for a sport or other muscular skill you would need to take things easily, exercising gently at first, and then when muscles strengthen, at a greater pace. This modern art of magic is planned to work in the same way. There is no point in rushing ahead with a new exercise until you are doing the previous one well and without strain. Magic is amazingly old, its arts have evolved over thousands, perhaps millions of years - no one can learn them all in a few weeks, nor be proficient in the many different skills of mind, body and spirit all at once. To work magic effectively can produce instant results, at the end of several years' training!

If you are studying alone, and trying out methods which are strange and new to you, don't worry if your progress seems slow and hesitant. You will not come to any harm, and the more thoroughly you learn the first techniques the firmer will be the base from which you can leap towards the heights of adeptness. Certainly some of these exercises will have strange effects - they are meant to! Magic is concerned with change - if you get *no change* you are getting *no magic* either - so look out for it, both within yourself and in the world around you. Your sight will clear, and reality will become more real and more obvious. Patterns will begin to emerge from the background designs and the path ahead will gradually become visible and attainable. It will cost you something, though. Even in magic you will not get anything for nothing. As your personal direction becomes apparent you will realise that you will have to lay aside other activities, or plans, at least for the present, but the rewards will be there also.

These Gentle Arts are presented in a way which will suit solo students; they don't require membership of a group, lodge or coven, and because they rely far more on individual experiences and skills than complex shared rituals, you will be able to progress as fast as you choose. This well-tried method of working uses the symbols and power of Natural Magic rather than of High or Ceremonial Magic. Many of the arts are those of the mind, and not techniques requiring elaborate preparation, equipment or regalia. You will learn to use methods which feel 'right' or 'natural' to you, and with which you feel secure and confident. Soon you will discover that you have all manner of magical talents which you had overlooked, and it is these which will take you as far along the path to adeptness as you wish to travel.

Because these are the arts of Low Magic or Natural Magic or Folk Magic, for the most part, they have not been recorded in books, but in the customs of villagers, folk lore and superstitions, the songs and poems of country people going back for many generations. Much of this material has been considered 'too trivial' to write about, for the simple spells and chants, the candle-burning rites, and the methods of healing all tend to be arrived at intuitively. The practitioners of ordinary magic in the past were seldom scholars, proficient in book learning, but common folk who developed their innate skills for the benefit of their families and those around them. Most of the spells were performed on a 'one-off' basis, or on the spur of the moment, rather than the carefully planned, rehearsed and scripted ritual of modern magicians. The immediate need was what caused the old witch to make a talisman, or chant a rhyme over an injury, or call back a straying cow to the shippon. The things they used to do were essentially simple, as are all true arts of effective magic. We have grown up in the age of speed and 'instant' everything; in the past events were slower, people acted in a more intuitive way, being aware of the phases of Nature, her times and tides which gave them power. We have to relearn this simplicity and the links with our ancient magical heritage, and walk slowly, at the pace of the horse not the sports car, along the traditional winding paths.

The Gentle Arts are for all. They are safe, although they may seem strange to us in the jet age. They will take us into wild forests where the Old Gods may be met on their own terms. They will guide us on the inward journey that leads to the stars that shine within. They will take us to the foot of our Family Tree, and reintroduce us to our Totem Animal that we knew as a child, or met with in dreams un-noticed. This path is not straight, for it follows the contours, but it is gentle on the untrained Walker of the Inner Ways. The beginning of that Ancient Track lies at your feet, wherever on the Earth's mantle you may find yourself. Will you come with me upon that Moonlit, Sun-bright road?

1.
PERSONAL ALCHEMY

... he answered me, I am Ion, priest of the sanctuary, and I have suffered intolerable violence. For one came, quickly in the morning, cleaving me with a sword, and dismembering me systematically . . . he mixed my bones with my flesh and burned them with the fire of the treatment. It is thus, by the transformation of the body, that I have learned to become spirit.

Zozimos, 'Alchemy', E .J. Holmyard.

The first thing any would-be magician must accept is that all things change. You may well have read that 'Magic is the art of causing changes . . .' according to Aleister Crowley, or that 'Magic is the art of causing changes in consciousness . . .' according to Dion Fortune - so it is, but it is equally important to recognise the potential for change, to see changes taking place, and most important to learn to control those changes.

Although the most obvious changes take place in the physical world - plants grow, seasons come and go, night and day alternate, and the moon's phases wax and wane (and you will soon learn all these will have an effect upon you and your life patterns) - others are harder to detect and make use of. Some of these relate to other than the physical world, they are evolutions that occur within the mental level, and in the realms of spirit, of which many people are totally unaware, and these changes go unnoticed. To become a competent and effective magician means that you will have to come to terms with the mental plane and the spiritual plane, for it is here that the seeds of the changes you wish to make must be sown. It is within the subtle levels of life that these can secretly grow and develop, so that only their ultimate flowering is perceived in the physical world.

If you apply patience and work gently on the raw material of your own life and ambitions you may be able to shape the changes which are bound to affect your path towards magical perfection in your own way. It is no good rushing at acquiring skills and launching yourself into high-powered techniques until you understand the basic themes that underlie occult law. You will need to learn to trust your intuition and find time to allow your psychic abilities to speak to you during meditations and other journeys on inner paths. Gradually you will discover your subtler senses coming back to life. Children can accept myths and real life with equal validity - adults have lost this art, and the first techniques of magic are aimed at recovering those child-like abilities. They cannot be bludgeoned back into use, nor called forth from the depths of your memory by brutality. You must awaken these forgotten forms of perception gently; as in the story of Sleeping Beauty. They will reveal to you long-lost insight and inner certainties of the meaning of life. This winding path to the inner mind is another aspect of reality, it is not an excuse to escape into daydream and hallucination. The methods you use will cause you to face situations, relationships and even feelings about yourself and your accomplishments. To many people this is a painful and disturbing process.

Training in magic should lead to inner peace and happiness. It is not reasonable to expect everyone else on Earth to immediately fall in with your whims and desires, nor will you gain power over the lives of others. True happiness is a state where there is no inner conflict, no feelings of guilt, regret or failure. A competent magician will fail many times during his training, suffer fears and disappointments, but to him these will be spurs, urging him on to seek understanding, courage and success on a later occasion. The most effective techniques will be gentle ones, for though there are many therapists and 'experts' who have systems of analysis and fault-finding, these are often brutal; if applied by insufficiently trained 'ologists' they can do more harm than good.

To perform your personal archaeological dig you will need the same skills as an archaeologist working on an ancient and delicate site - you will need patience, space to work in, accurate record-keeping and perhaps even assistants to help you clear away the debris of a life-time. You will have to be prepared to work hard and deliberately, just as the historian digs patiently at a concretion of sand before uncovering an example of ancient workmanship and great value. Like the digger, you will have to start at the upper surface, the modern state of affairs and work down and back, a little at a time.

The first thing you will need is space, both in the physical sense of requiring a quiet place to sit, and also a mental space, which will permit you to relax, free from the needs of others, for at least half an hour a day, to begin with, and later on, when you get into more practical arts, double that. The place you choose should be reasonably quiet, and completely undisturbed. Sometimes it is necessary to get up a bit earlier or make use of a room the others in your household don't use, so that you will have peace and stillness in your environment. You will need a comfortable seat, too, that will support your back and neck, yet allow you to relax physically and breathe easily. You will probably prefer to have dim light, or a candle, relative silence or quiet, non-distracting music to cover up intrusive sounds. You will also need to arrive at a correctly poised frame of mind so that, as your body relaxes, your mind and intuition can get to work on your history and situation calmly. It is a knack, and there is no short cut to continual practice. Try various ideas until you find that the 'stream of consciousness', those thoughts that flit through your head, are slowed down and can be stopped.

There is a way of doing this by imagining a dark sky in front of you, and allowing ideas to drift away until there is stillness and a feeling of anticipation. Only practice, every day, until it happens will bring this ability to you. Without a space of calmness you won't be able to gradually examine your life pattern, select the good bits - the skills, the successes, the happy relationships, and put aside the bad times, the failures, losses and periods of depression. These are the areas that will need the most work. You cannot sweep your mental rubbish under the carpet - you will never achieve peace, and so power, that way. You must gently, at your own pace and in your own way, look very carefully at this pile of past disappointments. By doing this you will uncover jewels in the form of lessons learned,

yet maybe not properly understood. You will find treasures when
you can use the tumbled feelings as a new foundation to a better
life.

Some people find it very hard to forgive other people for the
letdowns in their lives, and find it totally impossible to forgive
themselves! This is a very sad state of affairs, for every person on
earth is unique, and has inherent qualities (both genetically and
from his previous lives) which are far greater than he ever dreamed
of. Magic is the skill of accepting this individual uniqueness, its
enormous potential for good and happiness, and learning to make
use of it. Many people have been taught by their religion that they
have to suffer for their sins - but they can't see that feeling guilt-
ridden *is suffering!* You are *responsible* for what you do in life, if
you fail then you must attempt to put right what has gone wrong,
both for yourself and those around you. If you are convinced that
saying a prayer, or undergoing a penance will free you from the
feeling of guilt in a more certain way than actually putting right
what went wrong, then do that. On the whole the magician *works* to
put right his mistakes, he learns the lesson of failure and does better
the next time. Try to see that no priest, no God can suffer on your
behalf if you have not tried to make better what you made bad. If
you can forgive yourself, then the Gods of the Mysteries will forgive
you too, and restore their blessing. Once you can see that your own
failure is not world-shattering you will find it easier to forgive others
who have caused you pain or trouble, then you will rediscover love
- both of self and of all those around you.

It is often hard not to punish yourself, but time has passed since
you let yourself down, and in that time good things may well have
occurred which far outweigh the thing that went wrong. Concentrate
your sessions of self-analysis on what happened after a problem -
how did things work out? Work back slowly, recording in a secret
book what you discover, and what treasures you have unearthed
from your forgotten past. These are the prizes which life already
has awarded to you, yet you overlooked them because of regrets
and self-delusion. While many people are busy painting things black,
others are quietly, carefully peeling off the thick paint and seeing
gold and brightness, which the alchemy of passing time has mixed

with the darkness of the hour.

Unless you have some self-confidence you will never stand up to the great pressures of magic. It is a very rewarding study, but it is not for the fainthearted or the dabbler - those are the kind of people who play with the powers and when things start to happen, as they will, get scared and yell for help. No one can help them much, though, for the awakened dragons, the bad dreams, the 'things that go bump in the night' all come from within. If you handle your psyche gently and slowly, like a nervous horse, it will come to hand and serve you, work in harness with you, and carry you safely through the inner realms of the mind, its own land. If you try to flog power from it, want to beat it into submission or spur it to carry you to the paradise within you can be sure you will be in for a rough and frightening ride!

Calmness and self-awareness go hand in hand. If you can keep your head and think clearly you will travel safely on those inner paths, you will enjoy your travels and bring back souvenirs to complete consciousness. From the inner world which is also the past, as we generally think of it, you can bring to the present ancient wisdom and, more important still, the practical skills which can turn wisdom into the precious gems of personal experience. Once you can put aside your fears and self-doubts you will become strong and capable, and discover that you can succeed at things beyond your wildest dreams. Be patient with these first steps on the path of magic and you will be in for some very pleasant surprises. You will discover your memory for events and faces improves, the way you feel about people will become clearer, and your discretion will be sharper. When you need to be calm you will be, and if you need to show your temper it will be under your control - anger won't run away with you. Your softer feelings will surface too, those of love, compassion and sympathy.

Set yourself targets of time and achievement, small ones to begin with - five minutes a day of peace and inward-turned thinking; then, perhaps, five minutes of thinking about the needs and wishes of others. Allow a few moments to settle down, and a while afterwards to record in your secret book what you have discovered. Breathe deeply, drawing in the life-force to the bottom of your lungs. Feel the cool air penetrating your body, and imagine the energy of the sun permeating you to bring healing and strength, calmness and well-being. Dance about a bit, swinging your arms and bending all your joints, or if you have learned the slow art of Tai-chi, try some of those exercises. Be slow and gentle with your mind and your body, for these are both gifts of the Gods, and so they are precious. Treat your needs with consideration rather than greed. Learn to be physically still and able to listen to the inner voices. You will soon find a way to meditate which suits your nature and schedule. This is when you will discover the art of problem solving, of receiving intuitive information and awakening the magic of creativity that can transform the dullest life into a valuable one in the eyes of evolution.

Develop all your ordinary skills that are based upon your physical senses. Just because you expect to gain insight and astral vision from working with magic, don't overlook the fact that if your mundane eyes are shortsighted, your view of the real world will be distorted. Practise 'seeing' - that is, actually, consciously observing what is going on around you - so that when your inner vision starts to become clearer you will be able to recognise what you are perceiving. Listen to those who are communicating with you, not just to hear the words and make some adequate response, but actually 'hear' what is being said, implied and conveyed by tone, nuance and language. Learn to devote all your attention to any form of communication or perception so that you do not miss the vital clues of the message, often secretly embedded in the medium, both in real life, and in any kind of intuited material.

Open up your senses to the environment; sense the changes in weather, the phases of the moon and the changes of the sun through the houses of the zodiac. These subtle feelings will not come at once, nor necessarily, quickly, and they won't come *at all* unless you try to make them work. Reach out to those around you, friends or strangers alike, see to what extent you can judge their mood, their needs or unexpressed desires. Find out more about your physical environment, discover why you like to visit one place and not another, why you prefer one food or type of music etc. Often, and only by direct experimentation, it is possible to find that things that you have shunned, perhaps for many years, because of some childhood bias, are things you can actually enjoy! If you wish to walk the inner ways you will have to sometimes try things which you suspect you won't like, or fear, or are disturbed by, but that is part of the growing process. Coming out of the womb was a new experience, but you must admit that some of your life has had its moments of joy or fun!

The ancient alchemical processes as applied to base metals caused them to go through a number of distinct and definite changes. In the matter of personal alchemy these may be encountered as 'initiations'. However, if you expect some learned adept to enter your life (and after testing you in various ways and, of course, finding you more than adequate) conferring rank and honour upon you, you will be disappointed! The pattern of life itself will provide the tests, and the initiations will always come from within, if they are to have any validity. Certainly, if you strive to find the right path through the maze you may get through them faster, but just as the pace increases, as in the laws of physics, so will the pressure, and this can be very unpleasant indeed. That is why this book is about the Gentle Arts, rather than the greatest ones.

Magical expertise is not shown by the number of badges you can wear on your sleeve, the number of 'initiations' into a variety of groups, lodges, covens or whatever, but by your personal power, your ability to cope in trying situations and your genuine humanity to other people. In the last few decades, when 'instant' coffee, 'instant' food and 'instant' enlightenment seemed all to be available in packets, at a price, some students were taken in, and expected that, if they paid their fee, turned up at the right address, clutching a black cloak and a bottle of the right sort of wine, they would receive in exchange, the secrets of the universe there and then! All were disappointed. Some realised their folly and began at the beginning again, seeking the way for themselves and accepting only what they actually earned by hard work as their magical due. Some, having decided that Adept A was a fake sought out Adept B, Lodge C, Group D and so on through the alphabet of possibilities, and some even reached 'Z' before they either gave up, or finally decided that there must be something more to the initiation lark than strange rites in dark rooms.

Just as physical growth comes from within, brought about by natural, chemical changes, so spiritual growth starts in your innermost being. From babyhood to adulthood you have grown imperceptibly and you can really only detect the changes in retrospect. Spiritual growth, which can be sustained, is a slow and gentle process. There are arts which can apparently speed up some aspects of this inner expansion, but they do so at the expense of other areas of your nature. Left to themselves, the changes are slow, maybe, but they are balanced and controlled, and there is none of the 'leaping forwards and then falling back' syndrome which some outside influences can produce. Accept from the beginning that psychic growth and magical power, like oak trees, are slow to develop but, if left to themselves, will grow strong and sure, and often much faster than you could ever predict. The seeds need to be sown in the proper growing medium, tended occasionally, so that the roots put down are strong against the tides of the world, and then you will suddenly discover that your magical self has expanded, your inner vision become clear, and the changes you wished for have happened in your life.

Now it is time to prepare that seedbed, to decide which of the many 'trees' of magical experience you will cultivate first (the others will grow faster in the shade of the earlier ones!). You have plenty of paths or traditions to choose from. Today there is a great deal of literature available on the magical methods, both ancient and modern, oriental and occidental, simple and amazingly complicated, to choose from but that alone requires a certain insight and awareness which many novices don't have. Either you have a 'gut feeling' that you will get on well with Qabalah, Druidism or Tantra or you feel totally lost among the material which bombards you, from the library shelves or magical magazine 'small ads'.

Most older systems were designed for groups, and though the way of the Hermit is an ancient one, most of the people who chose the lonely path had a strong religious rather than magical dedication. To walk the paths of magic on your own, especially if you really are a beginner, is a daunting prospect. Although there are plenty of books on rituals, symbolism and theory, the greater proportion of them, by far, was written for people working in groups, or within the confines of a particular school of thought or tradition. Hermits, in the days of old, received their training among others before they discarded human company for their anchorite's cell or mountain retreat. Today, most lone seekers don't have this foundation to spring away from, and so often fall prey to the 'instant initiation' brigade, or a system which really doesn't suit them.

This book is written by an individual practitioner, for those who choose to walk alone, or who find that they are divorced from others by their lifestyles, philosophies, aims or ambitions. Any magical tradition requires hard work, but when you have a friend or tutor to turn to, somehow the burden seems less heavy and the night of ignorance, less dark. On your own you will have to develop that inner sense of certainty early on, so that you can rely on your own judgement, detect your own progress, devise your own path. It takes just as much dedication and courage to tread that path as to plunge headfirst, but blindfold, into the arms of some group which might promise all power and glory but only at the price of some of your own values or ideals. The solo path will never strip you of your own ethics, nor force you to obey some alien whim, and though your direction may change as your knowledge grows, it will always be in the direction in which you perceive the Light to shine.

The way forward may be slow, but it is safe, gentle and can be very rewarding. It will help you to rediscover your magical roots through the use of imagery, which you certainly had as a child. It will show you the secrets of the universe, well within your own grasp, and in the privacy and security of your own home, and guide you on voyages through time and space. By reawakening your store of awareness and perception to the natural world you will re-establish links with the Gods and Goddesses, both within and in the outer levels of experience. It will, in time, be these fragile links which will allow you to learn from their sources of wisdom and power, and which, in the end, will take you through the initiations of the elements of Earth, Water, Fire and Air. They will lead you safely through the arts of magic of the Earth herself; of the weird Moon powers which open the inner psychic eyes; the Solar healing forces of mind and body; the brilliant wisdom of the distant Stars and, perhaps, finally, the Cosmic magics which work with the act of continuous creation, to make the greatest changes of all.

As your knowledge grows, so will your understanding and personal power. You will change, becoming stronger and more dedicated, more selective and better able to cope with life. You will become an asset to humanity, not a drain on its resources, no longer a taker rather than a giver. What you learn will help you, but in turn it will help all creation, and the harder you strive the greater this return will be. You may find your objectives change, and that you begin to work, in a mundane sense, for ecology groups, or by teaching, or campaigning for what to you seems important. You may become angry at other people's insensitivity, greed or innate destructiveness, or you may find simple ways of redressing the balance between man and nature by healing the Earth, by redeeming the Wasteland on more subtle levels than those.

Only by daring to open yourself to the forces of change, by increasing your knowledge and understanding the perpetual cycles of birth, death and rebirth, as they occur in nature, and in yourself, can you gradually become a clearer channel for healing and energising forces to flow. This is a heavy burden. It takes determination and dedication, but its rewards can be astounding. By following the simple steps of coming to terms with the magic of each of the elements, by actually becoming fully aware of the earth beneath your feet, and her stabilising power; the cleansing and refreshing essences of water; the energy and heat of fire; and the life-sustaining breath of air; and within yourself and the whole universe, the spiritual force which all creation shares, you set free your own magic.

You need to accept that as a part of nature, you cannot divorce yourself from the ills of the world, but that by relearning some of these ancient arts you will be able to strengthen your own innate power for good, for healing and for life in abundance. It may take some time to master these skills and philosophies, it will take effort and commitment, it may even make you think anew about relationships, your own place in the world, and what you wish to achieve. It is never an easy option, to strike off on a lonely pathaway from the common road, but its rewards to you, as an evolving soul, can be enormous. It will teach self-reliance and offer you personal experiences of communion with the Gods and Goddesses, or their angels, representatives or energies, as you come to see them for yourself. It will show where in the scheme of things there is a place ideally suited to you, and if you have the courage to follow the star of your own inner being, you can rise to great heights.

Read through each section of this book carefully, and think hard about what is being said. It is a new approach to some very old arts and crafts, and some of the ideas expressed here may seem very alien to you. You should never accept anything you have doubts about, but consider the options. Try out any technique sincerely, but with a spirit of adventure. What matters are the experiences *you* have, not other people's theories, the contacts *you* make with the deities, and the new discoveries that you are able to make about yourself, the world and the future. Those have always been the gifts bequeathed by Nature to her children, yet many have become too wound up in the material world to recognise the value of a quiet heart, the gentle voice of the wind which lulls the troubled spirit and blows away the fretful mood. The song of birds can still enchant us, and in a child-like way, carry us to the Land of Faeries, to the Otherworld, wherein our dreams may be made real. The chains we carry around are of our own forging, and with the return to the Old Ways and the Gentle Arts it becomes possible to cut them away, link by restricting link, until our minds and souls are free.

Your success at following the ancient path will depend entirely upon your own efforts. The exercises and methods taught here are safe. Many of them are extremely old, yet their power and efficacy are for you to find and use for yourself. The work is hard and will require a fair amount from you, in time and effort, not in money or material items. You will have no handy Magus or High Priestess to turn to, as you might have if you were being trained in a lodge or coven, but that way may not be possible for you because of the way you live, or your own choice of the solo way. You will need to learn to trust your intuition, and once you have made personal contact with the forces of nature, allow them to guide, protect and teach you all the things you want to know. Again, it will be what you seek, as an individual, rather than as a member of a team or group.

Any good or evil you encounter on your travels to the inner worlds will be of your own making. The road within is neutral, merely a path of change, but what you find there, or bring forth into the light of your awareness will be for you to judge. There are no dark Gods who do not have bright faces hidden behind the mask you may choose to make them wear. There are no frightening Guardians who will overwhelm you in the other realms, unless you give them that power- they are there to protect all travellers, including you!

Certainly some of the experiences you will have will be surprising - that is an inherent part of magic. If it caused no sense of awe or wonder or surprise, then it would not be magic! You can use power to change your future, but you cannot dictate the exact manner of the change, only the outcome you desire. You will find that you can do spells for material things, but they will arrive as a result of coincidences. The luck or healing or knowledge will come to you through the post, or from a friend, or turn up in a library book. The outcome of magic is natural not supernatural, these days, but if you obey the simple rules, respect the forces, no matter how real you imagine them to be, act without greed or selfishness, there are few limits on what you can achieve. By using the gentle arts of magical alchemy on yourself you will begin to change the dark and leaden soul of the novice, or the student who has forgotten the path walked in an earlier life, into the bright gold of the controller of the forces of nature. As your inner light grows, it may light the path for others, who come behind you on the long road of spiritual evolution, and so, even in very small ways, you will help strangers on their journey, too.

2.
THE MAGIC OF EARTH

On either side the river lie, Long fields of barley and of rye, That clothe the wold, and meet the sky; And thro' the field the road runs by, To many towered Camelot. . .

The Lady of Shalott, Tennyson

Magic is as old as the hills and as wide as the span of the horizon of the Earth herself. To master its ancient arts and simple spells, to celebrate the traditional festivals and share the spirit of this inherited wisdom is a path that anyone may tread. There have been many books on various aspects of Old Magic, detailing its history, its persecutions and some of its modern revivals, but most of these books have missed out its inherent simplicity and power. From my own experience I know that you don't need artificial, modern, written sources to lead you to the Goddess of Earth, Mother Nature, call her what you will. Any walk among trees, over wild countryside or along a wintry, deserted beach will bring you far closer to the roots of the oldest religion of all than muttered rites in a man-made house, or words read from a page by guttering candle light.

To discover the Goddess of the Earth and her consort/son and lover, the Lord of the Sky, you will have to tread an ancient path, as I have tried to explain, by setting out from the bounds of civilisation and returning to that child-like appreciation of the world around you. You will not need to believe or accept set tenets of faith or practice. You will need to explore one step at a time, the clues that the ancient wisdom has left scattered in your path. The reason that there aren't rows of books written by the wise women, the cunning men, the shamans and the medicine men is that writing things down was not a natural part of their culture. It is not a matter of secrecy, nor of the danger of their knowledge, but only because much of it was so simple, so trivial that it didn't warrant the effort of setting pen to paper.

If you have a favourite recipe or knack of doing some basic task you don't write it down or hand it on as a great mystery - nor did our ancestors. Much of their knowledge, which when applied may be called wisdom, was a matter of knowing the best way to do the basic things of life, whether that was catching something for the pot, or curing the sickness of man or beast. Magic was a part of life, just as electricity is a part of our lives now. We don't necessarily understand how it works, nor do we study hard in case we need to turn on a light switch, we just do it! So did our forebears. You cannot separate the magical from the mundane, once you begin to open your eyes to the actual world around you. Consider a rainbow, the flash of lightning, the might of a volcano or the power of the sea. Each of these is the work of nature, often showing far more strength than we can reproduce, or more beauty and delicacy.

It is for this reason that it isn't possible simply to list a number of necessary items, describe the setting of a ritual, and write down the words which someone could say to call up the Earth Mother. You will have to set off from the place you are in on a personal journey of exploration. To a certain extent you will have to search your own land and locality for clues to the system of magic, as well as searching your own heart for what 'feels right', that intuitive certainty of the best way to go. Books may not help, but they too will contain fragments of this vast and complex study.

On trying to throw some light on the subject of the Gentle Arts it is necessary first to realise what a wide-ranging subject it is. Spreading throughout the whole of mankind's history on Earth, across the entire face of the globe, its span in time and distance is enormous. Some aspects of it seem to be able to trace their roots to the very beginning of humanity's evolution on this blue-green jewel floating in space, yet now in the age of computers and space shuttles, these old methods and ideas are still in use. Parts of the practice of Natural Magic will be found all over the world, shared by sophisticated/civilised people in concrete cities and simple folk in the wilderness, using techniques of dreaming and far vision in the same way. Time, too, does not limit the use of the magic of nature, for there are sacred centres all over the land masses of the Earth which have been gathering places for worship, magic or seasonal festivals for as long as anyone can discover. In other villages or on holy mountains there are new celebrations, or brief and sporadic rituals, perhaps limited to one tiny spot and which may be over in an hour or so, to be repeated the following year.

The celebration of natural events may entail gatherings of thousands of people, dancing, singing, walking in procession, worshipping for weeks at a time, or they may be limited to a family or clan or the inhabitants of a small, remote village asking a blessing on their well, or their crops and livestock on a certain day in the year. On an even smaller scale than that there are the individual acts of country magic where a family or small group of people have preserved 'superstitions' or traditional knowledge about certain plants for healing or 'far-seeing' properties, the use of particular stones, fossils or plants as charms against the 'evil eye', or specific diseases. These are all aspects of Natural Magic, from the grand scale down to the individual crumb of wisdom, from the unbelievably ancient to the new use of some natural substance discovered yesterday.

In the Gentle Arts, magic is the use of natural things, created by the Goddess of Earth or the Lord of Creation. The results of this simple traditional set of arts, crafts and religious experiences is still relevant in this modern time. The healing plants are being re-examined for properties long misunderstood; ancient traditions of knowledge, self-awareness and magic are being reassessed by scholars, scientists and philosophers, and many are proving to have values which have been put aside in the materialistic world. The magic of nature is for anyone who has the patience, daring and determination to look deeply into the mirror of self-knowledge and, where it is found wanting, be willing to study, practise and gain understanding of the very principles of creation. It is a long and sometimes lonely path but the rewards are limitless.

Natural Magic has always been the province of the Village Witch, the lone Cunning Man, the Shaman, the Medicine Man or the Wise Woman, and it seems likely that ever since humankind banded together to seek their living in a group there has always been one person who had some extra skills. When catching or finding food meant the difference between life and death such ability was obviously much prized, and it is probable that the shaman, in his stag-antlered, skin disguise found in the cave paintings at *Les Trois Freres* in France was such a magician. It is possible too, that these ancient cave drawings show the first sorts of 'Sympathetic Magic', when the hunter, disguising himself as one of the prey, could lead the deer or cattle to the waiting tribe's spears or pitfall traps.

Not only did certain individuals show extra skill in hunting live game but some must have discovered sources of roots and berries, leaves and fruits on which their people depended for food. This knowledge, like all magical skills, had to be effective. No one would wish to trek miles to discover the fruit had been eaten by animals, or the leaves or nuts were not yet ready. Recent research with chimpanzees and gorillas, who wander freely through their habitat, has shown that they know exactly where the next supply of wild fruit or leaves is to be found, and they don't waste energy visiting a tree with unripe food. The same applies to water sources - no one can survive too long without water and supplies are not always available. It must be from these very early and basic beginnings that the arts of water divining and clairvoyance needed to locate a vital source were developed. Someone whose guesses were most often correct would be a great asset to his or her tribe.

Such simple practical knowledge may well have been passed on both genetically and by instruction, practically up to the present time. Now we learn most things from written rather than spoken or demonstrated sources. If you think of how many bits of information you carry round in your head you will be surprised - telephone numbers, recipes, details of your car, brand names of foods and drinks, books and their authors, musical performers and the records they have made - all sorts of odd items, facts and figures are stored in your memory. In earlier times everyone would have lists of more important data stored in their memories, especially if they had never learned to read or write. The skills listed here are very modern in the history of human endeavour, becoming common in only the last two hundred years or so. Mankind may well have been around for 6,000,000 years or more!

When people lived in caves or simple shelters they were much closer to what we now know as Planet Earth. They had no clocks, no supermarkets, no books or TV but they had time to decorate the walls of their dwellings, and to chip hard stones into spear points, arrow heads, axes and scrapers. They also made beads to decorate their bodies, and many of the functional artefacts were ornamented with animal or abstract designs. Look in any museum and become aware of the skills of these so-called primitive peoples, anywhere in the world. Have a go at knapping a flint into a useful tool, try your hand at making a pot from river clay without a wheel, design and make a necklace of natural seeds, bones and wood strung on a thong and it will give you a little insight into the abilities of your ancestors, and bring you closer to the source of Natural Magic.

In every culture of mankind upon Earth there has been some sort of recognition of the planet as more than a dead lump of rock floating in the sea of space. Most of the knowledge we have about our ancestors comes from enduring works they left behind which have survived many thousands of years of time. We have not only examples of their tools and pottery, their homes and their ornaments, but in many places we have huge works of earth and stone, constructions the sheer size of which must indicate their importance to the folk who designed and built them. Britain alone has literally thousands of such monolithic structures still visible after four or more thousands of years. There were probably many more which have been lost, hidden or buried, and they can be seen all over Europe, the Mediterranean area and in America too. From the single boulder or rock, which may have been a plain boundary stone, to the vast and complex constructions of Stonehenge; the dozens of rings, ovals and patterns of standing stones, earth banks and ditches, some many miles long, the barrows, mounds, tumuli, cromlechs and quoits; all stand silent witness to our ancestors' relationships to the Earth on which they stood. Now these great sources of wonder and mystery may be encouraged to give up at least some of their secrets.

Once historians and students of the ancient ways are willing to abandon the notion that Stone Age people were dim witted, ugly and brutal creatures, ekeing out a poor existence at the whim of weather and fate, and recognise the complexity of their earthworks, the beauty and simplicity of their art forms, they will perceive with new eyes what lies before them. No one would spend years of hard toil building a stone circle unless it had some very important purpose, any more than roadbuilders construct motorways leading nowhere today. Heaving ten tonne rocks about is no light undertaking, nor is digging a ditch or raising a vast mound such as Silbury Hill in Wiltshire. We have been blinded by the logic which has taught us to imagine that these ancient peoples were woad-daubed savages, and it takes a long time to become aware of their technical and practical skills. We may not be able to discover immediately what their purposes may have been, at this great distance in time, but anyone who is willing to learn to become aware, can switch off the twentieth century and enter a timeless world in which it is possible to return to the past, and witness what happened at some of these sites. Certainly it is possible to argue that any such vision is mere imagination (imagination, derived from the same source as magic, the most powerful tool we have!) - but because it results in a personal experience, it will be very real to the 'time traveller'.

In all parts of the world people have sacred centres, whether associated with a teacher or prophet, or places of healing or inspiration. There are sacred cities, temples, springs and holy mountains. Many hilltops have churches on them which have replaced earlier pagan shrines, stone circles or other magical artefacts. Even today, if you can find a high and lonely hill, uncluttered with the works of the modern world, and you can climb it alone, you will soon sense a little of the atmosphere that such places have. The wind will feel different there, the silence or the sole intrusion of the sounds of nature, birdsong, the distant calls of cattle, may even seem to have a message for you, once you learn the art of attunement with the Earth Mother.

There is no set pattern as to the design of stone circles, nor even in the choice of sacred sites. Like the ability to find food some of our ancestors must have had a sense of place, the skill to discover some natural hill or hollow, mound or cave where the forces of nature were stronger, and so more available. Perhaps these people sought healing, or advice and guidance from the Spirit of the Earth.

Perhaps they could sense the upwelling of some energy which science has yet to name and unravel. Certainly there are places which do feel 'weird', where energy seems to tingle up through a stone or hill, or some calming balm in the very air brings peace and inward stillness. Everyone must seek these things for himself - one person's experience can only be valid for him, just as taste in food or dress is an individual choice.

Many of the oldest structures are classified by archaeologists as 'burial mounds' because bones or funerary objects have been found in these complex and elaborately constructed underground chambers so they have been associated only with death. If a stranger came into an old English village church he would also find tombs, memorial slabs, images of a tortured and dying figure of Jesus on the cross, but no one supposes that churches are only there as elaborate covers for the select dead - presumably the tribal chiefs - nor that they were places of punishment and execution, judged by the evidence of the crucifix. It is necessary to learn to examine these buildings, both ancient and modern, in the light of intuition, the magician's most valuable asset.

Why did those folk so many thousands of years ago carry stones to a particular place, set them up in circles or complicated mathematical ellipses, in straight lines or as markers, pointing to some other sacred site or to the rising point of the Sun and Moon? We can't be certain, but we can try to understand what the relationship between the people and the Earth Mother might have been. Some of the recent research into ley lines, power points, earth acupuncture and dowsing may be able to throw a little light onto the uses and patterns of design which conventional scientific methods may never do. Perhaps these unlikely arts are a way of getting back some of the senses which twentieth-century life has dulled in many people.

Alfred Watkins lived in Herefordshire on the borders of Wales and became aware that there appeared to be ancient trackways leading straight from one sacred site to another. Some of the marking points were single stones, set at the roadside; others were circles of standing or recumbent stones. From hilltop, adorned with an ancient mound or more recent church, to valley floor where a ford or pool of water made a way-mark, these old straight tracks ran for many miles. Some were marked with trees or small groves on hills, others were indicated by notches carved out of the skyline so that the traveller was always guided onwards. Despite the passing centuries, these lines may still be traced in many places. Some have become modern paved roads; others, across hill and moorland, are much as they have always been. Certain of the features on the lines have been changed, churches replace the standing stones, but often the churchyard wall retains the circular shape of the original sacred site. Walls have been built and the solo mark stones have partly vanished into their footings, but the keen eye, the intuitive walker on the Old Ways will find them again. Some stones have crosses carved upon them, particularly in Cornwall, as if the sign of the Anointed One would change their power and cut them off from their links with the Great Mother!

Although the stones are not carved with runic texts, nor do they bear symbolic pictures, for the most part, they still maintain their links with the Earth power of simple magic, and it is possible to learn to read them, not like a book, but rather like recalling a long-forgotten dream. You can't learn the techniques of Old Magic from the pages of a book because they are matters of personal experience. Nor can you learn to ride a bicycle or cook a gourmet dinner simply by reading how it is to be done. Get out there and try it. Find a quiet place, even on the edge of a town or city, and let the earth beneath you speak to you.

It is difficult to know how to go about describing the myriad aspects of the Gentle Arts, the religion of the Earth Mother with her many faces and the Sun God with his burning light, or to explain the old crafts in a way that will make sense to a modern reader. It is not that the knowledge is secret and may not be shared, it is not that it is too complicated to explain in written words (although this is much harder than having an expert actually show you) because, on the whole, the spells and charms are simple. But it is because there is such a vast array of wisdom, knowledge, data, information, practical ability and intuition that it is hard to know where to begin. Perhaps it might be best to start at the beginning, although to go on to the end will prove impossible in a growing and evolving cosmos.

Mankind has always been aware of the concept of motherhood. Women brought forth their children; cows, lionesses, mares, sows, - all, in their own way, brought forth young. From the earliest times of human consciousness each individual may have had an awareness of who his mother was because the bond, developed through the long years of childhood, taught him the relationship (the same awareness is shown among apes and chimpanzees, who also have long periods of growing up). The relationship with the mother was therefore a special one. Not only did people have this bond with their own physical mother but from the earliest settlements symbolic figures of fat, pregnant females have frequently been found. This seems to indicate another relationship.

At this distance in time we can't firmly say 'The ancient peoples of this or that land worshipped the Mother Goddess', but it does seem a reasonable surmise that motherhood was celebrated. As soon as any kind of records were kept, which have survived to this age, names of Goddesses and Gods are to be found among them. Mankind has tried to maintain a relationship, not only with his clearly acknowledged physical mother, and later on, father, but also with his Divine Parents. Many people who are turning again to the pagan religions and seeking to celebrate the festivals of the Earth cycle have done so because they find it easier to worship and communicate with the Great Mother and the Sun Father. If you are in trouble or pain it is often to your mother that you will call for help, and perhaps it is the Great Mother of All who answers your prayer.

No one who takes up the Gentle Arts should feel he has to abandon a long-held orthodox religious faith, nor should his aim be to wipe out the modern religions and replace them with some pagan revelation, but everyone should seek a personal and valid communication with God, Jesus, the Moon Maiden, the Great White Spirit, the Creator, the Mother, the Lord of the Sky, Krishna and so on, which is real to him. If the names you use or the way in which you worship is individual, so much the better. The inner working of any relationship, human or divine, is much better kept secret between those involved.

The Earth beneath our feet is not just a lump of assorted minerals whirling through the depths of space at the end of the sun's gravitational string; she is a living and aware being and we live upon her mantle like insects on a ripe fruit. Her bounty is endless but we can be greedy, destructive, selfish and shortsighted. We have plundered the minerals, defiled the pure air, polluted the waters, and our livestock has eaten bare the deserts, which were even in Roman times, the grain basket of the eastern civilisations. Now we are beginning to recognise these problems, and unless we act soon and decisively the raped and cruelly treated Earth will crumble beneath us. Once you begin to have some feeling that the Earth is alive and responsive to pleas for food, for safety and for sufficiency in many things you have to seek some other way of restoring the balance of man and nature.

There is no simple answer, but each person who turns from his own need to that of the Earth will be taking a step in the right direction. Anyone who can be bothered to learn some of the Earth magics, and who then uses them in a generous and responsible manner will be helping, albeit in a tiny way, to achieve the final and vital rebalancing of life-force and living individual. A first step is quite easy but it is something you will need to do for yourself. You will need to get to know the land upon which you are dwelling, be it city or town, village or remote farmstead. Find out about the soil and the rock beneath, what it will grow. Is it dry or damp, is it fertile or must it be fed to make the poorest plants flourish? How do the seasons pass there, dramatically or gently, spring fading into summer into the time of leaf-fall? Become aware of the strength of rock, the beauty of building stone, the colour of brick, the simplicity of older methods of constructing walls and homes.

In times past children learned from their parents and grandparents, not from books, which cannot answer questions. They watched and imitated and played at all the things which adults about them did in their ordinary lives. Gradually a great store of unwritten knowledge was gained on what things were, how they were used. This included not only working tools and equipment or foodstuffs, but the magical objects, the chanted spells and charms which made the butter turn or warded off harm and disease from cattle and kindred. Even now the horseshoe with its points upwards is nailed above the door so that the blessing of the Earth Mother, in her guise of a white mare, will not run out. Collections of naturally holed stones, called Holy or Hag stones are hung by red ribbons in byres and stables to prevent the cattle and horses from being ridden by demons at night, or milked dry by the elves. Fossils were strong charms which proved the intervention of strange forces. How else could the curled ammonite (which legend has it was once a living and venomous snake) have been turned to stone, or the arrows from elven bows (belemnites) have been harmlessly knocked down to be found in ploughed land except by the intervention of some protective deity? There are thousands of such ancient bits of lore, studied by learned people, reported in journals, and debated by professors who all ignore the basic fact that the country folk who have preserved these fragments of timeless wisdom have done so because they work.

We cannot tell what sort of people the designers of the ancient monuments were, whether they were priests or engineers, seers or scholars, drawing on some even more remote source of knowledge. We don't know if the stone circles, the earthworks and monolithic constructions were temples, dedicated to the Sun God/Goddess, and though more recent computer studies have demonstrated that the sun and stones align in a spectacular manner at certain times in the year, we can't be certain this was significant when they were built. It does seem extremely probable that the idea of the shaft of sunlight, or the dark shadow of a carefully placed standing stone into the centre of the circle symbolises the mating of the Sun/Sky God with the Earth Mother, whose womb or body is depicted by the earthwork itself.

From the scattered remains of once great and wise peoples we have little historic evidence of their religion, their festivals or their technology. We only have the carcass, as it were, of a huge and long-living prehistoric beast and we need to reconstruct the way it lived, the colour of its fur from just the fossil fragments. Now we only have legends of the giants who lived in the land and built the Giants' Dance, now called Stonehenge. We have their pictures carved on the sides of hills at Wilmington, where the Long Man with his two staves looks across the Sussex countryside, or the Cerne Abbas Giant with his vast genitals and upraised club, both clearly symbolising fertility.

To set up the alignments of stone and sun and moon would have taken perhaps hundreds of years of patient observation and the passing on of that data, so it is likely that some sort of priesthood or school of earth technicians existed. It is generally thought that ceremonies were performed at these sacred sites, and though they were set up long before the Druids came to Britain, around 1,000 BC, the idea of Midsummer and other seasonal rituals has stuck. Evidence from the pre-literate Roman period is scarce and we only have second-hand reports of the Druid priests upholding the law, teaching the children, studying astrology and astronomy, medicine and geometry - all the skills which had already existed in the construction of the great monuments - and looking after the people who built them, by muscle power and magic.

From these distant wise ones has come a scattered pattern of bits of lore and myth. We have read tales of the Druids burning sacrifices in wicker baskets - perhaps they were really making large effigies of the Green God of Nature, as people in certain villages still do. Many pubs are named after him - Jack in the Green, The Green Man and even Robin Hood. Each may be an almost forgotten allusion to the God of Nature whose image was borne through the fields and then burned, just as the chaff of the wheat was cast into the fire after the harvest. We don't *know,* but it is likely.

In mediaeval times the masons responsible for the great cathedrals and churches also had their magic and secrets. They do to this day, although most of the speculative Freemasons know or care little for the crafts of their forerunners. The cutting, shaping and raising of stone for such holy edifices was filled with traditional magic and lore. Even though the cathedrals were chairs of Christian knowledge, there is a strong pagan influence, which is visible even in this day and age, if you know where to look. The Green Man, a relic of the Druid's bonfires is to be seen on many a church roofboss, with leaves of oak or arbutus issuing from his mouth and hair. The pre-Christian equal-armed-cross or Celtic circled cross is often woven into the design, as is the pentagram, that magical symbol, which is so often seen these days adorning the modern occultist as jewellery.

The idea of a slain God is not only the province of Christians. As I have already mentioned, the Corn King is cut down each year, and rises again in the spring, about Easter tide. The Hero goes, travelling down into the Underworld to seek wisdom of his lady love or some treasure from the Otherworld in many mythical traditions. The Earth Mother herself as Demeter goes into the dark kingdom of Pluto to bring back her daughter Persephone, so that green and life may return to the upper world of men. King Arthur, with some of his knights ventured into Annwn, that Celtic Otherworld, to fetch a great cauldron- which may have become the Christian Holy Grail in a later turn of the spiral of legend.

Some kings and heroes, saints and travellers have gone to some other world, never to return - the list is long. There is Jesus, and Mary his mother, Prester John, Melchizedek, King Arthur and Merlin to name but a few. Each has sought either heaven, living, or gone to some 'Summerland', Avalon, the place of Apples of Immortality; Merlin to his cave, walled in by his lover, the witch Nimué. Legend has it that all will return when the hour of need grows strongest, but now they rest in the realm of the Earth Mother, undergoing some initiation or training which will fit them for the task to come. Most of the real initiations of the priesthoods of old enacted such a journey into the cave or sacred grove, so that the initiate would learn valuable lessons about the mysteries and about the mastery of his own fears and weaknesses. He was not taught from books, but from personal experience gained by going down into the dark places with only the torch of his own pure will to strengthen and guide him. That path to the inner realms is still there, more overgrown and harder to find without the pointing priesthood, but you can become a pilgrim and venture on the dark way, if you dare - although no one is saying that it is a physical cavern you will need to enter.

From very early times in man's history on earth he has interacted with the planet, not only deriving food and shelter from plants, animals and caves, but he has left his mark on the face of the earth. In many lands there are great ceremonial areas, enclosures, and arrangements of standing stones to indicate places of magical power or seasonal gathering. Huge figures have been marked on the desert floor at Nazca in Peru, and in Somerset the twelve figures of the signs of the zodiac have been discovered, marked out by rivers and streams, footpaths and hedges and the shape of the landscape itself.

One cannot be certain that this is not coincidence, but there are tales of giants and lions in the area. The figures around Glastonbury may also be equated with the central characters in the Arthurian legends, which, if they have a historical basis at all, may well have taken place in that same area of countryside. By shaping natural mounds, diverting streams and walking certain paths, perhaps driving flocks or herds, patterns have been indelibly made, and from the air they are still quite clear.

Glastonbury Tor, that English natural pyramid, has long been the centre of magical and religious interest. Its top crowned now with the tower of St Michael's chapel, the rest of which fell down in an earthquake in the Middle Ages, once had a ring of stones. Glass has been made there and its looming slopes must have been a green refuge above the bogs and marshes of the plain below. Around its slopes there coils a twisting maze path. Perhaps it is the pilgrim's way which, turning back on itself, yet even continuing to the centre, will lead to the Holy Grail, or Gwynn ap Nudd's castle. Gwynn was the Lord of the Underworld or Otherworld, and it is into his realm that those seeking initiation to the Earth Mysteries would need to find away. This is still true, for if you want to get close to the Earth Mother you will have to explore a cave, loiter in one of the roofed Long Barrows or sacred stone temples, above and below ground which can be found all over Europe.

Mazes are other ancient ways in which people may have sought communion with the forces of the earth and sky. Perhaps their spiralling paths copied the movements of the planets, those 'wandering stars', through the vault of heaven. Perhaps the 'cup and ring' marks which look like the pattern made by tossing a pebble into still water, are star maps carved by our ancestors to mark the pattern in the sky at festivals, or significant births. The spiral seems to symbolise eternity, and the cyclic nature of green life, of plants and trees which grow green and flourish, flower, fruit and seed and then cast off their leaves in winter's sleep, to begin again in the next seasonal cycle. Grass-cut mazes have often faded through time, but those marked in stone are found on ancient rocks, and mediaeval cathedrals, on coins from Classical Greece and the works of Native Americans. All over Northern Europe maze patterns still exist in a number of forms, some large enough to walk, others carved, painted, engraved or laid as mosaics on historic sites which we can still examine.

There is no way of proving what these earth and maze works were for, but anyone who is willing to set aside the notions of 'experts' and see for themselves can learn to read these rocks by a form of 'psychometry'. Just as a modern clairvoyant may ask you for your watch or necklace from which to pick up information, you can discover simple ways of allowing these old sources of wisdom to speak for themselves. Try to find a place and time when your chosen site is quiet and reasonably deserted. If you can sit down with your back to a stone or bank, or even ancient tree, close your eyes and senses to the modern world and allow your feeling to sink back through time. No one can say what you might discover - no one can say it is true or correct. Someone else at the same place may discover something entirely different, but that will not invalidate your experience with ancient magic, and the 'sermons in stones' which you may hear.

Another simple piece of Earth Magic you can perform is to find a stone you like, a pebble from a stream, a sea-washed rock or a chunk of coloured mineral and get to know it as a friend. Carry it round with you and feel its surface. If you become tense or worried stroke it and allow its density and natural inertia to calm you - you may be surprised how effective this form of earth magic can be. After a few weeks pass the stone to a friend and ask her to sense what she can about it, perhaps grasping it in her left hand, which we know links to the more intuitive side of the brain. (Dowsers have often used the left hand, if they are right handed, to feel for water or sources of minerals etc. Healers, too, use it to make diagnoses or locate the seat of pain or illness.)

Learn something about the geology of your home region - is it based on ancient rocks or more recent clays and gravels? Are there any useful mineral deposits, fossils, gems or anything else which makes it interesting? Do certain plants grow well there and others not? What weeds and herbs may be found on river banks, derelict sites or round the edges of farmland? All these are valuable clues which the old wise ones would have known about so that they could

locate a healing plant, or fungus, a tree or even mineral in case of
need. Many common weeds were a valuable part of our forebears'
diets, often filled with vitamins and trace elements that modern field
crops do not have. Nature has been very generous to her people,
but we have ignored her stores of natural wealth, preferring artificial
drugs and chemically enlarged food plants. It is time to revert to the
old ways before this priceless store of the Earth Mother's bounty is
lost forever. Examine old cookery books, traditional tales and local
legends of feasts and festivals, sacred sites and magical spots and
go and 'feel' them for yourself

Magic of every sort is not a matter of belief. You do not believe
a spell will work or a prayer will be answered - you *know*. Magic
gives you an ultimate certainty that a spell properly performed with
sincerity will have the desired effect, or you will immediately know
why not. There is no way to prove the truth of that statement except
for you to try some of these old arts for yourself. Magic works for
anyone, just as electricity does. You don't need to understand the
way it works nor speculate about what processes are involved in
the completion of your desire. But you must act with common sense,
in a non-selfish way, within the bounds of reason - for example, 'I
want a million pounds, now!' won't work, whereas 'I would like
the means to go on holiday for a week, find a new job or get a
reliable car' are all within magical reason. You don't find angels
turning up with gold bricks these days, and you may have to pay
actual cash for the new car, but somehow, if you go about asking
politely, and work (yes, actually work) towards achieving your
desire, then the chances are it will be accomplished, by one of those
strange coincidences that anyone familiar with magic will recognise
at once. If you *need* a holiday (note, need not greed!) it is quite
likely that an acquaintance will turn up with a spare ticket to some
delightful spot, or a relative will send you the keys to his holiday
villa in exchange for you painting the place while you're there!

Magic uses the forces of nature. If you work with the seasons
and tides, the energies and forces will be running in the right direction.
For example, you would not plant flowers in the autumn, or try to
row in a straight line across a fast flowing river - in each case you
would he advised to take note of prevailing circumstances. This is

very true with magic. Learn to recognise the signs so that all the known factors can be to your favour. Learn about the pattern of the year which changes every three months as the sun enters a new quarter of the zodiac, recognised in most parts of the world as spring, summer, autumn and winter. In the spring it is time to sow and begin new ventures, in the fall you can harvest the results. Winter and summer are times of waiting and resting or watching over the growing enterprise.

There have always been seasonal festivals, originally marking significant times on the cycle of the turning year. When the livestock gave birth in the countryside a festival was held. When the hay harvest was gathered the people rejoiced, and again at harvest time and the culling of the winter herds - each was dictated by the actual work and needs of the land. No one set dates on the calendar, as do the modern 'witches' to celebrate some of the Mother's feasts, but watched the growth of new plants, the completion of some phase of the farming cycle, and the ever-changing patterns in nature.

There are four main festivals in the oldest ritual calendar celebrated in Britain, based on the flowering of the Earth both as provider of food and livestock, and as Great Mother and Goddess, giver of spiritual gifts and fulfilment. The first in a calendar year is Brigid or Bride, early in February, borrowed by the church as Candlemas. At this festival the Earth Mother was given thanks and simple offerings of the first spring flowers as a 'thank you' for the return of her son, the Sun God and hence spring, to the land. A special place, known in Ireland as Bride's Bed, was decked with greenery, bright cloths and snowdrops by the women. It was a time of hope for the warmer days to come, and each person in turn, women and men, knelt before the shrine and after pouring a libation of milk or water (or these days, wine) asked for a special favour, particularly luck in farming, or some skill a person hoped to develop with the Goddess's blessing, like poetry or music. At this time the Goddess was able to return to her virgin state, the New Moon Maiden, who has many names; Diana, Artemis and Olwen or Rhiannon are but a few of the more widely used.

As the year turns and the grass grows greener the cattle and sheep are driven from the sheltered valley winter pastures to the higher moors and mountains. This time is marked by the fire festival of Beltane, the 'good fire,' and the Goddess, seen in the foaming, scented blossom of the hawthorn, weds her son. Hawthorn is sacred for it was often used to hedge magical enclosures, and a staff of May wood, such as Joseph of Arimathea may have brought with him to Glastonbury, was a wand used by magicians. Children used to eat the fresh green leaves and call them 'bread and cheese'. These were the first signs that summer was on the way, and the many festivals of raising the May Pole were held. The dance of the Padstow 'Obby 'Oss, with his sinister black circular costume and tiny horse head, in the Cornish fishing village, is but one celebration of life overcoming the black death of winter. In many towns and villages a tall pole, freshly felled tree or ship's mast was erected in the square and it was decked with wild flowers and ribbons by the local folk. This was a sign of the returning power of the sun and it was captured by the children who danced about the May Pole, binding in the spirit of the sky as they wove their spider-webs of coloured strands on May Day. Now these ancient poles are gone, forbidden in the Reformation, when singing and dancing for the Lord, or for pleasure even, was condemned. In some places the festival has been revived, and school children vie with each other to be chosen as the May Queen, the pagan virgin bride, wedded symbolically to the Green King, or Jack in the Green, or even Robin Hood, Lord of the Wild.

The mayflowers bloom in mid-May, or even later, in many parts of Britain, but often the date of the celebration is fixed by the calendar, not by Nature herself whose wedding in the greenwood is a real part of the proceedings. Gypsy weddings, over the broomstick, often took place about this time, for the travelling folk have not forgotten their links with the wild world. The May Queen already carries the son who is the Sun, newborn at Yuletide, to bring light and warmth to her people. She is the mother and creator of all living things, the Sun is their servant. Decked in ribbons and flowers the folk celebrate the wedding, and those human pairs who wish to unite, hold hands and jump over a bonfire. Cattle are driven between two smoking fires on which are burned herbs of healing and protection, and they are driven on with wands of rowan so that no evil spirits will follow them to the summer pastures. The Beltane wedded ones celebrate in the woods and follow the cattle to the high hills to live all summer in bothies of leaves, or in huts of wattle, thatched with reeds.

Kipling was well aware of this country custom, and his poem 'Oak and Ash and Thorn', has seeped into the rituals of modern witchcraft. One verse goes:

> Oh, do not tell the priest our plight, for he would call it sin.
> For we've been out in the woods all night, a' conjuring summer in.
> We bring good news by word of mouth, good news for cattle and corn,
> For now is the Sun come out of the south, with Oak and Ash and Thorn.

Even the folksong about gathering nuts in May is probably a corruption of 'Here we go gathering *Knots of May...* ' sung as people broke the taboo of having hawthorn blossom in the house, and brought the sweet-scented branches in as a welcome to the Lady of the Green Wood and her Lord of the Wild.

Summer heat waxes and wanes until the time of Lammas, Loaf-mass or the day when the corn is cut and the grain winnowed and ground and baked into the first loaf of the season. Like the festival which surrounds 'Beaujolais Nouveau' it was a time of great rejoicing. Everyone would work long hours, cutting, binding, stooking and carrying the corn so that it would ripen fully, become dry and easy to thresh from the ears, and so secure a good store of life- giving grain to see them through the winter. The name of the feast is derived from the Sun God, known as Llew, or Lugh, or Hu, and so it was the Llew mass, the mourning feast of the dead God, slain and cut down, as is told in the song 'John Barleycorn'. His spirit, the life of the land, had to be preserved and kept sacred during the long, cold winter. Often special acts were performed when the last few stalks of standing corn, and with it the 'neck' of the sacrificed God, were cut through. In Cornwall the ceremony of 'Crying the Neck' is still performed on some farms, when rather than a particular individual being the 'killer' of the Corn Spirit, all the farm workers, cutting the corn with sickles, stand a few paces away and throw their instruments at the 'neck' so that no one knows for certain whose blade made the fatal cut. The last sheaf of corn stalks is carefully gathered and then it is woven into a 'Corn Dolly' or 'Kern King' according to the local pattern. These woven corn ornaments, usually preserving the ears of corn and bound with red ribbons to signify the living spirit, are hung over the mantlepiece, the equivalent of the house altar in a modern dwelling. All through the winter this 'Spirit of the Corn' can be admired and then at the spring sowing the grain is stripped and mixed with the other seed corn to be planted for the new crop. Often the ears of corn were chosen for their size and health and so this ensures a really good seed as no one, no matter how hungry, would dare to eat the Corn King.

There are Harvest Suppers, special songs sung as the last of the sheaves of corn are carried in from the fields, and plenty of drinking of the local brew of ale or cider to celebrate the climax of the arable farmer's year. Although the church also celebrates a Harvest Festival this is usually a bit later on, when not only is the corn in, usually cut in August, but the fruit and perhaps grape harvest has been gathered in. It tends to be the end of the harvest, rather than the beginning, which the older, pagan feasts are concerned with.

The last of the most ancient set of festivals of the British Isles is generally known as 'Hallowe'en' and is frequently looked upon as the time when evil is abroad and all sorts of eerie and ghostly goings-on occur. This is a fairly faint memory of the old time of gathering. The flocks and herds which had roamed the high pastures under the watchful eyes of the young shepherds and shepherdesses camping out in their 'summer houses' were brought down to their winter quarters. Some of them would find their way onto the supper table of their keepers, for in earlier times, winter feed was scarce and only a proportion of the livestock would be kept. Because of this necessary culling of the herds a feast would ensue, as well as a great gathering of the whole tribe, family or village. People would be reunited with their kindred after the summer separation and there would be a great time of story telling, of introducing the new babies to the others, and the recollection of any old folk who had died in that time. At the feast the First Parents were made welcome, in other words a place was set out with the best dishes, the whitest bread, the sweetest honey and the strongest mead or beer for the

Goddess and the God of the people.

The doors of the house would be left open so that latecomers could see the lights from the house to guide them in, and perhaps a bonfire was lit to cook the feast, and burn away the troubles of the summer. There was a special ceremony of welcome for the Old Ones, and the ghosts of the clan who had gone before would be welcomed back, to give advice and share their knowledge with the living. From this ancient custom have come the various games associated with Hallowe'en parties, like ducking or bobbing for apples, 'Trick or Treat' and fortune telling with mirrors and apple peel. The apple is the Celtic fruit of Immortality. The Silver Branch, cut from a flowering apple tree in spring was the passport of the Underworld/Otherworld where a traveller might meet fairies, gnomes and the King or Queen of the Dead. The fruit was not only the fruit of Knowledge, but of Immortality, and so by plucking one up from the water with your teeth, or eating it off a string without holding it in your hand, you were symbolically eating the fruit of eternal life and so gaining that for yourself. Peeling an apple with a knife to give a single long strip was another test of patience and care, and the finished peel, thrown over the left shoulder into the dark might well form a pattern or letter associated with your future, perhaps the initial of a spouse-to-be! Mirrors, too, always items of importance and value, are used to look into at midnight, by the light of a single candle. If you carry out this piece of ancient magic you may well see your future moving before you.

Of course, there are many more festivals in the year, some borrowed by the church and so altered from their earlier, more pagan fertility related symbolism and the ones particularly associated with the movement of the Sun through the signs of the zodiac will be discussed later in the book. Equally, many of these really old celebrations have been changed, altered, attenuated and added-to over the passing centuries. Some are still great times of public feasting, singing and dancing; others are private, local or almost forgotten altogether. Many are being revived, for these are special occasions when the very forces of the Earth may be felt by even the most city-orientated individual, and something of the old ways sensed in a modern setting.

Probably the original outdoor rites held at Stonehenge, at Avebury or any other sacred enclosures will never be made completely clear to us, but through methods of meditation and time travel the dedicated folk magician may be able to get extremely close to the traditional uses of such places. There are plenty of circles of standing stones, mounds and earthworks to choose from, and a first attempt to get near the source of the greater forms of natural magic is well worth the effort.

We have legends and songs, myths and stories to lead us closer to the ways of the old ones, and to witness and communicate with the God and Goddess in the landscape. There are mighty hill figures, cut out of the grass to show the white chalk beneath which illustrate the tales of giants and horses, dragons and monsters who guarded the land. We have the artificial womb-caves of the Long Barrows and tumuli where surely the initiates of the old, wild magic must have gone to suffer their ordeals and be reborn of the Earth Mother. If you can visit any of these ancient structures with a clear eye admitting the light of intuitive vision you may be able to see for yourself what used to take place there. Many new seekers have done this and have brought back more vestiges of the traditions of the past and the rituals which today are found only in fragments and shreds, scattered among countless customs and local feasts.

Look at the part of the Earth where you live. Get to know its structure and its uses, its myths and local customs. Study the history of your town - how long has it been there? What was there before? Are there any ghost stories, processions, seasonal gatherings, festivals or sacred sites in the area? Is there a holy hilltop or a healing well, an ancient earthwork or a place with special properties? There could be one such under the very house you live in, if you begin to look. You might discover some other key to the mysteries of Earth Magic, but they won't be the only ones you might come across, if you begin the search for the arts of traditional magic.

As well as the large earthworks and massive sacred sites and public festivals watch out for the legends attached to a tree or grove or wood in your area. Study museum collections for the healing spells, the fossils which have been found and polished and used as charms to ward off harm or illness. Witch-beads sometimes turn up too. These are small fossil sponges of white rock, varying in size from that of a small pea to a walnut or golfball, each with a clear hole drilled neatly through it, which formed part of the original creature from which the fossil has been calcified. These were often worn as good-luck bringers by members of the Old Faith, and usually strung on red thread or wool. See if you can find any other fossils; those commonly known as fairy loaves, or gnomes' bread may once have been starfish in some ancient sea. Belemnites or Elfbolts turn up in sandstones, flints have many marine fossils which were thought to ward off attacks by evil forces. Ammonites are especially interesting, for these marine snails form the pattern of the spiral, both right and left-handed. This has made them particularly valued by ancient people who saw in their coiled shape the pattern of progress, through the twisting maze of life.

Stones with natural eye shapes, those with coloured rings or holes right through were all looked upon as special. Certain trees, like the ancient churchyard yews, or mighty oaks are also part of natural magic, and the legends attached to each, peculiar though they may be to the area, form aspects of a store of traditional wisdom from which the seeds of practical crafts and new areas of magical skills may be reborn. Try to look at these familiar things with new eyes and you may begin to see.

There are whole studies concerned with the use of gem stones or minerals in magic and alchemy, as well as vast tomes on the uses of plants, herbs, trees and fungi, not only for obvious uses such as special foods and wines but for healing, to give special visions or dreams, and as a form of divination so that questions may be answered and clues to the future discovered.

3.

THE MAGIC OF WATER

A City may be moved, but not a well!

Hexagram 48, *The I Ching*

Although mankind has to a small extent shaped the landscape, and been directed in his affairs by the Earth herself, another important factor in the positioning of settlements, of crop cultivation, and eventually towns and cities has been the presence of fresh water. Whether in well or spring, in lake or in river, a source of clean water has been imperative to any attempt to cease from roaming, even in climates as abundant in rainfall as that in Britain. Once people began to farm the land and domesticate livestock, instead of just following the herds of wild game or relying on the available fruits, grains, roots and greenery to feed them as they travelled about, a supply of water was vital.

Even in the earliest settlements on the banks of streams or lakes there must have been a feeling of boundaries and limitations. It is probably for this reason that it is generally considered that the power of magic cannot cross running water. This is not absolutely true, for it is possible to send telepathic messages right round the world (and to spacemen, in this electronic age) and acts of healing can benefit a patient on the other side of the globe, if the spell is worked correctly. The limitation of magic by running water most likely indicates that each Village Witch or Cunning Man had a territory, bounded by rivers and streams, and her or his power was strongest on the folk who lived in that place. Certainly much country magic depended on the Wise Woman's knowledge of the people and livestock on her 'patch', especially when it came to fortune telling, or sorting out love affairs. A detailed knowledge of the lives of the locals would be a great asset, and as it was difficult or sometimes forbidden for anyone to stray outside the parish boundaries without good reason, it would be possible to learn a great deal about everyone in the village. Often the house of the local healer was at the edge of the community so that she could get out into the wild woods to gather herbs or cast spells without having to pass another dwelling.

Water is fascinating. Listen to a stream bubbling over stones, or watch a wide, suburban river snaking its way among concrete banks - it has a life-force of its own, which was discovered a very long time ago, and with it a number of sorts of natural magic, usually concerned with healing or cleansing someone or somewhere of harmful influences. Many of the most ancient sacred sites have pools or springs of water in or near them, so that worshippers at a shrine, or petitioners asking questions of an oracle could bathe and be cleansed before entering the sanctuary.

In many places each spring or well had a guardian spirit or Goddess, to whom small offerings were made. Sometimes these were pieces of cloth or paper tied around the branches of a nearby tree, or stuck on the thorns of the prickly hawthorn which often grew near water. Although the idea of a water nymph attached to a particular stream or pool is ancient we don't know what they were called. In some places - Wales and Cornwall, in particular - it is likely that saints with strange names were actually the pagan spirits who kept the springs running. From this guardian nymph/saint idea has grown the tradition of Well-Dressing, which takes a number of forms, according to the location of the well.

In the north of England well-dressing consists of creating a picture with flower petals and greenery, set into a bed of soft clay, all round the facade of the well or spring. In recent times the pictures have become Biblical scenes, relating to water or wine, like Moses striking water from the rock with his (divining) rod, or Jesus turning water into wine at the wedding at Cana, but probably in earlier times these pictures or designs would have been of a more pagan nature, laid out by the village folk as a tribute to the Goddess of the Spring. In Cornwall the ceremony may take several days and, on the whole, it is far less organised and Christian than in the north. At St Ives, in Cornwall, where there is a well dedicated to St Ea just above the beach, a whole weekend in February is dedicated to decking the surrounding wall of granite with greenery and early spring flowers, and particularly ivy. St Ea, an unlikely saint if ever there was one, was supposed to have been washed across the sea from Ireland on an ivy leaf bringing the teachings of Jesus to the Cornish people. The well, which doesn't cease running even in the very dry summers, and used to supply the entire village until a few years ago, was where she (or even he) was washed ashore. It is reputed to heal eye conditions and poor sight.

There were a number of processions of people in disguise (an old part of many pagan festivals, more of which later), some at night by flaming torch light, dancing in the street, and several other activities which have become attached to the well dressing but may have other ancient origins. A silver ball is thrown to the children on the beach below the church, in the morning, and they have to hang on to it until twelve noon and hand it in to the Guild Hall, where the ball-bearer receives a small prize. The mayor also casts from the Guild Hall balcony handfuls of hot pennies to the children below, who scramble for them. Although the garlanding of the well and even the prayers from a local priest, of whatever faith, are certainly parts of the well-blessing, as is the flambeau procession and dance, the silver ball and the pennies are derived from some solar feast. The idea of capturing the spirit of the Sun, the silver ball, and hiding it until noon, when the sun is at his highest in the sky turns up in a number of festivals all over the world, as does tossing hot pennies, which used always to be brand new ones which gleamed coppery-gold as they flew through the sky literally 'pennies from heaven' to reward the keepers of the festival.

Many wells are famed for their healing or other magical powers, and many traditional spells advise the sufferer, perhaps of a skin disease, to obtain the water from three different wells outside his parish, and then add certain healing herbs, like eyebright, to the water. This would ensure that the sufferer took sufficient care to be worthy of his cure, which was possibly affected by the Goddess of one of the three wells. Three, of course is the number of the Great Goddess, either as maid, mother and crone, or in her triple form of Goddess of Earth, Water and Moon.

Certain watering-places became world famous, and, in the

eighteenth century particularly, these traditional healing springs or fountains became the centres of pilgrimage and expectation of healing by the sick. Many of these health resorts are still well known as spas, where people still flock to bathe in the waters, or sometimes mud, drink from the spring and lounge about where they can be massaged or showered with healing draughts. One of the most famous is probably the city of Bath, not far from Bristol in the west of England. It is usually supposed that the Romans discovered the place and turned it into a delightful watering-hole, but recent excavations have provided considerable evidence that the place was known as a sacred area by the ancient Celtic people who lived there long before the Roman invasion.

Bath is a particularly fine example of a sacred spa and it also has legends of people being cured, like King Bladud, who suffered a skin ailment which looked like leprosy. He is supposed to have been cast out as a leper and taken to herding swine in the steamy marshes in the deep valley below the Iron Age fortress on Solsbury Hill. His pigs also suffered some unpleasant skin condition but they had the sense to roam about the marsh and wallow in the warm mud produced by the seeping hot springs. They were cured and Bladud, taking the hint, also wallowed in the steamy mire, and he too came out spotless.

The Romans, delighted by an endless supply of hotwater - it rises at a temperature which is too hot to touch, about 50°C, dedicated the whole area of baths and temples which they built to Sulis Minerva. Thus they combined, in typical Roman 'If you can't beat' em join' em' fashion, the name of Minerva, Goddess of wisdom and perhaps healing, and Sulis, whose name is derived from the Celtic Goddess of the Gap, already associated with the place. The Romans named the place 'Aquae Sulis', the Waters of Sul, and because they so often took over the local gods, adding a Roman name by which the folks at home would recognise the deity, set about building the temple and various baths around the springs. The remains of the swimming pool, hot, cold and tepid baths and a range of hot and cool dry rooms were all part of a large temple with elaborately carved stonework. The centrepiece is not a representation of Sulis Minerva but is a huge male face, whose beard and long hair and wide staring eyes show him to be of native Celtic workmanship. In his beard there are twining snakes, or perhaps eels, for Aquae Sulis is close to the River Avon, and beside his prominent ears there are wings, and about his face there are flames so this is indeed the image of a powerful Celtic God of the Earth and Sky. History has not passed down to us his name, but the calm, vast pale stone face has a vitality all its own, and must have been an awesome sight for visitors to the temple and the bathing establishment next door.

There are a number of smaller, more basic carvings of three goddesses, very much in the native form, as well as a grand bronze head thought to be Minerva. A tall, standing bas-relief of a Moon Goddess, with her hair piled up in a sea-shell shape, with the crescent moon making a halo also gazes calmly down from the restored pediment on those who come to stare, or even to worship, to this day. Perhaps this is the face of Sul herself carrying in one hand an entwined distaff or a whip to drive on her horses, if she is Epona, the goddess of the White Mare, whose vast image sprawls across a Wiltshire hillside not so many miles away. Even now, trampled by the feet of many tourists, this area around the steaming hot springs is still a holy place. Its ancient atmosphere of worship and communion with the Goddess has not been wiped out by the decay of nearly two thousand years, and rude uncovering by the curious.

Any place where water issues from the ground is a strange place, if you think about it. The interchange between the source within the inner Earth from which runs forth clear water, the very elixir of life, at the centre of the monument at Bath, where the hot water rushes steaming through its ancient red-stained curved archway, is a sacred place indeed. We cannot now stand on the gravel where the hot springs rise, nor can we cast offerings of carved jewels, coins or symbolic parts of the body to ask for a cure, but we can still marvel and sense the awe of the place. Here the Goddess of the Healing Waters is very strong, her steamy perfume of the inner earth indicates a place of blessing and of initiation. Here there is clearly an entry into the other world, a gap through to the world within - but few know the way to go through nowadays.

No doubt, in earlier times, before the Roman edifice was carved from its quarries, there were priests and priestesses here, to see that those who came for healing, or inspiration, made the correct offering and behaved within the sanctuary with decorum and honour. Surely there was an oracle here, or a source of arcane wisdom which the people could visit. We do know that people came here to petition the Goddess, and some wrote petitions to her on sheets of lead, asking that divine judgement be made upon the guilty person. The ancient Druid priests were also known to be lawgivers and experts in settling their petitioners' problems. Maybe they had a school here, or a place of healing, worship and wisdom.

Where a spring of water rushes forth from the Earth it brings some sort of beneficence from within the body of the Goddess, either as her healing tears or some other life-giving essence. It is a place of communion with the most simple and ancient powers, a source of wisdom, for within a pool shaded by oracular hazels the Celtic Salmon of Wisdom dwells. Find his secluded river and see if he will rise up with the magical nuts in his mouth to offer you knowledge of hidden things. The Celts often associated water or watery things with wisdom. They probably originated the saying 'Truth lies at the bottom of a well' - perhaps it does, for in a deep well you can see stars, reflected, even in daylight!

Inspiration is another gift of the Celtic Goddess, Cerridwen, whose name means 'White Sow'. She was a witch and cunning woman who contrived to give her ugly son the gift of knowledge. For a year and a day she collected herbs in their hour and stewed them in an ever-bubbling cauldron stirred by a young boy. Just before the end of the process of herbal alchemy the pot boiled over and splashed onto the hand of Gwion Bach, the cauldron-cook. He put his burned finger to his mouth and so received three drops from the Cauldron of Inspiration. It may be from a similar source that many poets and painters, artists and songmakers have been granted a taste, for like the Holy Grail, it may be there for anyone to discover for himself.

The Cauldron of Cerridwen is definitely pagan, and there are other similar pots, one of which will cook the food best liked by anyone who dares to eat from it, in myth and legend. Another would restore to life those slain in battle but they would remain dumb though otherwise well. King Arthur ventured into Annwn, the Celtic Otherworld to bring away from Pwyll, its keeper, the Cauldron from the dark realm. Each one could be acquired but it would cost a high price. In the stone temple at Tarxien in Malta a huge stone cauldron, about three feet high and nearly five across has been discovered, dating from the stone age. This indeed was a cauldron into which people might go to be reborn, healed of their ills, or received into the company of the Children of the Goddess.

The Holy Grail is the Christian half of the design, supposedly brought from the Holy Land, after Jesus was crucified. It was the cup of the last supper and Joseph of Arimathea, Jesus' uncle, is said to have caught the blood of the crucified Messiah, which many legends tell he then brought to Britain or at least Europe. In the Middle Ages the whole matter or Arthur became the central story of a wide variety of tales, lays and history. Even now the idea of the young king brought up by a wizard, who gains his father's sword and unites his kingdom, and gathers round him a band of the best knights in the land forms the core of space operas and TV films. The wizard, Merlin, is the archetype for the wandering hermit, healer and priest of the Old Religion, not bound by the conventions of those around him. There is also Morgan le Fay, the Water Fairy, who in various guises tempts both Arthur, when he comes to power, and finally Merlin, dragging from him the secrets of his magical arts, and eventually sealing him up, either like Osiris, in a hollow tree, or in a cave, where he may still be waiting. Once again the theme of the underground place of magical significance occurs.

Arthur, having fought his last battle with Mordred, his bastard son, is taken by boat, tended by three dark queens, to Avalon, the misty island over the westering water. Perhaps it is the Island of Apples, where he may be fed on the fruit of immortality until it is time to return again. Arthur did not seek the Holy Grail himself but sent his knights out, on the instruction of Merlin. Some were lost in battle, others found the Grail, under the care of the Fisher King in his lakeland realm, but did not know the vital question, which would restore his virility and the fertility to the land around. Galahad achieved the Grail, but it was too much for him, and he died.

The quest still goes on, whether it be for the Holy Grail, the

Water of Life, *Elixir Vitae,* or the Philosopher's Stone, sought by
the alchemists, which turns base metal into gold, or rough humanity
into the dwellers in paradise. Much magic and chemistry has been
learned on these various quests. Alchemy, the art of the Black Land,
brought from Arabia or Egypt, uses not only minerals in its chemical
processes, but also plants and seeds, made into tinctures and
infusions. Again the thread of old lore was woven into another part
of the tapestry of ancient magic, and though it was not visible in the
main design, throughout the passing centuries wizards and witches
kept up the research and use of all kinds of simples, the spells and
pagan religion. Merlin may well have been a Druid, even though
history places his and Arthur's age in the sixth century AD, after
the Romans had gone home. Arthur's battles were against the Saxon
invaders, who were trying to over-run the fertile Celtic homelands.

Because these myths or histories, depending on how you look at
them, are filled with archetypal characters and symbolic acts they
are the stuff with which modern seekers of our traditional mysteries
should be really familiar. The tales of Arthur and his knights, Merlin
and the various witches are all valuable keys to the Old Religion
and system of initiation which the past has tried to convey to us.
The first book to come off Caxton's printing press was Mallory's
'Morte d'Arthur'. If you examine what is going on throughout many
versions of the Arthurian legend you will begin to see that there is a
path for the initiate, seeking the keys and symbols of his past
tradition. It isn't obvious to a casual reader, but anyone who explores
the material with an intuitive eye will begin to see the pattern emerge,
like knotted animal designs, so beloved of the Celtic peoples, or the
mazes which they have left on stone and hillside.

In many lands there is the hero who sails off into the sunset,
from Britain and from New Zealand, from Irish myth to the American
Indians' heritage. Out there, beneath the setting sun, is a sacred
land, of the Ever Young, where the Fountain of Youth gushes forth
its living waters, and the Apple Trees bear the fruit of the Hesperides,
sought in Greek myth.

Islands have always been rather special places too. Most of the
small islets off the coast of Britain have had monasteries or the
cells of hermits, dating back in some cases to long before the

Christian era. Here on a remote rock, cooled by the sea breeze and lulled by the voice of the ocean, those who have sought communion with nature and the power of the elements have waited for inspiration and the voice of God. Who can say that the crying of gulls did not convey its message, nor the slap and wash of the waves on the shingle speak in whispers of some ancient mystery? There is something very archaic in the sound of the sea. Perhaps it is for this reason that when people began to take holidays, even a day trip to the seaside was what they preferred. Something about the vast flatness of the marine horizon, or the power of the waves which can pound hard granite into sand affects the human emotions and opens up an awareness to the forces of nature, and the magic of wild forces which city life, or even inland village or farm life, cannot match.

Along the sea shore there is a special place, like a magical circle, between the worlds, of land and water, of sky and earth. To go there on a quiet winter day and wander undisturbed can bring a great feeling of peace, and you can recharge your spiritual batteries from the energy of the tides. Searching for shells or small pebbles which may be used for divination, or for sea wrack which can be used to decorate your home or magical sanctuary brings you close to the power of water. Mariners have learned just how far it is possible to use the power of sea and weather, how to sail with the wind and use the tides to advantage. Such tides also run through the affairs of mankind, but most people are too dense to perceive them. It is another aspect of Natural Magic, to recognise the ebbs and flows of nature, and make use of them to benefit your own path through life and that of those around you.

Sailors, dealing with such an overwhelming element have always been a superstitious lot, and there are many taboos about what you may bring on board a ship or do when you get there. No one would bring a rabbit, live or dead onto a ship, nor would they whistle, for that would raise a wind which would blow the sails and rigging into shreds. Women were not welcome aboard either, for some of them might be witches, ready to lay a bane upon the nets or gear so that the fishing would be in vain. Some witches were good, though, and would sell a sailor a rope with three knots in it, to set free a gentle breeze, a strong wind and a gale, respectively.

Around the shores and holiday resorts the fortune tellers set up their booths, and Madame Sarah would tell the tar's fortune from the lines on his hand, or from cracked playing cards for a small silver coin. Even now, on the piers and arcades all along the sea front such clairvoyants and fortune-tellers still ply their trade. Here at the edge of land and sea there is room for the arts of divination and foretelling, the selling of charms for safe travel and good luck. Even the sticks of rock are probably derived from some earlier fertility charm!

Inland, divination took a different form - that of water-witching or dowsing, which comes from a Cornish word meaning 'to seek'. Anyone can learn to do it, just as anyone can learn to swim or ride a bicycle; there is a knack which cannot be taught in books, only gained from practical experience. Dowsers used to use a 'Y' shaped rod, cut for preference from a hazel bush, which the Celts knew as the Tree of Wisdom, or from waterside-growing willow. Each had his preferred size and shape, but if you cut one such twig you can try your luck. The grip on the twig is all important, for it is by stretching certain muscles, which the presence of water somehow seems to affect, that causes the twig to move in your hands. The traditional grip is to have your hands palm up so that the ends of the Y rest across your hands between your thumb and fingers. By closing your fingers into a loose grip and bending your wrists you will find that the third arm of the twig will be made to point slightly upwards. There should be just a little outward tension as well, but do be gentle for woods other than hazel or willow tend to split apart. Walk forward to some obvious source of running water, be it a stream or fountain or even a running bath tap. Once you get the hang of the grip you will find the twig begin to move slightly, either up or down, twisting within your hands. Don't grip too tightly, because this twisting force, in sensitive people, can be enough to raise blisters! It takes a few attempts to get it right but almost everyone can do it if they have the patience to learn how. Gradually, with practice, it gets easier and the movement clearer. Sometimes the rod will twist one way for water and the opposite way for holes in the ground, or metal cables or pipes. Keep on trying until you achieve some sort of regular response.

Another outdoor form of water or mineral divining rods may be made from a pair of wire coathangers, such as you get from dry cleaners. Cut off the long bottom rail and one of the diagonal side arms into one piece of bent wire. Form the bend into a right angle and find a hollow rod, which could be a section of bamboo cane, elder or rose wood (these all have soft' pithy centres which you can push out with the wire) or even the discarded outer of dead ballpoint pens. Any sort of short tube which can be easily gripped, and inside which the wires can turn freely will do. Use your imagination.

To use this form of divining rods you will need to learn to hold them parallel with each other and parallel with the ground, which should be flat, to begin with. Walk slowly forward towards or over a water source, for example the known course of a waste water pipe or garden hose, and watch how the rods behave. On most cases they will swing together and cross as you go over the water and then swing apart again. Sometimes they swing right round and point outwards along the line of the water pipe. Most people can get some sort of reaction with this simple set-up.

Once you are getting a regular and reliable movement from whichever kind of rods you prefer you can start tracing underground or hidden water supplies. It is best to stick to water while you are learning, but once skill has been gained this form of Natural Magic may be applied to all kinds of minerals, lost objects or archaeological remains. Gradually you will find the reaction becomes much more precise so that the rod moves and then stops so that pinpoint locations may be achieved. This is only really the first part of this ancient and strange art, for an experienced dowser can tell not only that there is water present, but its depth, speed of flow and direction, purity and mineral content, and how much effort it would take to reach and use. That only comes with dedicated practice, usually over a long period, but for fun, for tracing your home's electricity cables or gas pipes, for finding the runoff drain for an outbuilding etc. this can be a handy skill. You can teach your children the same thing, which they will probably find much easier than you did, because it is not necessary to understand how it works for it to work. You can play 'treasure hunting' by hiding a coin or a small prize in a metal box in the garden, or under a rug indoors, and see who can find it, or perhaps have a row of similar cups, one of which contains water, set on a table and covered with a cloth. Get everyone to test each and decide where the water is. You can repeat this with different substances and attune yourself to each, by holding a sample in your hands as well as the rods. For example you could have a glass marble, a coin and a natural stone, some water and some oil. Holding a specimen of each, go along the row testing until you are able to locate each substance in its hidden container. You may well surprise yourself as to the way in which these ancient forms of Natural Magic will work for you. You will need to ask the question 'Is it water in this cup?' or 'Is there metal in this cup?' as you go along the specimens. That way you will get a certain response only at the container of that substance.

Many wise women and healers have made their own wines, from the wild harvest of free fruits, berries, leaves and flowers. Most of the trees and plants are sacred to a specific God or Goddess; for example, dandelions, which make a fine, golden wine, are sacred to the Sun, and their leaves and flower petals, eaten young, offer healing for bladder complaints as the leaves contain iron and other valuable nutritious minerals. Certainly our ancestors weren't to know about vitamins but they recognised that as a spring tonic both dandelions and stinging nettles, made into soup or cooked like spinach, were of good to the body. Today, homemade wine making is a growing hobby and as it can cost a great deal less to make wine than buy it, for people with plenty of time and little income, it can provide a useful pastime.

Elderflowers, gathered in early summer, make a fine white sparkling wine, often called elderflower champagne, with a rich fruity bouquet. Later in the year elderberries, blackberries, rowan fruit and wild whortle or whin berries can be gathered and, with the addition of a little sugar and some wine yeast, soon provide excellent wines for ceremonies, for feasting or simply, pure enjoyment. Elderberry wine is a deep, dark red; blackberry, somewhat more ruby; and strawberry wine can be a delicate pale pink, but all are delicious. Gathering the fruit, whether from a sacred wood or from a 'pick your own farm can provide an essential link with the bounty of the Earth Mother, and if the processes of wine making or baking ceremonial food are dedicated in her honour, the chances are that the final product will be excellent. Any good book on country wine making will tell you how you can make the best of your local wild fruits, and so long as you are not greedy and pick every single blossom or berry, thus preventing a new cycle of growth the following year, you ought to be able to master the magical arts associated with festive fare.

Back on the theme of water, you should be aware that even taking a bath or going for a swim could be a way of getting in touch with the Goddess as ruler of water. You will certainly find that if you look at books of local history there will be references to wells and springs which were reputed to be places of healing or comfort. Often it was necessary to bathe in the waters, and considering that for many centuries the idea of stripping off your clothes, all in one go, and washing all over was looked upon with dismay, such action was taken extremely seriously. There is even a case of a woman being accused of witchcraft because a neighbour noticed that when she was washing her Sunday best dress she turned the pockets inside out to wash them too! This was considered to be so sufficiently strange that the poor old dame was tried and hanged! In those days it was thought that 'cleanliness was far from Godliness'. St Thomas a'Becket was known to be very holy because when they stripped the clothes from him after his death they were practically walking with the number of lice and fleas in them!

That is not the case now, and bathing in the pure water of life can be a pleasing and even religious event. By adding herbs like rosemary or lemon balm, tied up in a muslin or linen cloth hung from the tap, you can scent the water and bring relaxation and calm to yourself after a hard day. Learn about the magic of bathing herbs, and grow them in your garden. Drink them in the form of teas which bring the natural magic of peace and tranquillity in a much safer way than taking chemical drugs. Herbs don't have side-effects; they either work, slowly or gently, or they don't. Only personal experience will teach you what works best for you and your friends. There are a number of excellent, clearly illustrated books on the uses of herbs and plants in infusions, in baths and in massage oils, yet another branch of the Gentle Arts. Wallow in a deep, warm tub of scented water, imagine your troubles floating free and away to a solution. Allow a prayer of thanks to drift up to the Great Mother for allowing you to bask in her womb of warmth and comfort, and for the good things in your life. When the suds drain away taking with them your fears and problems you may well begin to find you arise like a butterfly, changed and renewed by this simple process. You may very quickly discover that problems do find solutions while you are relaxing and thinking of brighter things!

People who live inland often do not have any feeling for the tides of the sea, yet the same sort of ebb and flow runs through everything. Magic is an art which learns of these tides and uses them to best advantage. They are ruled by the moon and will be discussed at length in Chapter 7 on Moon Magic, but it is worth harking on the words of an invocation, written by Dion Fortune in her mystical novel *The Sea Priestess*. She writes of the Goddess, known to many as Isis,

> I am that soundless, boundless, bitter sea.
> All tides are mine and answer unto me.
> Tides of the airs, tides of the inner earth;
> The secret, silent tides of death and birth.
> Tides of men's souls and dreams and destiny,
> Isis veiled, and Ea, Binah, Ge.

Ea and Ge are very old names for the Earth Mother, and Binah is the qabalistic name for the 'Dark, sterile mother', a seeming contradiction in terms, but she is the mother who brought forth creation, self-fertile and alone.

There are tides of ordinary life of which most people are never aware, but anyone who sets out upon the fairy path of the Old Ways will become more and more certain of these invisible influences, which change the dull pattern of everyday life and toil into joyous adventure, if you are sufficiently daring to look destiny in the face. You may well know of the pattern of your dreams and feelings which changes as the moon waxes and wanes, or perhaps you haven't yet studied this. It can be very important, for both men and women have cycles of creativity and expansion followed by quieter, inward thinking spells.

The water element is concerned with feelings and emotions, and it is the Cup of Love that every true witch should aim to fill, and spill over from her own heart. Only by giving out love and tenderness, genuinely, not in a dramatic way, can you begin to earn the love and regard of others. If you can't or don't love how can you be worthy of love from someone else? Like respect, it has to be earned and paid for, but you can never give out or receive too much. Just as a cup cannot be truly emptied (if you pour out the water or wine it is full of air!), no person who is dedicated to serving the Old Ones and learning their ways can ever be bereft of love. Love your Mother the Earth, honour her as you walk upon her mantle, treat her bounty with respect and not greed, give thanks for the sunny day, the sound of birdsong and all the little joys of life and these will redouble. Walk about in a cloud of misery, hating the world and its myriad wonders, and gloom will deepen. If you are assailed by misery or depression ask the Lady of Life to ease your burden and guide you to a natural healing herb or potion. She can open a book in your hand or bring a friend with the answer to your door, if you will ask her. From flowers and sunlight a whole range of gentle medicines can be made which will, with the moon's tides, shift the deepest gloom, the darkest despair and the longest anxiety if you can reach out for such help, and admit you need a little tenderness and care. The All Mother will never deny you. Gradually certain aspects of the significance of such ordinary things as the earth beneath your feet, the waters of land or sea, the endless sky over your head will take on a life of its own and you will begin to understand the mysteries which are all parts of Natural Magic. You may learn the Crafts, master the magical arts and discover a fulfilling personal religion.

Water has always been thought of as holy, and it is frequently used to bless objects or people. In the ritual of Baptism, the believer, immersed in a pool or river, came forth ceremonially cleansed and reborn. It is often used in a similar way in magic, but unlike the church's Holy Water it isn't made holy by a priest blessing ordinary water, but it is taken from a spring or well which is holy in its own right. Most places have a Holy Well or a spring or fountain, or the spa waters which have always been used for healing. You may not know about your town's well, but if you live in the country you are certain to be able to locate the local water source, which may well still be in use. If this is the case, you will easily be able to get water if you want to use it in your magical work.

You can cheat by using bottled spring water, or collect rain, so long as you don't drink this unpurified. (You can buy water purification tablets from any chemist - people take them abroad on holiday if they doubt the purity of the water!). But if you really do want to explore the natural forms of magic it is well worth the effort of locating a spring or well, even in or near a town, so that you can have water direct from within the rocks of Mother Earth. It will be far more powerful, and you can symbolically add a few drops when you bath before a special occasion, or if you wish to bless yourself, or magically cleanse a place. Then you take a bowl of water, give thanks to the Earth from which it came, and the sky, from which the rain that made it, fell. Ask that it may drive away all sadness and other unpleasant feelings, and then with a twig of rowan, the magical 'lucky' tree, or elder, the Old Goddess wisdom tree, sprinkle water clockwise around the room, seeing the dark clouds of misery roll before you, out of the door. Then go round again feeling that the place is clean but empty, and finally, a third time, so that you can welcome bright sunlight, good 'vibes' and peace into the place. Make sure you actually 'feel' these things before being satisfied.

Washing your hands and face before a meditation can be used as another way of switching into the relaxed frame of mind you require, for you can see the minor troubles of the day being washed away, so that you are refreshed and ready to search into other realms of reality. It is very important to do this if you get into the practice of performing rituals. Then you will probably change your clothes as well, perhaps into something special for your working. This should always be a garment which is only used for magical work, just as you would have a different apron or jacket for working in the garden to that you might wear while cooking. Not only is it necessary to keep things used in magic physically clean, but make sure you don't touch them when you are in a bad mood, or show them to strangers - then you will have to clean them again.

4.
THE MAGIC OF FIRE

I am the Flame of God, and the Angel of the Sword, yet Man has taken me and tamed me to his purpose. I am a Lamp to his Path, yet at my hour of noon is nothing hidden, for I am the Light of the Mystery revealed. I am a torch and by me is the path revealed...

Modern magical ritual

Fire is another archetypal principle whose magical associations must go back to the roots of human history. The first fire was a gift from the Gods, in lightning or bush fire, and the people took it and tamed it for the hearth fire, centre of the dwelling place. Fire is a male element, its radiant heat and energy so clearly linked with the sun in the sky, with summer, and also with the destructive principle. At first, like wild animals, the people must have feared the flames which leapt from the lightning-charred tree, or raced across the grassland, burning all that lay before. Perhaps it was from this conflagration that man discovered the use of fire to char or roast animal meat, or crack the shells of tough nuts. He would see how the wolves and predatory cats shrank back from the flames and heat, and how, if a pile of wood could be kept burning at night no harmful creature would come near. It presented a challenge for he had to learn how to keep fire, how to make it grow and share it, how to start a fire, one of his earliest technologies. From his knowledge of knapping flints he would have seen sparks struck from the hard stone. He would have seen whole trees reduced to black charcoal in moments and perhaps he put these two pieces of knowledge together, striking sparks from flint on to dry, charred wood.

Fire not only gave him protection when he dwelt out on the verdant grasslands but would preserve his people from the bitter cold, and when they began to settle in caves he had fire for heating and cooking. It was also a new tool, by which huge logs could be hollowed for boats, or shaped for building. Small poles could be pointed in the fire and the heated wood was found to be a bit harder than ordinary wood. Newly felled spear shafts could be straightened in the fire, and brush lands cleared and made fertile by the ash of trees and plants. By lighting a ring of fires he could drive game into traps or protect a herd and prevent it straying in the night. Fire gave him many new skills and taught him new techniques.

Fire has always been thought of as sacred, and it is sad that whole generations are growing up who have never had a living flame in their homes. Central heating may provide comfort and save the drudgery of hauling coal and wood about the house, but sitting and watching real flames can produce an ideal state for meditation and realisation. Seeing pictures in the glowing coals, or the wavering smoke was a valuable asset to the old witches, whose humble huts were always centred on a fire. It was the fire which heated the seething cauldron in which broths were simmered, or in which the magical healing herbs were boiled, or the potions cooked. In the bubbles of boiling water and the fire under the pot, patterns of past and future were discerned. If the hut door was closed the sacred herbs could be burned, as in the Sweat Lodge, so that true visions of encounters with the Gods could be arranged. It is also possible that some of the Long Barrows and ancient stone buildings were used in the same way. Some incenses were ways of opening doors to the Otherworld, and in the dark, fire-lit hut it must have felt like another world of shifting shapes.

Today there are children growing up who have had no experience of a living flame. They live in centrally heated homes, which don't even have chimneys, and even cooking is done by electricity or the invisible forces of microwaves! Some of them come from high-rise blocks of flats so they are detached from the earth, having no direct contact with it, and certainly no garden to play in. It is no wonder that they can suffer spiritual deprivation and illness of mind or body. We are all creatures of the Earth and should have direct contact with our mother planet so that our spiritual roots may be fed from her infinite source of inner strength. We need the experience of Earth, and Water and Fire, just as we need Air to breathe to keep us alive.

Think about your experiences with fire. Did you grow up in a house which burned coal or wood for heat, or even cooked by this traditional method, or have you, too, grown up in an electric environment, where the only flames you encountered were on a birthday cake, or the artificial candles on the Christmas tree? Did you enjoy lighting bonfires in the garden, playing at cooking over a smouldering pile of damp wood, or did you simply stand with a crowd of adults round a great municipal bonfire on 5 November, and stare fascinated at the fireworks, bursting into myriads of silver and gold stars? Did you take up smoking cigarettes or a pipe, or anything else? Have you got this taste for inhaling smoke under control? It is important in magical training to be fully in charge of your own faculties, and to avoid anything which you know to be physically harmful.

Perhaps you are in a position to light bonfires, or your home still has working fireplaces, on which you can burn coal and logs, and so indulge in the ancient art of pyromancy, seeing pictures in either the flames or the glowing embers. From the hot red and grey ash, through the patterns of the dancing golden flames to the twisting wisps of smoke there are many levels at which the perceiving vision can read the answers to questions. If you have never seen the shimmering heat palaces in the hearth, or the black and grey charred towers in the heart of a dying bonfire, you may have missed a valuable opportunity to awaken the gentle art of fire scrying, or of rebuilding those strange ancient links with a part of our heritage that is passing away.

Fire plays an important part of magic. It is nearly always preferred by those who use the old arts to light their meditations, to illumine the crystal ball they are scrying in, or to change the ordinary lights and shadows of a mundane room into a sacred, candle-lit sanctuary. It does appear that the gentle and moving light from a candle can help those subtle changes in consciousness which lie at the heart of true perception, effective magic and inner awareness. Just as the harsh glare of electric light is dimmed to a single candle flame, so the glittering distractions of everyday life are banished beyond the circle of flame-light. There is a tangible difference to the feel of the place, although nothing but the light-level has been altered.

Fire also has an important part to play in traditional celebrations, many of which were called 'Fire Festivals', like Beltane, from the words 'Bel', meaning either 'good' or 'lord' as in Baal, and 'tan' which is Welsh, and Romany, for 'fire'. Fires were used widely in agriculture; at first to clear the forests which once almost totally covered Britain, so that the fertile ash of the burned trees would enrich the land. Fires were also lit to celebrate any major event, either of a local nature or because it was a traditional date of celebration - the end of winter, the completion of the harvest, the longest day, Yuletide. All had their season and their reason. Even today, many a civic event is concluded with a display of fireworks, a much more spectacular but equally fiery demonstration of joy or excitement.

As well as the heat to cook food, warm the dwelling place and provide light from candles and simple dips, fire has a magical side too. We still find that special aromatic gums and spices are burned as incense in Roman Catholic churches, and in the rituals of Buddhists, Hindus and pagans. Traditionally, it was supposed that the rising smoke would carry aloft the prayers of the faithful, or that its scented fumes would drive away harmful spirits, or diseases. Today, most magicians and witches still burn some sort of incense, either the traditional grains, which are burned on charcoal blocks, or the familiar 'joss-sticks', obtainable in many a supermarket or healthfood shop.

As each tree or herb is associated with the power of a particular planet, and so God or Goddess, special fires were lit, using the symbolism of that force, so that the patterns in the embers formed an oracle, or the scent of the smoke attracted that entity before the fireplace. Shamans would be shut up in a small hut and a small smouldering fire of wood and herbs would be lit. After inhaling this magical smoke they would be able to communicate with their ancestors or receive information about the whereabouts of game, or a way to help their tribe. It is possible that some of the 'Long Barrows' or hollow 'burial mounds' found all over Britain and Europe served a similar purpose. Within the darkness and close confines, the drifting patterns of herbal smoke may well have taken on the form of an ancestor or spirit, or the effects of the concentrated, drugged fumes may have awakened inner vision on the part of the shaman. Certainly the narcotic effect of many herbs has been known for a long time, and there are a number of poisonous plants which are fatal when eaten, but their alkaloids may have a beneficial effect when burned. It is not a field of experimentation that the average novice magician should try for himself, however, as the difference between an ineffective dose of a particular herb and a lethal one can be very small!

It is much safer to leave this aspect of fire magic well alone, and concentrate on the gentler arts of candle making, burning sweet woods on a hearth fire, or magical herbs on an outdoor bonfire, rather than risking life and sanity on the effects of an unfamiliar plant. Because candles are frequently used in magical rituals, and in the more basic arts of meditation, or inner journeying, it is well worth learning how to make them for yourself. Although for magical use it is perfectly permissible to use ordinary white household candles which are known to burn steadily and not splash hot wax all over everything, sometimes it is preferable to involve yourself totally in the work and have a hand in making many of the items required for yourself.

The easiest way to learn about candle making is to get a book from the library on the method from a hobby shop. In this way you will have the basic knowledge before you as well as materials which are quite safe, and which will result in candles which burn properly. You can cheat a bit, by buying some ordinary household candles and melt them in a double boiler, that is a tin can floating in a saucepan of hot water. If you rescue the wicks and decide to make your own candles about the same size as the professional ones, then you have all you need. Colour may be added by shredding wax crayons and carefully stirring in the colour to the plain wax as it melts. This is rather rough and ready, but you can often achieve pale colours this way. Be very careful not to mix wax in actual cooking pots as it is very hard to get rid of, and tastes horrible in food! The same applies to using spoons, graters or anything else from the kitchen, especially if it isn't your own! You will still need to make suitable moulds out of metal or heat-proof plastic. Objects like cigar tubes or containers of a similar shape are the most conventional, if you want to burn your candles in ordinary candlesticks. Otherwise you can use yogurt pots to make short, thick candles, rather like night-lights. These really need a thicker wick than the finger shaped ones, and you will need to experiment before using these for meditations etc. as they might splutter or go out, or worst of all, flare up and be dangerous.

Candles are very useful when you are learning the Gentle Arts, for their dimmer, moving light somehow seems to help with meditations, and you can really feel that the small, defined circle they produce is a sphere of light and safety within the world's darkness. Not only can you see them just as a source of light, by which you may read the words of an inner journey narrative, but also they can become miniature friends from another level of existence. Flames have always been seen as living beings, born of darkness, and by becoming willing to try to communicate with them, you may awaken an ability to talk to the fiery spirits.

You will need a safe candleholder, a new candle and a little oil (almond is the best, but ordinary cooking oil will do). You can buy special anointing oils, but by adding a few chips of aromatic wood, like cedar or sandalwood, you can make your own. Allow the oil to stand in the sun so that it is slightly warmed and the scent of the wood is absorbed into it. With this oil anoint the candle from the base up, being careful not to get oil on the wick. As you do this, imagine that the spirit of fire will be able to inhabit the candle and when it is lit, to communicate with you. Stroke the oil in for a few moments, allowing yourself to become still and quiet, and then you may notice the candle starts to feel different, more 'alive' or charged with energy. Once it has that feeling you can carefully place it into the holder and light it. Let the flame settle down, and be sure there are no draughts which will make it flicker wildly. Try not to breathe on it as you ask questions, as this too, will make the flame unsteady.

When the candle is burning clearly, look at it for a few moments, watching the movement of the flame, the different colours within it, and any smoke or lumps on the wick, so that you can see what it does left to itself. When you are ready, feeling calm and alert, begin to see if you can get the spirit of fire to talk to you. If you ask simple questions to which the answers are 'yes' and 'no' you may well find the candle can express its answers by different movements of the flame. Ask if it will talk to you, does it have a name, is it a separate being, can it answer some of your problems? Be patient and watch, you may be very surprised at receiving a reply to your enquiries. If it doesn't work the first time, gently snuff out the flame with your fingers, and try another time.

Of course, if you have the opportunity to gaze into the embers of a hearth fire, or among the charred remains of a bonfire, you may well encounter other messages from the spirits of fire and heat. It depends on how well you feel you can let yourself seek such guidance from such an unexpected source. Wisdom is to be gained from each of the ancient elements, if you have patience and openness of mind to seek it. Our ancestors made friends with all the natural things around them. They could learn from animals and birds, detect the changes in the weather in the patterns of the clouds, and from the glowing peat or wood under the family pot, read aspects of the future, if they had a mind to.

To adopt aspects of the Gentle Arts will require you to change your views about the inanimateness of things, and directly ask them for help or information. Developing an affinity with flames, and being able to discover messages in their movements in answer to your questions will require a different point of view to that of most people. Only by gradually developing this kinship with natural forces and accepting that a two-way communication can come into being between you, will you be able to understand the forces in nature and so control or direct them at your need.

There are two main ways in which you can come to terms with fire and magic. One is to use a different coloured candle, of your own making, if your efforts are acceptable to you, for each day of the week, to ask for certain things associated with that day and its planet, and to give thanks for benefits which you have received. The other is to develop your own set of Fire Festivals, albeit on a small scale, unless you live in a village which is looking for ways of attracting visitors, or wants to revive ancient traditions.

If you have any knowledge of astrology it will help you to

understand the main principles of each planet, or you can read books which tell the stories of the Gods and Goddesses after which the planets are named, or you might find a list of the magical correspondences which link a colour, gem, plant and energy with each. You may well discover that no two lists agree, so in the end you will have to build up your own, based on what you learn by practical experience. In magic, practical knowledge is worth any amount of other people's theories or their experiences. You must have enough courage to try things, carefully, for yourself, and gradually build up data on what works for you, and what apparently doesn't. This takes time and commitment, but if you begin with simple things like the symbolism of each day of the week, and by burning a candle of the correct colour, you will make a firm foundation to other magical work.

As there are no absolutely fixed colours, you will have to decide for yourself which feels best. Also, unless you have had a lot of experience in making candles, it is most likely that you will have to buy new ones for any candle spell you choose to do, and you may not find the colour you first wanted in the shops. Black candles, which are sometimes used in rituals of the planet Saturn, or in Death and Re-birth initiations, are sometimes harder to find, except in the special occult suppliers, so use dark blue or grey instead.

Taking the planets in the order of the days of the week, you have the Moon, traditionally represented by white or silver or pale grey for Monday. Tuesday is attributed to Mars so scarlet, or any bright shade of red is best. Wednesday has changeable Mercury which can be orange, according to the Qabalistic Tree of Life, or pale blue, or even opalescent colours. Thursday is Jupiter, traditionally either clear purple or royal blue. Friday is Lady Venus' day and is usually green, but can be turquoise or even pink, according to some authorities. Saturn, the sombre planet of Saturday, is usually dark grey or black, but can be dark earthy brown, or even dark red, depending on what you are able to find or make. Last, Sunday for the Sun is gold or yellow a bright and healing colour.

If you cannot find all those different colours of candles and you do seriously want to explore the Gentle Art of candle burning, another alternative is to buy at least seven candle-holders, which take standard candles and are unlikely to fall over easily. If these are clear glass you can suggest the correct colour of the day or planet quite simply by standing the holder on a fireproof mat or plate of the right colour. You could get plain metal candlesticks and paint these to match the colour of the day, or, if you had the resources, you could collect a set made of the metal associated with each planet: Moon, silver: Mars, iron: Mercury: technically quicksilver, so unless you can get one made of dental amalgam, try aluminium: Jupiter, tin or brass: Venus, copper: Saturn, lead, pewter or ebony: and finally the Sun, gold or gold coloured brass or any other metal. Should you set about scouring your local junk shop or flea market you will be surprised how the Gods can help, and even the most unlikely magical object can turn up, when you need it, and at a price you can afford.

It is true that you will have to pay for your magical results, but it will always be a fair price. You can achieve many things in an occult way that your ordinary methods would not help with, but you will still have to pay in time, in effort, in commitment or by exchanging some item. Things will disappear, or drift out of your life, once your magical will awakens, for this will be the price for the thing you asked for. Magical results, like 'fame', cost and you *do* have to pay! In physics and in the occult realms you don't get anything for nothing. Energy may be changed but it can never be either destroyed or created. This may sound dull, but if you awaken your inner vision you will soon learn to trust it, and find that it will lead you to the opportunity or objective you are seeking. By learning to listen, being passive and patient, you will allow your magical faculties to work in harmony with the power of nature to help you accomplish your will. Divinations will reveal the best path to follow, intuition will open closed doors for you and the calmness you derive from regularly practising the Gentle Arts will give you confidence and inner strength, and you will find you can cope with any situation to your own advantage.

You can begin to awaken this perception by performing some candle spells. You will need a quiet, undisturbed place, a candle, either of a particular colour or with a corresponding holder. You will need some scented oil, a box of matches and a clear idea of a small problem with which you need help. It will be to your advantage to have tried 'talking to a candle' before, and got some idea of the responses that they can make. Some flame spirits can be extremely eloquent and convey information clearly, while others are reluctant or sullen. Treat them all like friends and, no doubt, communications will improve.

Choose a time when you won't be disturbed, and on a clean piece of paper, with a new coloured pen, if you have one, write your aim. This should be something simple, like 'Help me to find a book which will teach me about the Tarot', or 'Guide me to find like-minded souls in my home town', or 'Help me to cure my migraine headaches without drugs', etc. You will have had to decide which planet is most closely associated with the problem. The first of those above would be addressed to Mercury, the Lord of Communications, Writing and Thievery; the second request could be made to Venus, the Green Lady who rules partnerships, friendship, growth, gardening (you might meet a magical companion at a flower show!) and nature. The third matter, health, comes under the jurisdiction of the Sun, and often it is a good idea to walk in the open air and sunshine after doing a healing ritual, either for yourself or someone else.

When you are ready, sit still for a few moments and allow yourself to relax and become aware of your magical self. Take the holy oil and say quietly, 'Lord Sun, . . . or Lady Venus (etc.), bless this oil that it may help me to form a true link with this candle so that I may learn from it and gain my desire.' Make up any words you like, and if you like to use the qabalistic angels, or Christian saints or pagan Goddesses instead of the planetary names, and you are certain of what you are doing, use them instead. Stroke the oil up the candle, avoiding the wick, until you feel the change from an inanimate object to a living thing. Wipe your hands on a tissue or cloth, so that you don't get the matchbox oily, and then, again asking a blessing of light on your problem, light the candle. If you are a perfectionist, you might use red-headed matches and strike them on a rough stone rather than a matchbox, or even flint and steel, as these are the older ways of making a flame.

Allow the candle flame to burn steadily, and then read out your wish. Fold the paper and place it somewhere safe, but nearby. It has now become a magical talisman, and should be kept until it has been accomplished, or until you are certain that you asked for the wrong thing. Now, treating the candle as if it were a friend, discuss your problem, quietly. Allow plenty of time for the flame to give you an answer by shaking its flame, or stretching or quivering etc. Flames can be very expressive, if you watch them with awakened vision, seeing the bright aura of fine filaments reaching out from the burning core. Sparks might fly, or drips of wax form the shapes of answers, just as tea-leaves may reveal the future. Even the wick can seem to form a question mark or some other indication that communication has been made. Do not hurry!

Talk about anything you like, for a few moments, always trying to preserve the relaxed body but alert mind state which is the key to all magic. Become aware that you are both beings of light, you shining with Earth light, yet recognising you are made of the stuff of stars, and that the flame is a being of heat and brightness. Feel the warmth, examine the way the light differs from modern electric light, commune in silence until you are sure something has been told to you, or that the audience is ended. Say a few words of thanks, even if you are not sure what has happened. Always treat beings of other orders of creation with respect and honour. Wet your fingers and pinch out the wick. This is the correct way, for if you blow out a candle, on the mundane level you splash wax about, and on the esoteric level you are using breath, the element of life, to quench something. Learn to pinch out a candle or even a taper swiftly, showing the daring which, even in the Gentle Arts, is an asset to any magician. Remain still for a few more moments. Absorb the atmosphere, the darkness, the inner stillness, before getting on with life. Take your folded request and place it under the head end of your bed, until something has happened to demonstrate your magic is working. Then you can relight the same candle and burn it, as a 'Thank You'!

Don't expect spectacular results. The book you require will turn up in the library, if you make the effort to go there a few times. The companion may be on a bus, or in the launderette, or at a lecture on archaeology or mediaeval history. You may find that by learning to relax as for meditation and inner journeying you can take control when a migraine threatens and turn it aside, or you might encounter an alternative therapist who can teach you ways of coping. The results of magic will always look like coincidences. People, books, or objects will 'just turn up' if you have a need for them. Accept them in that light and always offer a word of thanks for the accomplishment of your desire.

As you learn more you will be able to discover what properties the other colours of candles may have to benefit you on your quest for knowledge. You will be able to decide whether the waxing, waning, full or new moon phase is best for your purpose. You will find that by using this ancient fiery art you may awaken parts of your own inner light which has been dimmed by modern life and its stresses, and so you can enlighten the lives of others around you.

Do be patient and don't rush out to the nearest shop and on coming home with a bundle of rainbow candles launch into rites for psychism (Moon), energy (Mars), intelligence (Mercury), success in business (Jupiter), luck in love (Venus), the patience of Job (Saturn) and total health from the Sun in a few days. You will end up with psychic indigestion for which the only cure is months of abstinence from any sort of occult activity! If you feel frightened, as well you might, remember that the Gods want to help you. Your fear comes from unresolved matters within you, and because magic opens these fast-shut doors, some of the experiences and feelings which ooze through are unsettling or frightening. It is all a part of learning about the inner realms, and you will simply have to put up with it, complete the spells, finish the meditation, and say firmly, to yourself as much as anyone else, 'It is my will that I master these ancient arts, may the Great Ones help me and keep me safe.'

Be assured, black magicians aren't lurking round every corner to latch onto the fumbling efforts of any novice magician; they are far too busy in politics and places of power over nations. Any upsets are your own and coping with them teaches you the confidence and strength which you have under your control. Act with common sense, slowly and carefully and you won't come to any harm. If there wasn't any strangeness in what you are trying to do there would be no magic either, and the faster pulse, the anticipation and excitement are all parts of the process. As you master the Gentle Arts they become signs that the work is going well, rather than hindrances. You would have the same anxieties if you had taken up parachute jumping or scuba diving, I am sure! In each case, it is part of the fun and the attraction of the activity.

As well as coming to terms with the magical applications of fire as a way of receiving communication or imagery it is necessary to understand thoroughly the destructive aspect, and to know what to do if something unexpected should happen. It is a sure sign that some magical energy is present if the candle flames are all fluttering in different directions, or if the incense sparks and crackles unexpectedly, when you know that the charcoal block is fully alight (as it should be before you add the incense grains). Occasionally the glass in a lantern or even the specially prepared coloured glasses used in sanctuary lamps may break with a loud crack and shattered hot glass shards may be flung all over the place, especially during very potent workings. You should be well aware of the best ways of putting out fires, if, for example, a candle falls over and sets fire to the altar cloth or carpet. You should realise how dangerous oil fires can be, for if you happen to be cooking chips after a hard rite, and not paying sufficient attention, you can find yourself in the middle of a fierce blaze. In both cases it is worth being very careful about what you are doing, and to be ready to act in case of emergency.

In the temple it is best to keep a bucket of water or even sand to quench the occasional candle fire, which can be surprisingly hot. A small flame such as this has been enough to melt the lead base of a silver candlestick, and burn half-way through a mahogany tabletop! If you cook with deep fat or oil it is well worth investing in a proper fire blanket, for throwing water on oil or electrical fires (again a hazard of plugging too many appliances, even in the temple, into one socket) could be fatal. Robes should have tight or short sleeves and any other clothes or gear that come close to the lights are worth fire-proofing with spray for your own sake.

If you light fires out of doors do take precautions there too. It is very important to realise how easily a grass fire can be started, which in turn can spread and set fire to fields of standing corn, cut hay or other combustible materials, including other people's barns or houses! Take great care if sparks are flying on the wind. It is far safer to build all fires on riverbanks, or the sea beach, well clear of anything which could go up in flames. A small mistake could cost you a great deal of trouble, or even your life, if you were particularly foolish. This warning is aimed especially at people who have not had as much experience with fires as had their grandparents, for a small bonfire, untended for even a few moments while seeking further wood can turn into a blazing inferno if the wind is in the wrong direction. It can rush through dry heather on moors, or through standing timber much faster than you can run, and thick smoke can blind you so that you cannot find a way to safety. If you are in the countryside and see someone else playing with fire, or younger folk with matches, do warn them, and in the event of trouble, be ready to call in the Fire Brigade. This may sound alarmist but it is far better to be prepared and always act sensibly, especially when you are dealing with potent and wild forces outside your everyday experience.

Indoors there are other problems, which although not specifically magical, might happen in your home. Much modern furniture burns with great speed and gives off highly toxic fumes. I sincerely hope your magical working never causes you to experience this sort of change of lifestyle first hand, but it could happen in a place you are in. If somewhere does catch fire, shut the doors, get all the people out of the building if possible and call in the experts. Dialling 999 can be a life-saving magical act, and is infinitely more sensible than trying to put out furniture which could easily be giving off poisonous fumes all the time.

You will need to understand how to master the Gentle Arts, but by common sense and working with the forces of nature, rather than by simply demanding what you will to come to pass and hang the consequences. Learn the dangers of the Elements, as well as their magical powers. Learn a few basic rules of safety which will apply just as much in the temple as they will picnicking in the country, or climbing mountains. Study things like fire fighting, first aid and the practical skills of ordinary life, for it will help you to become a more useful member of the community, and often you will be able to apply this knowledge where that about the meaning of the Tarot trumps would be useless. Always be alert and act with caution if you are trying something new, especially if you are playing with fire!

5.
THE MAGIC OF AIR

It was as if the strong wind had risen to a hurricane. You never quite
know how hard the wind is blowing when you are sailing with it. It is
a very different thing when you come to turn against it...

We Didn't Mean to Go to Sea, Arthur Ransome

It should be very obvious that Air is a rather intangible substance,
yet as we air-breathing creatures know, it is just as important to our
existence as the earth beneath our feet, and the water we drink. The
ancient people recognised that it existed and had certain properties
but did not know the chemical composition of our atmosphere until
the eighteenth century. In many of the earlier texts they talk about
'Ether' or 'Aether' and give it spiritual as well as life-sustaining
qualities. To the magician, Air is the element of intellect, the mind,
and so by learning to control our consciousness, again by the most
gentle methods, it is possible to work beneficially with the element
Air.

   In ritual work, Air is generally represented by something sweet-
smelling, particularly incense or joss-sticks, but out of doors you
can always use scented flowers, just as you can in your house, if
the family objects to the church-flavour of real incense. It is worth
trying out the different sorts of scents available to you for meditation
and the like, for just as altering the lighting to the natural glimmer
of a candle can help you put aside your mundane self, so by changing
the atmosphere by burning an appropriate perfume can you further
change your inner awareness. Scents are extremely evocative, and
though we humans have lost a great deal of the sensitivity of our
noses, memories of a very distant childhood can be instantly recalled

by the smell of a flower, the plastic that favourite toys were made of, or the perfume our mothers wore when we were very small.

The reason that scent does have a potent effect on recall is because the olfactory, scent-sensitive nerves, are actually a part of the brain just above the nose. The eyes are connected at the back of the brain by some quite complicated cross-over wiring, but the nose goes straight to the seat of consciousness. Even with our dimmed senses, we are able to detect hundreds of specific scents, and anyone who doesn't smoke and practises a bit can come to recognise even the faint perfume of many wild and useful flowers in a meadow in summer. You can play games with a friend or your children, by being blindfold and trying to identify objects just by their odour - you may be surprised how well you do. Sometimes, if you become very psychically sensitive, you will detect the perfume of a flower or incense somewhere quite unexpectedly, and there are many magicians who find that entities from the other realms of existence may make their presence felt in this way. Ghosts, too, can return to their old haunts and carry with them their particular favourite scent all around them.

Although incense grains are not so easy to come by as are joss-sticks, it is worth writing to one of the many occult suppliers for some samples of the real thing, if you are going to indulge in some of the more practical aspects of the Gentle Arts. You will need something to burn the incenses in; the most basic object is a good old fashioned terracotta flowerpot, filled to the top with either sand or dry, fine earth. You will also need some charcoal discs or blocks as the incense gums and resins don't burn without a source of heat. You can buy or make a chafing dish of glazed, fireproof clay, or obtain a thurible, either with or without chains. These can be quite dangerous in the hands of a novice, so do practise a bit with them empty, if you intend to start swinging them around to consecrate your room. Incense, burned on charcoal, gets very hot, so protect the table with a heatproof mat, or tile. Also, if any red-hot charcoal flies out of the thurible it can set fire to a house, or, if you are out of doors, the whole countryside. Always be very careful, both with candles and any other flaming or hot materials; also, if you use swords and daggers. No one wants to be directly harmed by any of these ancient arts, and any act which endangers other people or threatens animals or land should be firmly excluded from your activities.

Although many of the skills of magic go on inside your head, it is no less a reason not to be careful and thoughtful in your studies. The powers you may come to be dealing with run the entire universe, and to handle the forces that even a solo magician can raise takes considerable self-assurance and expertise. It is all very well deciding to light a Fire of Azrael, as is described in Dion Fortune's novel *The Sea Priestess* but you will have heart-failure when the Angel Azrael turns up to answer your enquiry! Always think very hard about what you are doing, and if you have any doubts, please leave well alone. Far less harm is likely to occur if you avoid action, and you can always ask either that your knowledge be increased so you can cope, or that someone else comes along who has the experience and skill to deal with the problem. When in any sort of quandary, ask for guidance; it is almost certain to be forthcoming if you lookout for the message in whatever form it may be conveyed.

The human mind, and the trained imagination of a competent magician, are the greatest tools we possess. The most basic techniques of meditation, the ability to still your buzzing thoughts and so journey through other worlds and to create in those mental worlds the images of what you wish to bring about are the true keys to the mysteries. There is no elixir which will grant you that control, however, except hard and patient work, nor can any other 'Mage' tap you on the head with his wand and grant you the power over life or destiny. These can be earned, certainly by anyone with a bit of patience, a bit of common sense and the interest to go on with the dull exercises until they work well. Magic does work instantly, but only after you have taken several years of determined study to make it do so! Also, you need to build up credit in the astral bank with the right sort of currency to pay for the results you are asking for.

Most of the traditional incenses are gums, resins or crushed shreds of scented wood, like cedar, sandalwood or pine. The gums may be collected from apple or cherry or pine trees, but most of the more exotic ones come from around the Mediterranean Sea. The very dry wood of apple, pear, cherry, pine and balsam poplar, and the dried sticky buds of this aromatic poplar make a very pleasant incense, if you want to use homegrown materials. The charcoal blocks on which the incense is burned are different from barbecue charcoal as they have a proportion of nitre or other chemicals added which cause the blocks to spark furiously when first lit, and then continue to glow for about half an hour per whole block. When you light the block, do so carefully, allowing space for the sparks to fly without harming anything, and once the line of sparkles has gone right across the block and it is seen to be glowing gently, add a few grains of the incense or a pinch of the crushed wood.

If you aren't familiar with burning scented gums etc. it is best to get your supplier to send you packets of individual ones, rather than a blend which might not appeal to you. Some of the resins have a warm and soothing scent, others are sharp and lemony, some are acrid and musky, some burn with little actual smoke and some, particularly myrrh, have a thick white or grey smoke which catches the throat of anyone who uses too much. Some ordinary culinary herbs will burn, and those woody ones like sage and rosemary are quite pleasant. You can try drying the unused stalks of any herbs you use adding them to incense, like thyme, oregano, lavender and so on. Have a hunt around the herb garden or local hedgerows to see what goodies might be useful if you wish to have a selection of scents traditionally associated with the various planets. Back up the local selection with a few of the more common imported gums, like frankincense, benzoin, copal; or the plants including Dittany of Crete, Lignum Vitae wood or sandalwood. Most suppliers have a long list of available gums and resins, but a small amount will be plenty for you to decide if you like a particular scent, or effect. Some will make you cough and splutter, others will have no particular effect, so beware the blended incenses for 'Midsummer Rites' or 'Healing the Chakras' as these could contain materials which upset you. It is better to work slowly and aim to mix your own from safe and pleasant ingredients.

Another factor, which might come to your attention if you begin to study incenses and their effects, is the simple and automatic matter of breathing. In the Eastern arts of yoga in its many forms, breathing in special ways plays an important part in the training. In the West, although the physical postures are not usually adopted, as we are more accustomed to sitting upright in chairs, rather than cross-legged on the floor, the way you sit for meditation and magical work is important. So is being able to breathe deeply and regularly during any exercises, and this means finding a seat which supports your spine and neck, so that even as you relax thoroughly you do not slump and choke yourself. There are a number of simple exercises which will help you become calm and in the right frame of mind to meet the Gods of the Old Ways, or to commune with your own inner perceptions. Different paces and patterns suit different people so you will need to try out a variety until you feel happy and achieve acceptable results. You will also need to be able to feel your own pulse, either with your fingers on the opposite wrist, or in your neck, beside your windpipe. Never press hard on any pulse point, but relax and allow yourself to feel and count without any pressure. If you concentrate you can often detect a steady pulse in your face without having to touch it with your fingers. You will need to be able to judge the beat to use it as a regular count for some of the breathing and concentration exercises as it is less distracting than actually counting numbers or seconds with a watch.

It is worthwhile finding out what your normal pulse rate is by counting for a timed thirty seconds and doubling it. When you do start the various Gentle Arts which require you to sit still for a while you will discover that your pulse, and heartbeat, will slow down, so long as you are not getting too excited by the images that you are working with, or too scared by what seems to be happening. Meditation is known to lower blood-pressure, and can change the chemical composition of your blood by allowing the adrenaline levels, those fight or flight stimulants, to drop to a more peaceful state. This can make you feel more calm and relaxed all over.

The pattern of breathing exercise which will have a beneficial effect on you is to try a 4-4-4-4 rhythm. This means that you breathe in for a count of four pulse beats, hold for four, breathe out for four, and hold that for four. This might seem too fast or slow, so judge for yourself a number of pulses which you can maintain for at least ten cycles. Gradually you will find the process becomes automatic and you don't need to count. Another pattern is the long slow in-breath counting up to twelve or even fifteen, holding this for three, then breathing out just as slowly for another count of twelve, and then holding your breath out for three, and beginning the cycle again. If you do this six times before you start meditation or any other work you will find that you feel much calmer and full of energy. It is also a good way of waking yourself up if you feel tired.

By experimenting with different patterns you will discover those which bring you peaceful inner feelings, and others which energise, some which help you to make the gentle, subtle changes of level of consciousness which can lead to sleep, or the most important meditative states of physical relaxation with mental alertness. You will learn that a good, deep breath will help you lift a heavy weight (so long as you remember to bend your knees, so that your strong thighs take the strain, and not your much more delicate spine). You may find, if you get very involved in an inner journey, that you seem to be hardly breathing at all. This can give you a surprise, and it is important that you don't get sudden disturbances or noise, as this can give a shock to your whole system. Obviously, if you have a companion this is less likely to happen, but as this book is directed particularly towards solo students, it is something to take into consideration.

In 'olden' days the weather was a far more critical matter than it is to us in our centrally heated homes and offices. We may have information beamed to our TV sets from satellites, and long-term weather radar may show cloud formations which will affect our land in the days to come, but most of us only take note of the weatherman if we are planning to go out and need to take an umbrella. In the past those who were 'weather-wise' would be able to plan their agricultural activities to suit the expected conditions. Not only would farmers and stockbreeders be concerned about what the gods in the sky were throwing at them, but sometimes they had elaborate rituals to try to change things in their favour. Many of the folk customs which we today imagine are 'fertility' rites are really concerned with changing the erratic summer weather, or driving away the 'evil' of snow and frost. The cycle of pagan festivals was originally set up to celebrate, not particular dates of the calendar (that was the regulating force of the Church), but clear changes of season, or the conclusion of a harvest of some sort.

Although weather magic can work it is an area of great responsibility, because one man's holiday sunshine is another farmer's drought. Too much or too little rain, high winds, or scorching heat can ruin a wheat harvest, or threaten the lives of stock, which in turn affect the well-being of the entire community. To our rural ancestors the weather was accepted as a gift from the Gods. If the villagers and farmers had made the right kinds of offerings, the first fruits or bread, and performed the right sort of ceremonies, which included Well Dressing, dancing round the Maypole, torchlit processions to the local sacred place, bonfires and so on, the Gods of the Sky would be willing to bless them with enough rain and sunshine to bring in a successful harvest. If the rites had been forgotten, or incorrectly performed, or not enough attention had been given to the various offerings, the weather would be foul, the crops and stock fail, and the people would starve.

In Britain we seldom have such a bad harvest that there is a fear of starvation, but we can have a year of glut and overflowing corn stores followed by several years of wet weather, cold winds and dull skies, which, in cosmic terms bring balance. You cannot expect a jackpot every turn of the wheel, yet people do! We still have many of the traditional local customs, forming a varied and fascinating sequence of events throughout the year. Although the local vicar maybe in the crowd, and bless the Cornish Midsummer Bonfire, the words said as the Lady of Earth casts the offering bouquet into the flames is a pagan invocation, asking that the weeds in the field may perish and the valuable crops give a good return. In the Midlands and North they have ceremonies of Well Dressing, where pictures, usually nowadays from the Bible, illustrate one of the stories about water. The idea was to decorate the local spring head with an offering of flowers so that the spirit of the waters (in earlier ages a Goddess, after whom many of these wells are named) would ensure a regular supply of clean water all the year.

In Gloucestershire, about the time of the Spring Equinox in March, or at Easter, there are old rites like Cheese Rolling, when a huge round yellow cheese, a symbol of the strengthening Sun, is rolled down a steep hillside, young men scramble to get pieces of it as it breaks up, for luck, or to ensure that the Sun will shine on their farms or enterprises. In some Cornish villages a dancer is disguised as a horse or there may be a beribboned boat dance in early May to drive out the last of the winter cold, and welcome the first wild flush of green growth in the woods and fields. In Padstow the 'Oss is a sinister, black, circular beast whose dark skirt entraps the watchers, bringing luck, which in the past was called fertility! He is beaten down, and the song changes into a minor key, for he is the spirit of cruel winter, overcome by the bright solar power of the burgeoning spring. Like all dying and reborn heroes, he leaps up and dances on. His heartbeat is echoed by the bass drum, and the singers carry on with their ditty all around the village streets.

Wherever you live in Britain there is certain to be some sort of traditional festival carried on, from the New Year feast of Up Helly A'a in the Shetlands, the Mari Llwyd in South Wales, the Feast of St Ea at St Ives in Cornwall, Rush Bearing in the churches of the Midlands, Plough Monday when the ploughs were blessed, Easter Egg rolling- another Sun-come-back rite - the Midsummer Bonfires, and so on around the country and the year. In each month, in each county there is certain to be some ancient or revived festival which may well have pagan roots, and anyone who seeks to understand the relationship between the people and the land which lies at the heart of the Gentle Arts will need to explore these, and where possible join in.

Morris dancers, becoming even more popular outside pubs in summer and in village halls in the Yuletide season also dance weather magic. Their stick dances show the agricultural processes, somewhat disguised, maybe, but if you watch and listen you may learn from their actions what is really being done. The dancers wear white costumes which link them with the Earth and Moon Goddess, who in all lands and cultures is white. The bells and ribbons, again shared by shamans, dancers and magicians the world over, drive away evil spirits, and symbolise the growth of green nature. The handkerchief dances are plain weather magic, the hankies symbolising the clouds and wind and the leaps help to drive these away from the fields of wheat.

Some Morris sides act out the Death-Rebirth story, often in the winter, which tells of St George or King George and his battles with a variety of nasty challengers. There is a long list of these as they vary from place to place, but there is usually a Turkish Knight or Moorish Knight, Beelzebub or the Devil, Bold Slasher and a variety of other characters, including the bi-sexual Betsy, Father Christmas, and the Doctor, who restores the slain protagonists to life with a magic potion. All the actions of fights, deaths and restoration to life mimic the life of the land, and these ancient Mumming Plays hold other keys to the native mysteries and folk magic, if you seek to understand the myth within.

Although individuals can learn to control the local weather it is an art which requires responsibility, and should never be tried out for fun, or to demonstrate your ability, only in time of need, in a small area for a short time. By developing a relationship with the Earth Mother and the Sky Lord you can ask for a good day for the village fete, or rain to water the garden, now and then, but to ask for more, unless you are a farmer, is unwise and greedy.

You can certainly have a go at 'cloud splitting', on a warm sunny day, when small clouds drift across an azure sky like fluffy sheep. That requires only patience and a bit of determination. Choose a thin cloud and watch it for a while and then begin to will it to part in the centre. Imagine you can spread it apart in the middle as you would to stir washing-up liquid in a bowl. Push hard with the edges of your aura, or mental hands, or whatever you imagine will do the trick, and soon you will see the cloud start to drift apart. You can further divide one part into smaller fragments until it has gone. You will notice that other clouds remain the same and so it is your will which is causing your chosen cloud to fragment, not upper atmospheric winds or the sun on the vapour. Try once or twice the first time, as it does use mental energy and can give you a headache through concentration. This is one of the few things in magic that you can show off to your friends, but the chances are they will be just as good as you are, with a bit of practice!

The other area of Air magic which you can grasp are mainly concerned with mental powers, those of concentration, of focused attention, of an altered state of consciousness, which sounds so strange and yet is a very normal phase in your everyday life, for you pass through it each time you go to sleep. The Gentle Arts teach you to control those states so that you can enter them at will, and more important, relinquish them at once, should you need to. Most practical magic goes on in levels other than the mundane world, and it is only 'reality' as you know it that changes as the last link in the chain of changes, set up by a magical art. By learning to enter other states of reality, planes of existence or 'the astral world' you will discover that you can personally experience communion with the Gods, the Angels and spirits of nature, and arrive at the place where lies the roots of the reality you know. It is at this level that changes have to be made which will cause your spell to work, the information you require to come to you, and any other work you have set in train to come into being.

By starting to watch your dreams, noting these down meticulously each morning, even if you don't at first remember details, you will gradually awaken the subtle aspect of memory which is so important in meditation and magical work. If you don't recall dreams, how are you to remember what you saw in a meditation or at the end of an inner journey? These all use the same delicate parts of your memory and it is that which you should try to strengthen, by simply remembering dreams. Although there are many books on dream interpretation, because your experience of life is different to that of anyone else, the pictures, scenes, symbols and activities in your dreams are personal to you, so, in effect, only you can really understand them. You will become aware that you have a number of different sorts of dreams, and the patterns of these may vary with the phases of the moon. It is a good idea to try to analyse the different sorts of dreams into categories to suit your own notions. Just as some dreams seem to be very vivid in colour and full of activity, others are more imaginative and vague. Some people find they are merely witnessing whatever is happening, as if they were watching a film, while others are fully involved and take part in the action. It is well worth looking at this as far as your own dreams are concerned and see if there is any recognisable trend. Also see if any of your dreams predict the future, either in personal terms, or to forewarn of natural disasters, air crashes and the like. This too is one of the

Gentle Arts, to come to terms with this aspect of your inner life, as it is projected on the screen of your sleeping consciousness.

Another aspect of your own state of awareness which you need to look at closely, and which may never have been brought to your attention before, is the way you actually think. When thoughts enter your point of consciousness do they come as spoken words? Or as pictures? Or as dim feelings which you have to turn into actions? Does the stream of material flow steadily so that you are just continuously aware or do you find it comes in fits and starts, like a bad film, stopping and starting abruptly? When you think about a problem, how do you go about finding a solution? Obviously the method will vary from person to person, but in general terms, do you only accept what is most obvious? For example, say you want to go away on holiday but are hard up, how would you tackle that? By giving up the idea for the present? By trying to earn some money? By asking friends or relatives in distant places to put you up for a while? By entering a competition with money or a holiday as a prize? By offering your home in a holiday swap? Or what? Like the games you might have played as a child, try to think of twenty uses for a metre of garden hose - and not only write down the ideas, but watch how they are formed. It is by the subtle process of information-gathering that the inner world communicates - it doesn't send along an archangel with a trumpet!

Just as you need to observe your own conscious thinking processes so you will need to watch, in the same way, what occurs during any meditations, inner journeys or other magical musings. You will always need clear data communicated in such a way as not to frighten, upset or confuse you. It is no good at all being wildly psychic, if when a date on a calendar is shown to you, or something equally important, your inner sight is hazy and the pictures dim. Gradually you will need to gain as much control of your conscious thoughts and meditated information as you would have of your video films, so that you can stop a frame, go back and even hold a picture still while you examine it in detail. All this can be achieved by practising the seemingly uninspiring, but gentle, arts of meditation.

Recent research shows that the two hemispheres which form the main part of our brains each have different functions. The left half, which, in fact, controls the right-hand side of the body, is apparently concerned with language, logical thinking, mathematical and sequential matters and so on, while the right-hand half is more concerned with intuition, spacial understanding and patterning, imagination and pictures. Most of the skills of Natural Magic rely on the awakened insight of the right-brain being transmitted and understood by the logical, speaking left-half. Many of our modern skills of reading, writing and arithmetic draw primarily on the left side and so the many important links with the more receptive, intuitive side have been used less and need encouraging to reopen as clear and direct channels. It is no good at all having a totally logical mind which will not accept the validity of hunches and guesses, just as it is equally useless to have that sort of dreamy feeling which cannot communicate its information to balanced consciousness. Most forms of Western meditation, be they those which are simply a matter of sitting down, musing about a particular topic, or the more directed 'inner journeys' or even the much older walking meditation, all reopen these inner paths.

In the past our ancestors didn't 'meditate' as a separate activity but one which went hand in hand with everyday tasks. If you were hoeing a field of cabbages your mind was free to wander into the hidden dreamscapes of the infinite within. While you were rocking the cradle, or stirring the pot, or weaving or spinning, or following the sheep and cattle over the hills, all the time your awareness could easily be focused elsewhere. This is still true today, and many people with boring and repetitive jobs find they can day-dream for long spells. You can soon learn to meditate while walking or gardening or hoovering the carpets; it just takes a small effort of redirection of awareness. I think many of the hours we spend in front of the television are actually a form of meditation, when the moving pictures allow us to explore the distant worlds or far-off shores without our being really aware of it.

The Old Wise folk knew the value of these arts. There are many herbal potions, dances, chants, even the idea of 'broomstick riding' which allow awareness to be detached, under control, from the physical location of the practitioner, and glide away invisibly, through time and space. Flying through the air certainly was possible, but most of the time it was the consciousness or the 'astral body' which did the travelling, rather than the physical body, which was to be seen sleeping 'like a log' at home in bed. Many of the traditional Flying Ointments contained the juices of poisonous herbs mixed with fat and these would cause a number of different effects, from numbness of the limbs, dizziness, feelings of drunkenness and disorientation, which could be interpreted in the mind of people who did not normally fly, as the sensation of flight. These methods are extremely dangerous and should never be tried as many of the plants are very poisonous. It is far safer to master the safe and gentle art of meditation so that you are in control of your wandering consciousness and can return to full awareness instantly, under your own command.

If you do want to learn to project astrally be prepared to work very hard and patiently, because, like scrying in a crystal ball, it is an art which requires persistence in the face of failure, plenty of time and a relaxed yet alert frame of mind to do it. If you have been meditating for some time, and can genuinely recognise the change of focus of awareness you can train yourself to imagine yourself standing in front of your seated body, facing away. Try this only in very calm and distraction-free conditions, as there is nothing more frightening than having the door open and someone ask you a question, or the phone ring, just as you relax into making the shift! Keeping your physical eyes shut, build up your own standing image and when it has become solid and 'real' transfer your awareness into the figure. If you succeed you will be astounded at being able to see the familiar room from a different standpoint - this usually shocks you straight back into your body. Ideally, you should have a reliable companion for these experiments, and if they are at all psychic, they will also be able to see your 'astral form'. When you can fully transfer your awareness to the other figure you are getting somewhere. This is not easy and takes a lot of dedication.

Simply shifting your awareness out of your body is much easier - you imagine that you are where you wish to be and will find with a little practice, that you seem to be there. In this state of projected awareness you can still speak and so describe your view of the other location. In the case of a true astral projection you have little control over your body and so cannot speak or move. If you do find you can project your awareness, do be careful, because a loud noise or any disturbance can give you a nasty shock. For this reason a companion is a great help.

All the magics of Air, be they something as simple as breathing, or as elaborate as real astral projection, as common as the use of incenses or basic meditation, can effect you quite profoundly so take care and work slowly at developing your skills and assessing your reactions, even if it does take ages. You won't be wasting time, for these are the basic foundations of all magical powers.

Once you have studied, meditated and come to terms with each of the four tangible elements, you may wish to 'Cast a Circle' using them to provide a magical space. Casting a Circle is a very old magical act, and a great deal of fuss is made about it by witches in covens and some other occult groups, who have lengthy speeches and a love of waving swords and wands about and so on. Certainly the ancient Shaman or Village Wisewoman wouldn't have dared have her kitchen full of 'magical knives' and carved wands or pentacles, kept specially for working spells. Each individual would probably have had some special, natural objects which were imbued with magical power, like polished stones, strangely shaped wood or corn dollies, but these would not be noticed in the event of a 'witch finder' choosing to search the place. Today, many people forget how little privacy and wealth to buy possessions like expensive iron knives the old Cunning Men might have had. In their simple cottages and huts there just would not have been ample cupboards to keep swords, wands, chalices, pentacles and all the other paraphernalia that many modern practitioners find so vital to their rituals. None of this is actually necessary, although a sharp knife for cutting divining rods without harming the tree is useful, as are coloured pens and clean paper for simple talismans.

The oldest and simplest way of creating a circle is by setting up 'wards'. These are four objects, which can be as simple as twigs cut from a bush and stuck into the ground, at the four points of the compass, or they might be four items which represent the elements, Earth, Water, Fire and Air. If you are indoors these could easily be a stone or piece of wood for Earth, a glass dish of Water, a candle in its holder for Fire, and a pot of burning incense or even a few sweet-scented flowers for Air. Most followers of folk magic attribute the elements with Earth to the north, Water in the west, Fire to the south and Air in the east. The object of the four wards is that they help to purify the atmosphere and cut out distractions by being the edges of a circle around you and the work you are doing. This is only a temporary defence, though, and it is necessary to banish the power of these at the completion of the work or you will become mentally and physically isolated, because you banish all feelings, communications from people and useful energies too.

When you have got ready the Tarot cards for a divination, or the materials to make a talisman, based on the number, colour, metals and so on associated with a particular planet, you will need to see that you will not be disturbed for about an hour. There are two ways of placing the elemental wards depending on how much space you have to move about in. If you are out of doors, there should be no problem. It is best, if you are a novice, to start from the element Earth, as is described here, as you will see it is the safest, most solid basis for any sort of magic. You should take your stone and hold it upwards towards the north and ask the Lady of Earth (or Saint, Angel or Elemental etc.) to bless the symbol and bring you security and protection while you are working. You should then walk clockwise around the circle until you arrive at the west, where you take up the cup of water and ask the Lady of Water to cleanse and sanctify you and your working space. Then you circle round to the south, pick up the matches and light the candle, then raise it to the sky, and ask that the Lord of Flame will illuminate and purify your efforts and bring you clear sight (if you are divining). Go round again until you arrive at the east, light the charcoal, allow it to get thoroughly heated through before adding the incense, or lift up the vase of flowers and ask the Lord of the East to breathe through you the power of Air, and sustain your work both day and night. You can then walk round to wherever you are going to sit, stand or kneel during the working and get on with it.

At the end of your spell or divination, you should always allow a few minutes of silent meditation so that if the Gods and Goddesses you are working with wish to speak to you, or teach you anything, there is an opportunity for them to do so. It is always important, too, to say a fervent 'Thank You!' even if you have felt or seen nothing. Something will have happened, even if you are too inexperienced to sense it. Start in the east, raise the incense or flowers again, and say 'Lord of the East, thank you for your light and power. Please be in my heart always.' Then go to the south and thank the Lord of Fire in a similar way, taking into yourself the power of Fire. After that give thanks to the Lady of Water, seeking her inspiration and purity, and finally, the Lady of Earth, Mother Nature, and give her thanks for providing your home, base and food, throughout your life.

If you are able to share your work with a companion you can divide up the Elements between you, or take it in turns to say the opening or closing. When you are finished, take away the wards, and put them in 'mundane' places so that no one will notice. Magic is best kept secret for that is where it gets its power. For this reason what you choose to say and do must be invented by you for it to be successful. Just reading words someone else has written in a book will have little of its original magic or energy because they work best for the specific person and circumstances that they were originally written for. Allow the gods to inspire you and your friends, and you will certainly find that poetry or prayers, inner-path narratives and ritual speeches will all be taught to you, if you learn to trust your magic.

You will soon recognise the difference between the place when the wards are up and when they are down. It is possible to imagine a ring of flames of golden-white light around the perimeter of the room, or in the open, forming an invisible wall around you during your ritual. It will feel calmer within, and it will help you to awaken all those subtle senses which the Gentle Arts are designed to increase. You will discover that the symbols of divination make more sense, and that when you ask for help in empowering a talisman, by focusing the energy of a certain planet into it, you will actually *feel* the power flowing into the talisman. You can devise a simple version of putting up the wards to use on your own before meditation, and a more complicated and ceremonial version for rituals to celebrate festivals or when performing acts of magic.

You can collect suitable stones, cups (preferably either glass or silver, to link in with Water) candlesticks and incense-burners as you go along. Be prepared to make as much of your own equipment as you can, or adapt something you have bought. If it is second-hand you should cleanse it with water, by passing it through incense smoke, and by asking the God or Goddess to clean and bless it before use. You may also wish to make a working robe or cloak. Although many modern witches like to perform their rites naked, or as they call it, 'sky clad', there is no tradition for this in Britain, where among other things, the climate is against it. It does make working out of doors difficult, and if you are following Arts whose roots are in nature, having to be inside a building is immediately cutting you off from the very source of much power. It takes only a few hours to make a simple kaftan-shaped robe from any suitable coloured material, which is for preference a natural fibre. Cotton, linen, silk or wool are the most comfortable to wear, are safer handling lighted candles and hot incense, and come in many different textures and colours, to suit personal aesthetic taste. You can embroider, decorate with fabric paints or appliqué designs according to your artistic and magical aims. Even men ought to be able to sew the single seam up the side of the garment, which should be loose and comfortable, and can be tied in at the middle with a coloured cord or belt.

You will find that even for meditation, changing into a robe will help you get into the right frame of mind and adopt your magical personality and during festivals, ritual workings and divinations, you will discover that you see more clearly your purpose, and are less liable to be distracted by external worries, or sounds, or anything else which takes your mind off the work in hand. In dressing up, you become a magician, or whatever term you have selected to call yourself.

6.
THE HIDDEN PATHS

Only you can hear and see, behind the eyes of the sleepers, the movements and countries and mazes and colours and dismays and rainbows and tunes and wishes and flight and fall and despairs and big seas of their dreams.

Under Milk Wood, Dylan Thomas

In earlier ages when people lived much closer to nature, relying totally on the seasons to provide their change of diet, and the forces of wind and tide to direct their lives, they had no need of the artificial skills which we, who are trying to walk again in the ancient ways, strive to master. We are now accustomed to our entirely man-made cities, with their electric lights which rob us of the light of the stars, and protect us from the forces of the wilderness, tame our inner nature and blunt our true vision. Those who seek the magic of the past must find new routes to that lost freedom of spirit. It is all very well reading in books, seeing on film or video, or sensing at second-hand the power from the past, but those who are serious in their desire to learn must find ways to experience too. We have to learn these techniques just as the modern child has to master making letters into words, and words on the page into the thing they represent. The word tree is not a tree; it doesn't look, or feel, or grow like a tree, but we can recognise the concept and if we had to use the word as a label, we would all find a real tree to pin the label to. The old ways we have to relearn as modern literate people are very similar.

In a time when books were just for priests and monks, all records were kept in the memory. History was shared in song; language included mime and gesture, chant and all those silent forms of communication which modern psychologists classify as 'body language', which even an hour-old infant can recognise and respond to. Because the workers of magic and healers and wise women didn't leave us their words in books and papers we find it much harder to relate to them than we do to literate people who speak and write another language. There is a gap which only personal experience can fill, and as we are used to obeying the instructions, in writing, on a packet of cake mix or a new electrical appliance, where this is missing we may find ourselves at a loss to know how to proceed. We don't recognise a gesture, poem or chant as a way of recording and sharing information, we do not see beyond the entertainment value of hearing someone relate a story or sing a ballad - we are now going to have to learn those lost arts again.

One of the most effective forms of magical training is the use of 'path working', which is a form of symbolic story-telling which helps the listeners enter that altered state of consciousness in which they can reopen many aspects of inner awareness in a gentle and controlled way. We all heard stories read to us as children and in our minds conjured up the characters, the scenery, the happenings, even if these were not described in detail in the words. The same applies to listening to radio plays and sung narratives but is lost when the play is on film and the images are supplied for us. As more and more of our entertainment is taken from moving pictures on television, film or video, and less from the spoken or read word, so our inner capacity of 'imagination' becomes weaker, along with our innate ability to recognise and act upon intuition, or feel the tides of sun and moon, which were an integral part of the daily lives of our ancestors. We have to learn again to rely on memory and imagination. We, who have access to forms of record keeping, data storage and retrieval, instant world-wide communication which were undreamed of in the days of the Old Wisdom, still have to rediscover the basic aspects of awareness which we had as pre-literate children - and *it isn't easy!*

In our electronic civilisation we may have advantages which our ancestors would envy but we do sometimes look back with regret; perhaps through rose-coloured spectacles, it is true, when we think about their intimate association with the countryside, with the forces of nature, the ancient powers of magic, with the elemental beings, with animals and with our now lost heritage of psychic awareness. Many of these forgotten aspects of knowledge and perception can be recovered, but it is painstaking work, largely along overgrown pathways through the inner levels of our own minds, as well as through the woods and wildernesses of the real world, where the energies and shapes of nature are unfettered by human intervention. We do not see the guiding stars, the street lamps' glow gets in the way. We do not recognise the shapes of winter trees because to our world that knowledge has little application, although we might well pick out the shape of our own make of car in the distance. Herbs come in packets from the supermarket, knowledge comes in the pages of books or periodicals, the tools we need for handicrafts come from specialist shops - we don't have to go out and make them! So much of the material of practical magic has vanished from the lives we live, and there is no instant way we can retrieve it. The Gentle Arts have to be learned; there is no pill, no tape, no book which can truly impart to us these antique technologies - we have to start from scratch.

The area in which the most work needs to be done is that of the mind, the awareness, the expanded perception. Although most followers of the Old Religion may not see the value of regular meditations and directed inner journeys which are a vital part of the training of any Ritual Magician, ancient or modern, it is the surest way to reform the subtle links with the unseen, with the world in which the Gods and Goddesses live and have their being. To encounter them you have to go to their places. You have no right to command their presences in your man-made house, or demand that they attend your circle to share and bless your workings, unless you are more than willing to seek them out where they are most likely to be. You cannot 'evoke' elementals, although you can cause your blurred sight to envisage shapes which you take to be elementals, unless you are in the place it is natural for them to be. Go to any wood at twilight, still the thumping of your civilised heart, and call upon the Lord of the Wild to become visible to you. Walk among the sea-wrack on a deserted shore and invoke the presence of the Lady of Water, and listen with all your senses. Climb to the airy heights of some mountain peak and seek out the Lords of Air to reach out and touch you, but be ready to cling to the rock in surprise! Delve down into the depths of some cave womb and listen to the beating of the Earth Mother's heartbeat, feel her overwhelming presence, smell her earthy perfume, and come forth reborn and changed. If you are still and patient the elemental children of the Gods may appear from the bonfire, not as salamanders, but in their own flame-forms, darting and dancing in the glowing embers.

Put aside the preconceptions as to the forms of all elementals for they have been shaped by previous seekers minds and abilities to see. In their own shapes you will still know them, for you will sense them with awakened perception and know them to be truly of the elements of Earth or Water, Fire or Air. They are beings of another order to ours and the words we might use to describe them are misleading. Seek them out with clear eyes, and an adventurous spirit, in the last wild places, and they will come, they will communicate and perhaps even teach you about their worlds, if you have the sense to listen. Remember, you have no right to demand them to appear, nor can you command them to obey your wishes, any more than you would come at the beck and call of a stranger, and immediately do whatever you were asked. Learn to share with them that earthy, watery, fiery or airy part of your own nature, let that form a link of friendship and communication so that both sides can come to know the other for what it is. They may help you on your journey through the Gentle Arts, and it is surely through those same old skills that you might make contact in the first place, but you may have to listen to them if they are to bring you gifts from their level of existence.

Once you have made a real and direct contact then you can take back the image to your home and store of experience, and recall it, and so reawaken their presence beyond their normal place of being, but you actually do have to seek out the lonely countryside, the deserted hilltop, or the winter seashore. This takes courage, but unless you have both courage and determination, even with the Gentle Arts, you will never make any progress in magic. You will need to learn to allow strange things to happen to you without fear. You will need to be able to sense those presences and powers which never come into visible appearance, and feel safe and at home with them. You will gradually find your 'psychic whiskers' will become sensitive so that you can judge the moods of others, receive hunches and inner guidance. All these things are outside the scope of normal awareness, and because they are subtle and vary from person to person, it is not possible to list causes and effects so that you can assess your progress.

Many of the Gentle Arts have been lost in time because the magics were trivial and the methods of their use so ordinary no one bothered to write them down, so like children going to school we have to start with the first lessons. And, just as it may be difficult for a child to comprehend the sound and the letter which becomes a word we have to learn again the correspondences to build up the symbolic language in which the Gods and Goddesses communicate with us. In the Old Arts these include colours, times of the moon's phases, tides of the sea and sun, shapes, images and a whole variety of peculiar ancient links by which an inert stone can be seen to have the protective power of a ring of steel, or a drop of water the cleansing and blessing power of the Goddess of the Sea.

Today we see things as they appear to be and accept them only as what they seem. In the past people would look at the objects around them and be able to sense other layers of being there. A stone with a hole in it was not just a lump of flint which our scientific minds might explain to us as the results of volcanic heat on silica in which bubbles were embedded and later eroded. The old folk would recognise this as a charm against evil, and pick up the stone, bind it with magical red wool and hang it over the doorway of a house or byre so that no harm could enter. We can't say that it wasn't effective!

The whole of the inner landscapes is dotted with such symbolic objects. Within these integral worlds of the trained mind there are many animals, plants, trees, hills, caves, castles, chapels, mythical beasts and people who are more than their individual images might suggest. Some are guardians (this applies equally to features in the landscape as it does to more obvious animate beings!) some are messengers, some are dangerous and need to be overcome. All are stored within the infinite and usually totally unexplored regions of our memories and personal 'Akashic Records'. Often it only requires us to close our eyes to be able to examine this magical universe, but that too has to be done with daring and a spirit of adventure. By learning to use the keys to the doors to those unknown places, which all of us have brought into our present incarnation from the past, so that we can open and *close* the doors at will, we can gradually explore the inner countryside, befriend the guardians, meet the teachers and overcome the dragons which are just as much real parts of our psyche as our ability to sing or dream.

True magical systems, of any tradition, teach their students to examine their own lives, ambitions, skills and failings before they go on to the more exciting rituals and celebrations. This is just as true of the Gentle Arts as it is of qabalistic training or any other practical form of occult work. Unless you have some idea of what scares you, excites you, drives you onwards against the odds, those inner beings who are there to help you will not be able to communicate, for their language is the use of symbols. If you are afraid of deep water, for example, to perceive a fast-flowing, deep river will easily be seen as something to overcome and struggle against. If you like cats then the tiger you see may be a guide rather than a threat. Only by making short and controlled safaris into those inner realms and judging what you discover from your own experience can you understand what is being shown to you. Unless you have read the map, done a bit of personal 'psychic archaeology', examined your dreams for the valuable clues they give, you will find you are just as lost in those unseen worlds as you would be if you woke up one morning and found yourself in the middle of a jungle instead of at home in your bedroom.

The magical inner journeys, known as pathworkings, are usually designed to lead the listener through a changing landscape of a particular sort to a meeting with a God or Goddess, or to a place where new knowledge may be received from some inner-world being or situation. The original journeys were through the symbolism which links the spheres on the qabalistic Tree of Life, each of which has specific images, angels, colours, symbols and Tarot attributions, for example. These have all been recorded within the writings of modern qabalistic students, although the original source was a verbal one as, roughly translated, qabalah means 'from mouth to ear'. You learn the symbols of the spheres and paths by being told, making your own internal pictures and concepts, rather than reading some vast and ancient tome in which they were all displayed in glorious technicolour! Today qabalists derive the attributions from a variety of comparatively recent written sources, and so again, a tradition which was dynamic, growing and changing as each generation of qabalistic students built up their personal symbolism, has been fossilised through the use of written words and pictures.

You will find there are plenty of books on pathworkings, there are cassette tapes and illustrated periodicals which give you the background of a particular journey, and these can all be of great value to beginners in the Gentle Arts, but ultimately it will be far better for you to write or record your own narratives, which will take you to the specific place or symbolic situation which you need to discover answers to questions, or instruction of some sort, as your need dictates. In fact, it is an often overlooked aspect of magical inspiration to be able to shut your eyes, relax, and find a new path unrolling before your inward vision, without any effort on your part. Once you have learned to find and then unlock the many doors you will see how simple it is gently to change your awareness from the world you call 'real' and travel through other realms, meeting the pagan Gods and Goddesses, the heroes, the witches and wizards and keepers of forgotten knowledge at will.

Certainly, you will need to begin with very basic paths which will lead you safely into the other world. Often the memory of a familiar and pleasing landscape will be a sufficiently gentle introduction to this important skill. Relax and close your eyes, allowing your breathing to slow and become regular, and conjure up the sensation of revisiting a favourite holiday location. You might imagine yourself wandering along a cliff path above a Mediterranean-blue sea, or exploring again the mountains of Wales, or simply lying on a sun-scorched beach, watching the colour of the sun change through your closed eyelids, and feeling its deep penetrating warmth. Perhaps as you wander idly the images of people, trees and events will begin to intrude upon the picture, but not on your memory or creation. This is where it starts to get interesting for it demonstrates that the inner worlds are trying to communicate to you, albeit in a very minor way to begin with. Learn to still the running commentary, simply watch and observe so that you will be able to recall the details when you have returned to the 'here and now'. From the safe and familiar recollected landscapes you will eventually be able to wander in freedom in the weirder places where unicorns run wild, and dragons fly overhead, where the heroes have gone when their first task was completed.

Later you will find it useful to have a symbol for a particular change of location. In most of the published pathworkings this means your journey takes you through a door, gate or curtain. Often, if you are trying to build up such inner explorations for yourself it is enough to choose a door in a wall through which you have never passed. The outside of it may be familiar, but you can't be certain that it doesn't lead to fairyland if you have never crossed its threshold. You may find this sort of thing happens in dreams, that you find yourself walking along a well-known road and then by going through a door you have previously never entered, or which you seem to have overlooked in your waking life, you then encounter a totally different, and in come cases, even alien world. Doors have always been magical places, often the haunts of photographed ghosts, or the places where symbols of protection and religious significance have been placed, from the humble yet potent Goddess symbol of the horseshoe to the Hebrew texts used in the Jewish tradition.

Once you are through the entrance into the other landscape you will need to see clearly what lies before you. This may be a wild vista, far divorced from the streets of houses and shops, or factories and man-shaped landscapes of your real world. Here you may find the Wasteland of the Grail stories, still barren and derelict, for it awaits the return of the King and the Finder of the Grail. You might discover you have entered an untamed jungle, thick with greenery and creepers, bright with flowers and strange butterflies, and echoing to the cries of animals and birds. The door might open onto a desert scene where you are overwhelmed by the heat and dryness, or you may find yourself among the Nile Temples of the Egyptian Old Kingdom, or the Mayan pyramids of Mexico. Only by venturing through those closed doors with your inner vision, and so at the same time unlocking the closed doors within your memory or perception, can you hope actually to meet the Gods and Goddesses of whichever pantheon you feel most at home with.

Certainly, not everyone sees as clearly as they do with ordinary vision. It may take time and constant practice to clear the channels of inner sight which derive their reality from the less frequented byways in the brain. At first, many people who have not needed to use the intuitive, sensing right-part of the brain because in their lives numbers and words are more important, find that they do not see moving, realistic pictures. These people tend to see still images which may be blurred and indistinct, yet they may clearly sense the atmosphere of heat or cold, country or city ambience. They may hear sounds which are obviously not those of the world around their resting body, they may smell scents or simply become aware of the 'otherwhereness' that they are perceiving in some unspecified way. Everyone is different, each will find some of the Gentle Arts difficult; other skills may come easier, or even seem to be remembered from some previous life. Ultimately the only answer is persistence, even in the face of results which are not satisfying. Gradually the faint notions will turn into clear and real images, and the experience of walking through an alternative world will become apparent. There is no short cut, and there is no certain way which will unlock those doors for you, except the ways you discover by trial and error.

Once you are fully within the other timescape you may encounter a variety of characters there, just as the person playing a computer maze game, or 'Dungeons and Dragons'. You might meet wizards, witches, heroes, Gods and Goddesses, talking creatures, mythical beasts and a variety of beings who offer a threat or situations which frighten you. You may be emotionally moved, even by the dull-seeming words on a page of descriptive narrative, or those spoken on a pre-recorded tape. Within the alternative realm you may experience things which you do not feel in ordinary life. To be affected by strong feelings of love, sadness, sympathy, anxiety, passion, anger or any other vivid reaction is a sure sign that you are awakening those regions of awareness which slumber most of the time. To be truly at one with the Gods or characters of myth often leads to such feelings, for the oldest and most powerful source of magical energy is driven by our emotions. In many group rituals it is the dancing, chanting and imagery, shared by the group, which causes heightened feelings, whereas the individual, treading the lonely road to the inner worlds, has to discover these sensations for himself. This, too, can be a strange experience, especially for people brought up in cultures where the natural expression of feelings is suppressed and any kind of emotional outburst is looked upon as something strange. This restriction is weakening quite a lot in our society, but people are still embarrassed to be seen crying or laughing because of something they are being told. If it should happen to you, take it as an excellent indication that you are getting to the roots of your own power, and that when you have learned to control this, you will have a very useful magical talent.

The characters you encounter on these journeys all have a purpose, even if you are not sure what it might be to begin with. You need to treat all of them with respect, ask them questions or test their reactions to your presence in what, after all, is their world. Some will guide you along the path, though some might mislead you if you aren't careful. Some will instruct you, others protect you or offer some valuable asset which you will need on your travels through the unseen. Certainly, there are dangers there, but these are far less than those you might encounter crossing the road outside your house. What you might lose in any such encounter will be only your pride, or any false barrier between your consciousness and your inner perception which time and mundane life has caused you to erect. Be prepared for surprises, and apply common sense, and you will gain a great deal from the curious friendships you are able to make with the people of the Otherworld.

As you progress through the landscape you may discover treasures of various sorts, items of information or knowledge, jewels, or symbolic objects which have a meaning and value far greater than their seeming purpose. Collect all of these into your memory so that you can look at them again, in meditation, by seeking their meaning in books or by questioning your friends, if they are able to share some of these paths with you, for by comparing experiences all of you will learn. Like the images encountered in dreams their precise value is of personal meaning to you, and one traveller's experience is as important to him as another's even if they may differ greatly in content and imagery.

Often another door, gate or clearing in a forest, temple or sacred site is discovered within the journey, and here a greater gift of wisdom may be given. It is a kind of 'inner sanctum, within the landscape where the really important matters may be conveyed to you. Often in taped pathworkings there is a pause so that direct communication, over and above what has been written or spoken is left, and it is as well to take a short break in these ramblings to listen and receive, rather than go blindly on, perceiving or creating the landscape. Sometimes a character of the Otherworld will bring you a symbolic gift which you may be surprised to discover is somehow absorbed into you, breathed in or eaten, so that it becomes a part of you. This has to happen as it is not possible to bring back physical souvenirs from the other realms, although, strangely enough, actual representations of the magic gifts do often turn up in your life, soon after they have been given on the inner level. It is another way in which the secret, hidden things come forth into the light of the everyday world, and considerable amounts of knowledge can be brought out and shared, as they always have been. Today we have to use the language of psychology to describe our musings whereas our ancestors looked upon these aspects of the Gentle Arts as mere day-dreaming, but benefited none the less from guidance from intangible teachers.

After the pause you will start the return journey. It is not necessary to retrace every single step, down the mountain, across the desert, through the cave and so on the way back. With practice, it is really only necessary to focus on what you have gained and open your eyes, but for students with little experience of the magical ways, it is best to follow the way back, more or less as you went, once again 'seeing' the various stages and so remembering them, to be recorded as soon as you finish the journey. A gradual return will help you recall many details, just as waking slowly and gently in the morning is the surest way to help you remember your dreams. The sudden switch from sleep to wakefulness or relaxed concentration on the inner landscape is the most likely reason that you forget what you were dreaming about, or the images, conversations with guides, or useful information you gained has vanished completely. If you regularly meditate, or use creative visualisation or pathworkings you will find that your mental muscles begin to strengthen and your attention span and concentration also increases. Gradually you will be astonished to discover that not only can you believe you are walking through some other realm, but that you can recall the kinds of trees you see, the wild flowers, the intricate details of some work of art you examine. You will be able to call to mind the words and the tone of voice and accent, even, of any beings you encounter, and learn a great deal more in retrospect.

Record-keeping is also an important part of the Gentle Arts. Although many of the original crafts and skills were mostly used by pre-literate people, we are living in a world where reading and writing are important and we no longer have the kind of verbal and pictorial memories which record all that is necessary to know. To jot down aspects of a dream and then compare them with later events may uncover an unexpected clairvoyant ability, to 'see' with inner vision some place may lead you to understand your own past lives and position in the community. Recording the results of meditations is especially valuable for it is in those notes that you will see that patterns of increased awareness and understanding may be found. Meditation should bring forth 'realisations' which are those flashes of understanding and sudden increase of knowledge which defy description, except to say 'Aha!'. It is almost as if some connection in the memory had clicked open and a flood of comprehension about even the most trivial matter, pours forth. Not all realisations are earth-shattering, but they do demonstrate that you are making progress, and are a sure sign that you have mastered the Gentle Art of meditation, at least.

Pathworking, too, should help expand your understanding of the symbols you encounter on your journeys. As you will come to recognise, each God and Goddess of the pagan pantheon, each elemental, angel or being, each level of initiation of the inner worlds has specific images which your journeys will reveal to you. Only by treading those strange paths and seeking to understand these many aspects of symbolic knowledge regularly and consistently will you be able to clear out the channels of understanding, so that they become easy to go through, and fully comprehended by you.

You might find it simpler to explain this art to yourself as a form of directed and conscious dreaming. You set the scene, describe to yourself the landscape, the characters you may meet, but like a dream you will not necessarily be able to shape the end result, the vision seen through a previously closed door, the conversation with a guide or the practical instruction of a teacher. You may find this technique will help you if you cannot sleep at night, for you can choose a peaceful journey to the Land of Nod and walk its dreamy paths until you fall asleep. Many of the more formal magical schools teach their students regularly to examine the events of the day, working backwards from bed-time to breakfast, before sleeping, in order to sort out memory and not leave unresolved inner conflicts floating about in your mind which may spoil your sleep and cause you to worry.

A journey which you could take is one which many people find quite difficult or painful, for it is a look, backwards, through your own life. You can work at it a bit at a time, as if it were a series of scenes in a long play. Choose the location where you have spent your time, be it home, at work, at school or college and so on, and carefully see where you had the opportunities of which you either took advantage, or missed out on. Gradually you will begin to see a strange line of seeming 'coincidences' running through your life. The highlights of this might be casual encounters with people, who, in time, became very important in your life, or the book which fell off the shelves at your feet, and changed your path through life. Start with this book, for example. Something must have attracted you to read it. Maybe a long unanswered question in your mind, maybe a remark made by a friend, or some magical experience which needs further investigation or explanation, even if it is only for your own satisfaction, has caused you to search library or bookshop shelves. No one can guarantee that the answer you need will be here, but there are certain to be some new questions, to which you may already have the answers.

The invisible, inner worlds are endless. They are filled with exciting informative and magical places and characters, both human and of other orders of being, and only by daring to explore these for yourself will you be able to benefit from the many valuable insights which are to be found there. Secondhand information will never be much use to you for, as with dreams, the symbols, the images and the characters relate primarily to the dreamer. Certainly, you will share some of the same underlying concepts with many others on the path, but what matters most is that you are learning and understanding for yourself.

It is a good idea to practise deliberately taking notice of all the things around you. Try to discover three new pieces of information each day. This doesn't mean having to learn answers for a 'Mastermind' type quiz, but to become aware of the exact colour of the curtains to your room, which shoe you put on first each morning, how many steps from your door to the gate, or the nearest lamp-post. These things are not of great importance in themselves, but it is the simplest way to learn to increase your attention span, to help you recognise information of which you may only get glimpses, in some inner journey. This is how true clairvoyance works. If you later turn to the use of the crystal ball or black mirror, or even with the Tarot cards or the I Ching, you are only going to be shown snatches of the full story. Your increased perception will have to fill in the gaps and make the pattern of images in the glass or the symbolism of the divinatory system turn into a real and complete revelation.

Certainly, if you are hoping to be able to predict future events by any occult means you are going to need to be able to assimilate and comprehend tiny fragments as they zoom past your point of awareness, so that you can snatch them like arrows out of the air, and turn them into useful and accurate information. There is nothing more useless and dangerous than an inaccurate diviner! Suppose you saw a plane crash which you took to be happening in the future, then every detail of the type of plane, its coloured markings, any numbers or letters on it, and information about the place it was in could all help to turn a vague blurred blob into an accurate description of a particular plane landing in a specific place. You might even see the day on the calendar, or a sign with the name of the airport etc., if you tune up that aspect of your intuitive sight. Only by steadily walking the paths of the mindscape and learning how that reality differs from that of the world you perceive around you now, and recognising the value of each (and being certain not to allow yourself to retreat into the cosy inner world and never come back, which is a temptation some unhappy people try to indulge in), you will suddenly find your powers of vision and awareness expand in leaps and bounds.

You will find that there are many pre-recorded cassettes of a wide variety of authors and teachers which will spell out for the beginner the different stages of the journey within, and if you don't feel able to design your own paths, and dislike the sound of your own voice on tape reading those that are already printed in books, this could be a way of mastering this particular art. Even so, it is worth the effort of trying to invent your own paths. A way which you might find helpful is to collect a series of suitable images from magazines or travel brochures which represent the particular stages on a typical journey - a door or gate; a winding path; a wood or forest; a mountain; a lake; a cave; a spring or fountain; a garden; as well as pictures which to you represent the Guides of the Inner Paths, the guardians and so on. You would be able to draw these or perhaps simply write descriptions of a good number of these on separate cards, so that you can shuffle them and select a path to work at on each occasion. This way it would always be new and so would continue to expand your perception, which, it cannot be stressed enough, is a vital key to the Gentle Arts. If you have a camera, even a simple one, you could build up a collection of photographs or slides which depict the various stages on such a journey. To travel along these hidden roads of another dimensions is not a trivial pursuit, and the answers to the questions you discover will be of great value to you, in your mundane and magical life.

The often difficult and occasionally painful art of self-examination has always been one of the first criteria of practical magical training, for if you don't know much about your own inner life, how can you hope to understand, and so advise, through divination, anyone else? One way of looking at your spiritual ambitions, inner strengths and weaknesses is by working with the four elements, Earth, Water, Fire and Air. By meditating on the actual physical element, or using it symbolically in a simple ritual, or by making up a pathworking journey which takes in many of its aspects, you can soon find out which elements are easiest to work with, and which harder. This is likely to be further confirmed by the planetary positions in your natal chart.

Always start with Earth, as it is the densest and safest element. Use images and symbols, pictures and sounds to assist your awareness of the qualities, power and destructive force of each element in turn, taking plenty of time, certainly weeks, and possibly months over each, to come to terms with it. Facets of Earth which you should look at are natural landscapes of farmland, orchards, gardens, moorland and forest. Look, too, at rocks, minerals, gems and polished jewels, for these have great and ancient powers which few understand. Examine fossils, natural stones and river and beach pebbles, learn from their stability, resistance to change and destruction and see what can be made of them. Think about caves and mines, tunnels and caverns, potholes and gorges. Consider, too, the wild places, the scorched deserts, the icy arctic wastes, the barren mountain heights where rough rock is shattered by frost, and the dense impenetrable jungles where light does not reach the ground and no human foot has trod. Compare and contrast the sensations of hot-dryness and cold-dryness, of icy-coldness and steamy heat, and see how these are also aspects of your own temperament.

Look at Water, as rivers and seas, as raindrops and as surging tides. Flow with the water and sense your own life as a river of experience, flowing and filling until it re-enters the ultimate ocean. Study snow flakes and waterfalls, lakes, pools, puddles, cataracts and springs, wells and fountains. Many of these have ancient magical and alchemical significance. Study your own feelings and emotions, cupped within the framework of your life. Understand the tides of the sea, and of the year, so that you can always take opportunity of the flood and use that power to aid your work.

Study Fire, in the hearth and the candle flame, in bonfire and in the kitchen. Read the embers of a sinking wood fire, and the smoke of burning leaves which can speak with silent voices if you attune yourself to them. Look at volcanoes and forest fires, lightning and burning incense. Learn how fire has helped us on our long journey from the cave to the city, and how in its ultimately most destructive nuclear form it can destroy our entire world.

Take note of the weather, the winds and the clouds. Learn about the gases in the atmosphere, the way satellites look at developing weather systems and see what is happening. Notice the way birds fly and see again the pictures formed by summer clouds, just as you did when you were a child. Study the way you breathe and as you relax in meditation vary the pattern of breathing in and out to find a way which is calming and restful and another which recharges your flagging energy and gives you health and vitality. Stop smoking and give your body a chance to become fully fit and capable of working with nature to be strong and healthy. Fly kites and look at fields of growing grain or grass caressed by the hand of the Gods of Air. Develop your mind and memory, cultivate your intellect and learn to tune in your most subtle senses of intuition.

When you have had a go at all those things, both the forms of the elements in nature and in yourself you will have developed a great deal of useful practical knowledge and experience which will help you master the Gentle Arts. Gradually you can balance your lack of Fire or Earth or whatever element you personally lack or have difficulty with, and so you will grow in power and knowledge.

7.
THE MAGIC OF THE MOON

O Isis, veiled on Earth, but shining clear
In the high heaven now the full moon draws near,
Hear the invoking words, hear and appear . . .
The Sea Priestess, Dion Fortune

The Moon has always been seen as something strange, for her changing nature, her irregular shape, and the way she may follow or precede the constant Sun must have fascinated those earliest watchers of the skies. Her light is very different from the bright glare of sunlight, her effect is tangible to those who have at least partially awakened their inner sight. She has power but it is subtle, just as her light is cold and gentle. In many lands, from the earliest times she has been seen and worshipped as a Goddess, either in her own right, or as the messenger of a hidden or veiled Goddess. Today we are gradually understanding in our marred scientific way some of the effects her light and tidal pull can have on more lowly creatures, fish and the growth of plants. It was not idle superstition that taught the Old Wise Ones to gather plants in moonlight, or to scry in that artificial moon, a mirror, to see the future or to interpret moon-led dreams. We have lost that wisdom and though many magical groups more or less time their meetings to coincide with a full moon this tends to be for the convenience of having meetings every four weeks rather than to make the best use of her light and power.

Living in neon-lit cities, and in places where the night sky is shrouded in clouds or industrial steam, we can see little of the vast array of nocturnal lights which our ancestors knew, and named and used to guide their travels, or awaken their more psychic senses. We seldom look up at all, and then only to see if it is raining! We have lost, for the most part, the night-vision which allows us to look up into a dark sky and see the patterns of the stars and know them for the signs of the zodiac, to recognise at a glance the phase of the moon, and to tell the hour from the position of the constellations. If we want that knowledge back we have to turn to books or films or visit a planetarium, for our ancestors also grew up in houses, and it is two generations ago since they left the night to the light of the stars and changing moon. If we wish to use the Moon's magic we are going to have to dare to visit the dark lanes of the countryside beyond the loom of the town's illuminations, we are going to have to discover places where the upper air is clear, or devote some of the dark hours on holiday in different lands to looking at the sky rather than the dancefloor lights flashing on and off.

It is necessary to start from the beginning and understand the various aspects of Moon lore before we can establish that inter-relationship between our own hearts and the Moon Goddess, whose magical arts have been long recognised and recorded in the religious history of many lands. We need to know about the phases of the Moon, both waxing and waning, and the effects these have on our blood tides, for like the sea, much of our physical being is water, and like the oceans, we are moved and directed by lunar gravity. We have become too dense to recognise this, but if we relearn to watch the patterns of our dreams, the rhythms of our bodies and thoughts, and the passage of the Moon through the night sky, a new relationship will begin to emerge.

Anyone can see that the Moon changes her shape with the passing nights but people today do not really notice that she also changes her rising position in the sky each night, unlike the regular Sun, who edges gradually and steadily along the horizon as the months pass by, and pausing at each equinox, retraces his steps along the edge of the world, to the north in summer and to the south in winter. The inconstant Moon dances along the horizon, returning only to her starting point in eighteen years, against the Sun's regular path. Our ancient forebears knew this and set stones to mark the coincidences, as well as circles and ellipses to show the Sun's movements against the gnomons of standing stones aligned to the horizon. This was magical knowledge, for the usual interpretation of timing in agriculture doesn't really make sense. You don't plant seed on a particular day of the year - the ground could be sodden or frozen, or baked dry by unseasonable drought - you sow seed when the soil is ready, and has been ploughed and harrowed. You don't mate animals by the Sun but by their natural inclinations, when the ewes are in season or the cows bulling or the mares in heat. You may select one time of fertility rather than another because you prefer your flocks to multiply in the late spring when there is enough grass to feed them, but Mother Nature will dictate the animals' cycles, not the Sun in the sky.

Each of the four phases of the Moon has its magical potency, and a wise student of the Old Ways will learn to watch for these and focus occult work, psychic development and inner journeying to the period of time when the Moon's tides are most beneficial. You can discover, too, your own times of mental, spiritual and physical fertility from both observation and studying the Moon phase at the time of your birth from your horoscope. The lunar cycle provides a valuable and natural way of allowing any woman to assess her fertility if she wishes to conceive a child, or prevent this without any sort of intervention or drugs if she does not want children. Simply by finding out the precise phase of the Moon at the time of her birth, and avoiding making love during that phase, without taking some other precaution, any woman can remain childless. If a couple wish for a child then the woman's moon phase is the most likely time for her to conceive. If the Moon is then in a positive sign (Aries, Gemini, Leo, Libra, Sagittarius and Aquarius) then the child is more likely to be a boy, and in the other signs it will probably be a girl. If the Moon is only just into a sign then the child could be either. Of course, it is necessary to study your menstrual cycles too, to discover when you are most fertile, but using some very basic knowledge of your horoscope combined with common sense it ought to be more than 90 per cent effective, and is as safe a form of birth control as anything else. There is a lot of published work on this by Dr Eugen Jonas (viz *Natural Birth Control* by Sheila Ostrander and Lynn Schroeder, Bantam, 1972) which explains it very clearly.

Probably the ancient people who kept verbal records of their clan's history would know at which phases of the moon the girl children were born and so could give useful advice about bearing children, or not, when an individual woman asked. Some of the earliest carvings found on small items of bone, dating back to the Stone Age, appear to be Moon calendars, showing the changing shape of the moon over thirty nights, so it is clear that our ancestors were interested in what was going on in the night sky. Certainly the nomadic people of the desert areas were well aware of the movements of the 'travelling stars' which we now call the planets, of the time of the solar year and the moon moods. Many of the stars in the constellations we know as the signs of the zodiac have Arabic names, Aldabaran, Deneb, Betelgeuse and so on, and they would certainly have observed the moon too.

We tend to take the Moon for granted and ignore her ebbing and flowing light, except when a casual glance at the calendar or diary tells us she is new or full. This often only applies when people are trying to fix the date for meetings, which from their roots should celebrate the Goddess of the Moon in one of her distinct phases. Lose touch with the reality in the sky, and you lose touch with a great source of power and intuition. Carry out rituals like 'Drawing down the Moon' without understanding what you are doing and the end result is that nothing happens. Learn to make again the contact with the ancient wisdom and this and many other ancient ceremonies take on real meaning and can be used to heal the soul, and enlighten the spirit. The power is not lost, it is just that we have forgotten how to call upon it, to direct it and make best use of its variable qualities which can awaken or send to sleep, which can reveal the truth, or hide it in a web of moonlight. The Moon influences us whether we recognise it or not, but if you work with the Gentle Arts you should soon be able to detect the delicate influences which work on your emotions, intuition and inner vision. The clearer this perception grows the easier you will find it to control and develop your inherent skills to divine, and other psychic talents.

The Moon has been seen as a Goddess from very early times in many lands, although in Norse mythology there is a Moon Man. In modern pagan workings she is often seen as the personification of the Triple Goddess, who as Young Maiden is the new and waxing moon, as Mother she is the full and brilliant moon, and as Crone she is the last slender crescent of the waning dark of the moon. In many traditions she also has three names, the Celtic ones being Rhiannon, Arianrhod and Cerridwen. If you wish to add into your practices of the Gentle Arts a religious side you will need to meditate well on all three aspects of 'The Lady of the Night Sky'. You will also need to understand that although the moon is her symbol, she is not a lump of dead rock floating in the Sun's gravity and lit by its light. You will also have to work out how a Goddess who is associated with the moon can also be the Earth Mother, and the Ruler of the Sea.

The Moon Goddess is very approachable, but again, you must make the effort to find a place where you can see her light plainly, without any man-made things getting in the way. You must learn to become still and receptive and open to any response you may receive from her, which may vary from a vague feeling of unease to a clear and real vision of her as Isis, as described by Lucius Apuleius at the end of his ancient book *"The Golden Ass"*. Working with the moon powers in any form means that you are willing to be guided by intuition and gentle hints. Although the message may come to you in a delicate and almost intangible manner, this doesn't mean that the power is less. The soft touch of the Moon Goddess's mantle may set you off on a long hard journey, or lay upon you with the kiss of moonlight a great and heavy responsibility. She is always willing to awaken your abilities of inner vision, and the art of scrying, for she rules over crystals and pools of water, mirrors and all forms of glasses used for far seeing, for she is a mirror of the Sun's light. She also has the power to disguise, to hide, to shade and enchant, and the visions she may choose to show you can be hallucinations just as they may be true sight. Only by daring to go out into her haunted silver light, far beyond the city's glow, and commune with her will you come to understand the two sides of her silver coin, one of which shows reality and the other illusion.

To the qabalist the first path leads from the earthly Malkuth to the lunar Yesod, and on this purple and silver road lies the double power to bespell and to reveal. Here you may perceive the vision of the Machinery of the Universe, and watch the creation of the cosmos shaping out of the dust of stars. You may, in vision, tread upon the silver sands of the Moon and experience the indigo and violet images of that sphere. It is a path which leads through the conscious transition between life and death, waking and sleeping, and it may well be guarded by Charon who rows those souls across the river which divides the Lands of Time from the Timeless lands. Here you may encounter Anubis, that other ancient Guide of Inner Travellers and keeper of the gates of death. At the end of the silver road, where the sky is velvet black and the great orb of the moon stands silver bright amidst the star-spangled darkness you might be blessed with a vision of Isis herself, or any of the other aspects of the Moon Goddess which you seek within your heart.

If you go out on a moonlit night and call upon the Goddess as the One who inspires vision, the Keeper of Dreams or as She who can bless you with clear sight you may well be rewarded. You will still have to master the Gentle Art of scrying in a glass or crystal ball, of seeing in a black mirror or a pool of water in a dark bowl. You will have to find a way to switch off the pressures of the world before the Lady of Midnight will swirl her misty cloak across the speculum before your seeking eyes, and cause your vision to change to other times and other places. You may have to work hard, for a long time, simply to find a suitable instrument, or discover a way of making a dark glass for your own use. Certainly you can buy many such items, but they then will need twice as much work to tune them in to your own frequency and that of true vision than one you make. You can seldom simply sit down before a new crystal ball and scry in it, just like that! It takes a great deal of persistence and determination to get all the conditions right, but if you ask the Moon Goddess to help you, and if you will serve her, she is certain to give you some guidance.

There is a very old ritual called 'Drawing Down the Moon' which is misdescribed in some books - the ritual they mention with a cup and a dagger is a solar rite, for a totally different purpose. The old moon ritual involves three ladies or at least two ladies and a man who have between them a bowl for water or wine, preferably of silver or glass, a small round mirror, and a bottle of white wine, apple juice (the clear sort), or spring water. This ceremony must be performed out of doors during the first three nights of a new moon, usually soon after sunset - as you will discover the new moon is only visible just as the sun is setting! Find a place where you can see the moon clearly. One of the ladies takes the bowl, another pours the wine into it and the third person holds the mirror so that the crescent moon is reflected into the bowl. It may take a bit of juggling around to get this to work properly, but once the image is there in the silver dish it is necessary to call upon the Goddess as Diana, Isis, Rhiannon or Artemis, etc. to instil into your offering of wine her blessing and magical power. You may well find that each of you will be inspired to sing or chant, recite poetry or prose or pray out loud for the sort of moon wisdom which is on offer. As you will see, the new moon in the sky, the symbol of growth and revelation, becomes the old moon in the bowl, the bringer of wisdom and understanding to the brave. You will also observe that the image will quiver and blur and you may find that the wine seems to become almost luminous if you do the ritual wholeheartedly and with intent.

Once this has happened give thanks, again in word or song, gesture or dedication and pour a few drops to the Earth so that divine wisdom may descend on all below the moon. The wine may then be drunk as a communion between you and the Moon Goddess. If you use water it may be taken away to be used for blessing items to be used for scrying, or even for scrying if poured into a black bowl, or mixed with black ink, but its magical virtue will only last until the moon is full, and then it will be gone. If you are having a communion with the moon-blessed wine, you could make some shortbread biscuits in the shape of moons with hazelnuts in them, and again scatter the crumbs to earth as an offering of thanks. This may sound simple but, like all old magic, it is a potent ceremony and it will influence your dreams and visions in the days to come, so don't rush off and do it unprepared.

Because the moon has changing phases and each of these is best for some special, mundane and magical purpose it is well worth the effort of getting to know what happens in the sky between the Sun, by whose light the Moon shines (and the Earth and the other planets, for that matter), for only the Sun is actually luminous as it is a star. The Moon is held in the balanced gravity of Earth and Sun and turns always the same face to us. Learn how this inter-relationship leads to the phases of the Moon, and how eclipses of both Sun and Moon are caused. You will find plenty of simple books on the universe, written for children, and so you will understand how things at a distance can influence each other, and cause changes, just as magic causes changes at a distance. Look at the sky, notice where the moon rises each night, see how vast she appears when standing on a low horizon and how she seems to shrink to her zenith above you. See how much she changes from night to night so that a mere glimpse will tell you her age from new, or how many nights until the dark of the moon. You can look this data up in a diary or ephemeris but as one who is learning Natural Magic, you should *know*.

Because the Moon is seen as a Goddess in the Western Mysteries it is obvious that she is concerned with women's magic. Her power is slow and subtle, her influence gentle but potent, none the less. She will open the doors to dreams and you will begin to see that your dreams go through phases too. Some people dream vividly during the full moon nights, others during the dark of the moon. If you can sleep with moonlight pouring on to your pillow there is a good chance you will find her light will have strange but useful effects upon you. It will certainly increase your psychic faculties, and gradually allow you access to skills of the mind that you don't already control. You might find some of these strange and unsettling, but that is the nature of magic. If it were not so, then magic would have no meaning. Note down any feelings and experiences you have in a Moon diary for this is the surest way to judge what is going on in the realms of occult learning.

It is generally thought that the waxing phase of the moon is best for healing mental conditions (physical ills come into the province of the Sun), and for working positive and growth-orientated magic. It is a time for mastering the practical psychic skills like psychometry (that is the art of sensing information about the owner of an item which you hold in your hand), for scrying in any sort of crystal, glass or dark mirror, or other forms of divination with Tarot cards or the I Ching. You will never have too much skill in these arts, and some folk find them easier than others, but then some people may well have been trained in such magical arts long ago! The waxing phase of the moon is a time for planting flowers and crops which produce their harvest above the ground, or for beginning mystical exercises and continuing workings.

The time of the full moon, preferably before the change of tide to the waning phase, is the best opportunity for getting out under the moon and holding meetings, gathering herbs by moon-light, and communing with the Lady of the Moon alone. It is not the most potent phase for magic, as, like the full-blown rose, the beauty outweighs the scent or the lunar tide, which is still, just as the sea tide pauses between ebb and flow, and between flow and ebb, and the water is still.

As the moon's curved light starts to diminish you will find you can use the outflow to get rid of anxieties, problems which weigh heavy on your heart and 'female' troubles. You can also use the waning light to develop inner awareness, for just as the moon's shine is less outward, so her power becomes more inwardly focused. Meditations in the waning phase should be easier and more rewarding and the realisations they produce should be more profound and helpful.

In the dark of the moon you are dealing with the Wise Crone who is lonely and sometimes seemingly callous. She is the Goddess who will not suffer fools at all, let alone gladly! She has no time to waste on explanations, but her power and knowledge are endless. It is she who provides the ecstasies, the flashes of blinding insight, the certainty of received knowledge, but her power can be greater than we are, and she can dazzle and so blind our sight. Many pagans who try to worship the aspects of the Moon and Sun ignore her and imagine that she will not affect their lives if they leave her alone, but she may have other ideas! You cannot ignore her, nor can you somehow deflect the bolts of understanding which can turn a difficult situation into a hopeless one, for true wisdom is not gentle. The truth that shines in the dark of the moon has to be illuminated by its own light, and we are not always prepared for its brilliance, nor the power with which certainty can be forced upon us. There is nothing stronger than knowing what is right, and often this can totally upset our previous knowledge. If you can make your self go humbly towards the feet of this seeming ugly, unlovable, black, old crone, and become her long-lost grandchild, offering care and consideration, her dark and wrinkled face can change and you can behold the face of the Goddess of Wisdom, as she sees herself, unveiled.

If you want to communicate with the Moon in all her phases there are a number of things you can do. The first is the obvious one - go out at night, when the calendar indicates a new moon, and watch as the sun sets for the fine crescent falling into the pale sky in the west. Speak to this most beautiful aspect of the Goddess as Maiden, a child just becoming a woman. Learn to become her friend, her playmate, her spiritual lover, even, and see what sort of power she bestows upon you. Later, seek out the waxing phase, the quarter light of silver in the dark, rising later each evening and showing more of her face, to you. Speak to her as the maturing one, the young woman just about to bear her first child and learn from her the power of love and partnership, of sharing and giving. Offer her your time in exchange for her gifts of understanding and control of your dreams. As she grows and shows more light feel her energy awakening levels of your own insight and awareness.

When the Moon is full, rising late in the night, see how she edges over the rim of the horizon and momentarily seems to pause before her upward, shrinking flight. Speak with her as the Mother, bringer of the Light of inner understanding and common sense. Be prepared for some sharp answers if you ask questions to which you already know the answers for she will not tolerate stupidity. The full moon may be motherly and warm, but unless you become as one of her children she will treat you like a stranger. To really share her magical powers you will have to make a personal dedication to serve her in exchange for the inner light she may give you. You will have to acknowledge her bright disc and walk in her purple-shadowed landscape, where the reality of the day takes on a different face, and where certainty can change to doubt, and dream become more real than thought. Many claim to be priestesses or priests of the moon, but unless they have made that inner commitment and have her dark light shining in their eyes, theirs are empty words and her mystic power will not be in them.

In the waning phase of the Moon it is time to plant those seeds which produce their vegetables below the ground, the carrots and parsnips, the potatoes and onions, many of which you will see are white. The moon power will draw the seeds into the earth and nourish them so that the roots are full and juicy. Often it is necessary to look at an old herbal which will tell you to gather herbs or seeds or rose petals by the light of the moon, and wash your face in the first dew, before sunrise, to cure spots and pimples. Magically it is a time to look inward and find those skills and arts which come from within. For the ladies it is a chance to renew their links with the Goddess as priestess, serving her purposes as they see fit in the world, but at this time drawing strength and seeking guidance. Men will be able to use the waning moon phase to form links with their Anima, the feminine side of their souls, through which the Goddess works in them. This takes far more courage than performing some ritual in the light of the sun, in the eye of the day. Most pagan priests have never reforged this connection and they find it hard to visualise, to perceive and to accept the reality of visions which do not enter awareness through the open eyes. Again, it is a time to get out into the high hills and talk with the Lady as she matures in her wisdom.

At the dark of the moon you may again learn great secrets if you have the daring to approach the Moon Goddess in her Hecate form. She is dark and sinister, wise and unforgiving. Now is the time for the magic of banishments, particularly of your own accepted faults, the stubbornness of mind which will not accept alternatives to reality, the anxieties which have no real cause, the 'me first' attitude which is destructive to your very spirit. Ask this Goddess for help and she will advise you, for she brewed the Cauldon of Inspiration long ago and her knowledge is infinite. She may offer you the strange gift of prophecy as she did to Merlin, wizard to King Arthur. She may grant you true visions in the crystal or black mirror which are her instruments, and she may haunt your dreams with the future of the world, and she will astonish you by revealing to you your own depth of perception and inner awareness. Treat her with respect, draw down the light of her thin crescent into dark wine so that the hidden springs of clairvoyance may be opened inside you, but be sure you are prepared for the force with which she may answer your plea. Unless you are well skilled it is not a good time for working magic under her auspices for, like the rising tides of the sea which she controls, she can overwhelm the unwary, and wash them away.

There have always been priests and priestesses dedicated to the Moon. Dion Fortune, in her two novels, *The Sea Priestess* and its sequel, *Moon Magic,* describes how the first schools of magic were based on lost Atlantis, and that there were three temples, one a Sun Temple, and another a Moon temple. The third was usually known as the Withdrawn Temple and those priests worked their magic with the power of the stars. Because no written records of what went on in those hallowed halls have come down to us we have to use the methods of Moon magic to seek out such knowledge as may be given to us. Throughout the ages there have been Seers and Scryers who have used the ancient crystals and black mirrors to search back through the records to regain that lost source of instruction and healing. Many wrote their findings in code, or taught them behind the closed doors of a magical school or within a lodge. Some interpreted them in strange ways. Dr Dee, in Elizabeth I's reign, was convinced he was talking to angels, yet he was bringing through into his own time fragments of a long forgotten lore. Others before and after him have made contact with these timeless sources, as we can today, if we are able to set aside the limitations of sequential time and explore through the doors of ancient symbols. We can re-experience this fount of ancestral wisdom.

Certainly, our ancestors didn't imagine their journeys took them across the fields of time to some long-lost land, yet the myths, the songs, the inherited prophecies and tales all have references to older sources, now lost beneath the waves, or withdrawn into some other level of being. There is a long tradition of heroes and adventurers entering 'Fairyland', the 'Otherworld' or the 'Underworld' and gaining some strange gift there, or the skill to prophesy, or magical jewels which turn to dust when brought into the light of the sun. The gates to the lost land are still with us, maybe more overgrown, or hidden under the crumbled ruins of some long-neglected place. Yet in the moon's lambent beams those secret inner ways, those entrances which take the daring traveller under the hill, or across the subterranean lake, or into the innermost Earth, can be found.

They will never be encountered in your house, though there could be a path that leads to 'Faery' at the bottom of your garden.

As the circle of the moon's full face seems to diminish as she rises from the black line of the horizon, so you may find you too need to be able to shrink, like Alice in Wonderland, and enter a different world, both close and familiar, yet seen from the viewpoint of a small creature, perhaps a hare or a frog. This, too, is within the scope of moon magic and it takes real daring to follow that path on some moonlit night. Legends tell how the witches used to change themselves into hares and dance in the light of the full moon, and attend secret meetings on the heath. We cannot say this is untrue, but we can try for ourselves to use the magic ways to become as hares and experience it at some level for ourselves. When Cerridwen brewed her magic potion one of the effects it had on the boy Gwion was to turn him into a hare, and then a fish and then a bird, so it is clear that a draught from the Cauldron of Inspiration could still transform those who drink from it, if they are able to find or recreate it in the landscapes of the mind.

The easily seen changes of the moon were the only calendar the country folk would use. Feasts and festivals of the church were things imposed upon them, but they would name each full moon from some local happening like the flowering of a useful plant, the time to cut the hay or reap one of the green or white harvests which alternate throughout the farming year. When the snows melted there would be a time of seeing the first white flowers, usually snowdrops in Britain, and take this as a sign that the Green Goddess was about to return to her chilly land. There would be the first white lambs and the milk from the ewes, far more widely drunk than it is today (although its richness is beginning to be recognised as a valuable alternative for people who are allergic to cow's milk). This was when the people celebrated 'Oimelc' which means 'ewes' milk' but like all traditional festivals it was celebrated when it happened, not when some man-made calendar said so. Once the lambs were safely born, the first flush of green grass was eagerly looked for and the water meadows, flooded in the autumn to stop the soil from freezing were drained, and the warmer earth began its early growth. Although many modern pagans celebrate the solar festival of the Spring

Equinox when the Sun, in theory, enters the sign of Aries, there was an older lunar feast which was held when the seed had been sown, probably with the full moon in March.

As the green buds opened on the trees and the grass in the sheltered lowlands became sufficient to support livestock the more hardy beasts were driven higher up into the hills, moors and mountains, after passing between the magical herbal Beltane fires. Each moon was a time of recognition of a new aspect of the farmer's year and each had its particular festival, its tasks and activities, guided only by the pattern of the weather and the hand of Mother Nature. There have been various attempts to reconstruct this ancient Celtic calendar but most of these seem to be based on regular days in specific months as we know them, rather than from new moon to new moon. In fact, there is some evidence that the ancient Celts worked their lunar months from the sixth day after the new moon, or the first quarter, as we would see it in the sky.

If you want to work with lunar periods you will need to begin to observe what in nature comes to light with each moon. Look at the plants in the garden, the animals in the fields, the crops in the farmlands and the fruit in the orchards.

What you see may be local; the date of the flowering of hawthorn, for example, doesn't happen even in balmy Cornwall before mid-May, so May Day which celebrates the White Goddess's return with this strange scented blossom cannot really be held until the flowers appear. This is later in the east of Britain and later still further north. The same applies to the various harvest moons. If your corn isn't ripe and ready to be gathered in you cannot celebrate a harvest festival, if the grapes are still green, or the apples unripe there is no way that you can rationally hold the harvest home. Become observant, examine the flora and fauna so that new arrivals and harvests can be feasted in due season, but the season is of the making of nature and thus variable, whereas the calendar is man-made.

Once you begin to adapt your cycles to the moon's you will find all kinds of things start to fall into place. You watch your dreams and can judge the validity of any predictions there because you have discovered these come during the last few nights of the old moon, or your creativity and mental/physical fertility surges and new concepts are born. Learn to sense the subtle daily changes, which some people have tried to classify as 'biorhythms'. We do have cycles of mental, physical and emotional states but these are personal to us, just as any of our other natural cycles of blood-pressure and pulse-rate, each of which changes during the day and night, and at different times in the lunar month. It isn't simply a matter of charting regular ups and downs of each of our levels of being so that they match those of everyone else. Each of us is different and our personal rhythm may vary a day or two in each direction, depending on many external and internal factors. Only by patient observation, combined with an understanding of our true feelings, psychism and physical state can we identify and so predict the ups and downs of our biorhythms, and those about us. If you devote a little effort to understanding these phases in your own inner and outer life you will find it easier to make use of the upsurges and ebbs of this tide, and you will also be more able to judge the moods of other people.

If you also begin to learn the Gentle Arts of scrying you will also find that the moon's changing energies will help you. If you make a black mirror from a piece of shop-fitting black glass, or from an old-style alarm-clock face coated with several layers of matt black model paint on the convex side, each set into a rim of wood or plaster, you will find it a useful tool to learn on. Certainly a crystal ball may look more exotic but it is really quite a modern invention, introduced in Tudor times. Before that the scryers would have used a bowl of ink, or a piece of shiny black stone, wet slate or even coal, or anything else which would glitter and distract the normal vision so that inner sight can break through. Often a polished fingernail reflecting a speck of moon or sunlight could act as a focus in this way. As each person's ability depends a great deal on their particular mental and intellectual make-up it is best to try a few simple and cheap methods before you are driven to pay many pounds for a glass or crystal ball.

Choose a night of bright moonlight for your first experiments and if you can be out of doors or at least in a room with open windows through which unaltered moonlight can pour, allow it to fall upon the scrying glass or speculum for a while so that the instrument begins to feel filled with moonlife. Light a candle and a little incense to help alter the atmosphere to a more magical feeling, and then become still and relaxed. It may take many attempts to be able to see anything in any form of scrying mirror but, like all the Gentle Arts, persistence will pay off. You can't force yourself into the poised form of consciousness which is vital to all successful meditational methods, but only get to it by finding the balance between curiosity and relaxation. Eventually it becomes second nature and all sessions, be they pathworking, meditation or some form of divination prove rewarding because you have gained the knack.

As you watch in a calm and distracted sort of way you may discover the moonlight seems to have seeped into the glass and misted it' and in the midst of the swirling clouds a clear path begins to form, sometimes glinting with starlight. Once you have got that far regularly, it is only a brief step onward to the state where moving pictures, images, symbols and even dialogue into which you fully enter, or even seem to fall, occurs. It isn't easy and many people find this particular skill evades them no matter how hard they try. Usually it is at that moment when your patience seems exhausted and you begin to lose faith in the process that you somehow let go of whatever mental block defeats you and suddenly, for a while, you get a clear sight. Do go on with the basic exercises until you find that distinct and steady images of some sort happen under your control. Keep on with all the other studies of time and tide, of dream and divination, of moon surge and ebb in your life, and establish for yourself a true and effective communication with the Silver Lady of the Night.

Although we usually think of the moon as a purely night-time phenomenon, in reality she shines by day and night, rising later and later each evening. Her mystic effects can be felt on those days when she is but a faint glimmer in the dawn or dusk sky, and on those long summer evenings when rising full as the Harvest Moon, or in November as the Hunter's Moon she has variable influences upon us. Each of us has to find a way of understanding this, either seeing her as a Threefold Goddess, or as a tidal power which can alter our chemical make-up, or as the Anima in men and the eternal

Goddess in all women. We can build up a series of lunar festivals, each celebrating a different face of the Goddess, or drawing on that particular source of psychic energy to use in our magical work. We can use her light to bless the wine in the Moon cup, or her power to enhance divinations and bring us clarity of vision once we have built up the initial communion with her, in the familiar way with which our ancestors would have done.

8.
THE MAGIC OF THE SUN

Homage to thee, O thou who risest in Nu, and who at thy manifestation
dost make the world bright with light: the whole company of Gods
sing hymns to thee after thou has come forth each day. . .

Egyptian Hymn to Ra

Just as the ancient people were interested in the movement of the
moon and the patterns of the stars, they could hardly overlook the
brighter, more constant light of the sun each day. Traces of Sun
worship are found all over the world, and in many places temples,
pyramids, sacred mounds, circles, ellipses, rows and dolmens of
standing stones have been carefully placed to act as focuses for the
Sun's brilliance at certain times of the year. Even here in mist-
shrouded Britain, famed throughout the Roman empire for its
dreadful weather and magicians under every tree, many of the oldest
elaborate earthworks seem to have solar alignments, some of which,
like the Midsummer sunrise point over the Hele Stone at Stonehenge
are still correct. Think of any other scientific instrument which is
still functioning correctly after about 4,500 years! Certainly the
Sun now only peeps over the stone instead of standing   for a
moment as a disc above it, but the alignment is still to the rising
point. This is certainly true of many of the other less famous circles
and ellipses which are to be found in all the rocky landscapes of
Britain, and in Europe, and probably both South and North America,
North Africa and elsewhere.

These ancient structures teach us a number of things, many of
which have a magical significance. The first is that in very early
times (and some of the structures date back to 3,000 BC or even
before that) people watched the movements of the Sun against the

earth's curved horizon, and marked these positions, probably with movable wooden posts and later great stones, earthworks, rings, mounds and dips in the horizon. None of these excavations or constructions was a light task. In most cases the standing stones have been shaped with harder stones, and set upright or leaning to mark the skyline, with accuracy which our metal-wielding technologists might find hard to match. Only by being willing to see all these constructions as a part of a long-forgotten culture, whether they were designed as places of worship, or as parliaments or gathering places, markets for local produce, schools or merely as great calculators which portion time by the movement of the sun and moon, can we marvel at their endurance, and maybe, one day, helped by the Gentle Arts, rediscover their purpose and methods of construction.

We are used to information being encapsulated in words. If we could open our inner eyes we might just be able to recognise that similar stores of encoded information might be magically impregnated into rocks, crystals and the very landscape itself. We can all accept that the microchip can hold vast stores of data, imprinted electronically into its structure. Is it so large a leap of the understanding to be able to accept that the Wise Ones of the past were somehow able to impinge their thoughts or ideas magically onto the crystalline rocks which are commonly used for the construction of their elaborate monuments, which have survived the ravages of time? It is our mental dullness which prevents us from reading those encoded messages, not the originators' archaic and forgotten methods of encodement and storage. Certainly we don't *know*, no ancient text has spelled out for us the methods of entrapping information, but there are many hints in the words of prophets, and within the oral traditions, in songs and ballads, poems and seers' visions, that 'stones shall speak across the oceans', that sacred places would talk to the initiated with the voices of the Gods and Goddesses, and that trained scryers would be able to speak 'sooth', or the truth, if they could learn how.

By working with the moving patterns of shadows made by the sun on a gnomon stone falling on marks on the ground, the passage of observed time could be seen but solar time is far more relevant to the recent ages, where industry, mechanisation and railways need a timetable to allow us to determine how far behind schedule the services are running each day. Farmers, herdsmen, agriculturists, herbalists, wise men and women did not need the hours of the passing day marked by some form of clock. The movement of the sun round the sky, or the behaviour of the animals, or the warmth and dryness of the soil indicated the moment for some future activity. Time is an illusion which all true practitioners of the Gentle Arts will learn to see through. The magic of the sun may be just as misleading as those things seen in the mystical light of the moon. At night we expect to be lost or confused but by day, when the sky is clear, we imagine our path will be safe and clearly seen. Sometimes this is not so.

We have to learn again the perception of what matters, and this is particularly true in such things as the allocation of dates for celebrating various ancient festivals. Most of the dates we have are fixed by the Church, with the sole exception of Easter, actually originally dedicated to Eostra, Goddess of Spring, and which is still fixed by the Moon, even though it is the most important Christian feast! Christmas, and all the saints' days are aligned to a spurious calendar, and many other older gatherings and celebrations have been forced to follow suit and fossilise their position in a pre-determined place. In the older times each feast was dependent on whatever it celebrated. Seed time could *only* be celebrated when the seed was in the ground, late or early each year, as nature chose. Harvest festivals happened when the grain and the fruit from the orchards were safely inside for the winter and so it could be judged a good or bad harvest and celebrated accordingly. The lives of the people depended on their harvest in those aeons before Euro-grants, and food mountains and wine lakes! If the yield was poor the people could starve, and they would have no produce to sell or exchange for other goods, but if there was plenty great rejoicing was to be heard throughout the land, and the feast of harvest home would be abundant. When the animals were brought down from the hills there was another harvest, this time of flesh and hides, offal for the pot, and a great time of salting and preserving, so that there would be food through the hungry and barren months. Again, there would be good years and bad ones, when the ewes had dropped weak lambs, and the cattle had been sick, and the wild harvests of rabbits, geese, ducks and birds were small, so the people went without. If the grass was late there would be little milk, and so no hard cheese, stored against the cold days, and if the year was wet there might not even be fish for the streams would be too turbulent for them to breed, and too fast flowing for the nets to rob them of their waiting harvest. We have forgotten how cruel our climate can be to those who live from nature's variable bounty.

As the Moon was seen as a representation of the Threefold Goddess, so in most cultures, the Sun was seen as a God, or sometimes just the symbol of Godhead. The Norse folk have a Sun Maiden, but they tend to have rather different views in their wintry lands to the more southerly tribes. Like the Moon Goddess, the Sun has many names and attributes. Here in Britain he was usually looked upon as benign and kindly, whereas in the deserts his power was that of scorching heat and destruction. In Britain most of the oldest earthworks are attributed to some solar function, although many of the oldest single standing stones, the mounds and sacred pools are dedicated to the earlier Goddesses, of Earth or Moon. As bringer of light and fertility the Sun was seen as a healer and restorer of life, and these aspects are still part of our inherited magical tradition. The Sun God is always, however, the Son of the Mother, Mabon ap Modron, and her consort, lover, husband and father of her children, yet she attends his funeral rites, his entry into the Underworld, and again she bears him, each midwinter, as the Child of Promise, the Star Child. Although the Moon and her Goddess may wax and wane, She is eternal and undying, whereas the Sun grows strong to midsummer, but fades away to his autumnal death, departure and eventual return.

In some cultures, and in the rites of many modern pagan groups, there are two solar heroes. One is the Summer King and the other the Winter King, each with his symbolic tree, the summer Oak and the winter Holly. The story of their twice-yearly battles at Yule and Midsummer have become a part of the tradition of the ritual cycle. Looking back to earlier myths there are tales of the dark and light lords. In Egyptian mythology there are the twin God-forces, Horus the bright sun and Set the dark aspect who tricked and defeated Osiris, green-faced god of the Underworld and of growing things. In many traditions the bright Son of Light has a dark twin, bringer of chaos and destruction, and ruler of the shadowland which is always below the horizon. In the Christian tradition this dichotomy has become, in some branches of that faith, symbolised by Jesus and Lucifer, the fallen angel, who became *Rex Mundi,* Lord of the World to the Dualists of the Middle Ages. Belief in an actual source of evil and a personified Devil must be a matter for personal meditation and consideration. It may be hard to decide if a God who allows such suffering and hardship to occur is unchallenged for the throne of heaven, and if there is some Lord of Destruction abroad who is undoing the eternal peace and plenty which a Good God should provide.

The ancient people, to whom religion and worship were natural parts of everyday life, had a variety of ways of construing this division of light and darkness, and there are many ancient ballads and 'mumming plays' in which the Hero and his Shadow battle for the prize of the world, or the direction of the lives of humankind. Usually in the modern forms these have become such saintly figures as St George who kills the pagan dragon, or a probably older form, the Archangel Michael who overcomes but does not kill his devilish adversary. There is an important point here, for in one the hero is ultimately and finally triumphant, and in the other version there is the conflict which is to be refought for balance. In nature summer doesn't entirely overcome winter, nor day night. There is a continuous balancing throughout the year. Recognition of this fairly obvious fact is extremely important for anyone making use of the Gentle Arts in the New Age, for we have to balance our doing by our ability to wait and watch. We need to learn when it is right to give aid and bring light to those in darkness and when it is better to be still and await the coming dawn of a light far brighter than we can bear.

Because the seasons are fixed by the movement of the Sun through the sky the festivals which are solar in nature are more easily set within the year. In midwinter the days grow shorter and shorter and it must have seemed to our ancestors that the welcome power of the warming sun was to be withdrawn from them completely. At the death of the year there were gatherings of the whole household to light fires and pray for a return of the Sky Lord. Many of the customs which we recognise as part of the Christmas festivities have pagan roots, and are founded in these much older beliefs and practices - the decorating of houses with evergreens and coloured ribbons and charms, the singing of special songs which we still call carols. Originally a carol was a round dance, and in some places the circles of standing stones were known as 'carols'. Even Stonehenge was once called 'the Giants' Dance'. It was customary to bring in the root of a great tree, oak or ash for preference, and have it burning on the hearth throughout the entire old festival of the Twelve Days of Christmas, even then being able to save a piece to rekindle and so light the following year's log. The rich ashes of this fire were sprinkled on the fields to ensure fertility at the end of the celebration.

The mysterious mistletoe, still banned from many churches as a pagan symbol, was sacred to those Sun Priests, the Druids, whose ancient law dictated that they should hold their public ceremonies 'in the Light of the Sun, in the Eye of Day'. Much of their knowledge, faintly echoed in the expurgated relics which have come down to us from their enemies, the literate Romans, telling of their teaching, healing skills, arts of divination, magical power (which the Romans feared most, as their hot Gods did not function in these misty and damp places), and their knowledge of the stars. To the Druids the oak tree was the sacred dwelling-place of the Gods, and in the rare cases where mistletoe actually grows on the oak, as opposed to its more usual host, apple or lime or poplar trees, they knew they were in a sacred place. The Druids preserved the sacred teaching that the Gods would only manifest in natural surroundings, in sacred groves, on the shores of lakes, rivers and pools, in caves or by the sea. As much of Britain was a huge untamed forest jungle in their time, there were plenty of places in which the Great Ones might make their epiphanies. The Druids, both men and women, were Seers and Prophets, historians, keepers of the genealogies of the Chiefs' clans, judges of miscreants, and probably, in this particular context, executioners of prisoners, rather than cruel sacrificial priests, slaying struggling victims, bound within baskets and cast into a fire, as Roman records would have us believe.

The Sun Priests and Priestesses were healers, using both the natural life-giving power of the Sun, as it edged through its annual journey, and those special plants, each appearing in its season, probably when the ills it cured were most likely to be rife. Most yellow plants are dedicated to the Sun, and many have healing power recognised to this day. Greater celandine, marigolds, yellow dock, cowslips, broom, gorse, St John's wort (that midsummer flower), yellow flag, mullein, dandelion, tansy, elecampagne, honeysuckle and many of the cabbage tribe are still part of a modern herbalist's repertoire, as they must have been to our less scientific ancestors. Even in the famous Culpeper's day, each plant was attributed to a particular planetary power, of which the Sun and Moon (neither, in fact, planets, but counted so for symbolic reasons) are important members. This is another aspect of the ancient wisdom of which fragments have come down to us, in written form, in the old herbals, spell books and even the writing of the alchemists, who as well as making chemical changes, used plants, and astrological data to time their mysterious processes.

From the movement of the Sun we have our seasons and their festivals, of which there are a great number, in Britain and Europe. Many have become disguised as Saints' Days, or local gatherings to bless the well, the crops, the horses or the ploughs, but in their older guise, these were the days our ancestors allocated to thanksgiving or asking requests of the Sun God or the Moon Goddess, for it is she, as Lady of the Sea and all the waters who lays her blessing on the ever-running springs and wells, in whose depths lies truth. If you decide to celebrate some of the ancient feasts in an earlier form you will have to look at what is actually happening in the world, and what sort of harvest or good gift is the underlying reason for the modern church or village festival. Many of these have shifted away from the original date owing to the various changes in the calendar, and, in any case, the oldest feasts were fixed by the harvest or activity they celebrated, not by an arbitrary date, set by the Church.

Take New Year's Day, for example: if you follow the Celtic

calendar this ought to be the day after Hallowe'en, because Samhain (pronounced Sowin) means 'Summer's end' and it was the natural time to bring in the animals from the mountains and gather the members of the family who had herded them over the unfenced heights all summer. Once everyone was at home, and the necessary beasts had been killed, there would be a feast and to this the Ancestors, the First Parents, the God and Goddess, of the tribe would be invited. The best meat and beer were placed before them in offering, and the doors would be left open to the night wind. Fires were lit to burn the husks of the winnowed wheat, and with it, the failures and symbols of those things not needed to be kept through the winter. The people hoped that the light and flames would help to lure back the Sun God who had then commenced the long journey through the world below, while the sleeping ancestors were awake and stirring. It is at this feast that their wise and ancient counsel could be sought, and in the Moon Hag's dark mirror, glimpses of what was to come might be discovered to guide the people through the new year.

Another modern festival is New Year on 1 January, but it ought to be on the sixth, because that is the last of the Twelve Days of Christmas. You might prefer to celebrate the new year on the spring equinox, in March, on about the twenty-first each year, when the Sun in theory enters the first sign of the zodiacal year, the first point of Aries. However, this doesn't actually happen any more, due to the precession of the equinoxes. At that time now, as opposed to the time of Ptolemy who gave us the zodiac we use, the Sun is somewhere in the sign of Pisces, and in the next couple of hundred years, when the Aquarian Age is truly born, it will be in the constellation of Aquarius at that moment.

Of course, many other religions and other lands have their New Year on different dates. Many of us are aware of the Chinese New Year fixed by their lunar calendar to fall in mid-February, and the Jewish New Year is celebrated in September, and that of Muslims in August. No doubt there are plenty more, once you start looking for them, all perfectly valid times to begin new cycles, just as the Sun begins his annual journey through the fixed stars. Your own New Year may well be seen as your birthday, or if you have been through the ritual of rebirth at some initiation ceremony, then you have a 'Re-birthday' with a new horoscope and life pattern derived from it, if the ceremony was anything more than a ritual sham, or a good time among friends.

Although the Moon's phases are short, they are very easily felt in the inner levels of our being, whereas the Sun's coming and going is a much more outward, worldly experience. He, too, has waxing and waning tides within the great cycles of spring, summer, autumn and winter, as well as the very apparent growing phase and then fading time. Each quarter has a magical tide, and each can be used beneficially or to sweep away unnecessary things. These tides act in our lives whether we recognise them or not, but if we can see them coming, we can be prepared and ready to make the best of whatever opportunities or magical energies that come with them.

Taking the ordinary year, which is divided by the solstices and equinoxes, the winter solstice, falling about 21 December marks the turn of the tide of the solar year, and the energy is waning then. This is known in occult circles as 'the Cleansing Tide' and it has the power to wash away all sorts of things, people, events and possessions beyond our ken. Most people aren't aware of this, yet they feel depressed, run down and miserable after the bright lights of Christmas have given way to the phoney bargains of the January Sales, and when the weather here is cold and wet and generally horrid. Many people seem to die at this time, between early January and mid-March, and often domestic rows end up with separation, or the loss of possessions or some other seeming disaster. It is actually quite a helpful time, magically, for it does give us a good excuse to turn out those cupboards of our minds and turf out all the junk, the useful item whose use never seems to be required yet has been safely kept for a long time. If you don't clear out voluntarily, then the Gods have ways of doing it for us. The early spring can lead to all sorts of changes in our stable life-patterns, relationships and situations, as well as the sudden disappearance of material objects, or well-founded friendships. The rains and snows wash and purify our inner selves too, and it is a valuable time to perform divinations to explore possible paths forward. Often it is clearly shown that certain parts of the pattern will have to go, and new ideas grow in their vacated place. The Gods seldom waste any human talent, no matter in which field of practical experience it may lie. If we listen to those silent inner voices they can save us a lot of pain by explaining what is to change and how to do it the simplest way. If you just won't hear the gentle advice, that is when the chains of stability are broken by force, because change is magical life, stagnation is death.

Once the spring equinox has arrived in late March, when if we were living two thousand years ago the Sun would be entering the constellation of the Ram, the tide can easily be felt to turn. Now it is 'the Growing Tide', a three month time of expansion and outer gain. In the months of spring there is a feeling of new life arising from every plant and aspect of nature, and that too can work in us, but mostly on the level of gaining knowledge and experiences. It is a good time to get out and about and begin to observe the Sun God at work in the countryside, turning the dark fields green, and yellowing the pale primroses, golden daffodils and forsythia in gardens. As the wild flowers change from yellow to blue, and bluebells, scabious and other mauve, purple and azure hues spring amid the grasses, the days and nights unbalance in the direction of light, and the stars grow dim in the twilight sky.

The third solar tide, from the summer solstice to the autumn equinox, is the 'Tide of Reaping', when the ideas and material skills you have learned will offer you their various harvests.
You will begin to reap the rewards of your psychic visions. The many exercises which you are mastering will begin to pay off, the practical crafts and experiences will start to show a profit on that internal, invisible bank account. Any external seeds you may have sown will, by this time of year, be showing their fruits and you should be able to gather in whatever they have produced, on whatever level it has become manifest. This can include the solidifying of friendships, the building of relationships and the recognition of your worth in the material world too.

The fourth tide is of 'Self-Examination' or 'Formulation'. Here, between late September and Yuletide you will need to look closely at the harvest of your year's work, on the levels of spiritual, mental and physical gains, and judge for yourself how well you have done. Only you can do this in life, as only you can truly judge your entire life in the Halls of Death where others will ask the questions, yet it is you who makes the reply and so judge your own worth. The Egyptian priests of the Sun Temples at Heliopolis knew the forty-two questions, often referred to in the texts as the 'negative confession' which asked such things as 'Have you wronged any person?' and 'Have you stolen offerings from the Temple?' or 'Have you caused anyone to weep?' To each question the spirit of the one who has come to the Hall of Ma'at to have their soul weighed against the feathers of her symbol needs to be able to say 'I have not offended this law.' The same ought to be true at this solar tide of summing up and self-discovery. It is far less painful to look at your own failures and faults than to have some other individual point them out to you. Few on earth are perfect, but there is nothing to prevent anyone who seeks wisdom from the old ways striving for perfection as you determine it for yourself.

Once again the outward-going tide after Yule picks up its power and carries off all those abandoned or discarded aspects of our lives, for we have opened the hidden doors, and walked the secret paths, and there can be no turning back.

Once the material world is seen to be only a part of reality, and its value to us diminished, then these secret tides will affect us, whether we will it or no. We can only survive their power by being prepared, by casting off all that is outgrown and unneeded, or by binding with unbreakable bonds of love, of kindness and of trust the links which fasten us to our nearest and dearest.

Many followers of the pagan paths see the turning year as the continuing cycle of interaction between the Goddess of Earth/Sea/Moon and the Sun and Sky God who also rules in the Underworld. At Yuletide the Mother, sacred in all true faiths, bears her magical Child of Promise, often alone or cast out, and the Child is nurtured among strangers or under some other disadvantage. In the Old Religion this was the first day of twelve days of feasting, celebration and storytelling, and on the last of those days, Epiphany, the Astrologer Kings came to offer the symbolic gifts of sovereignty, priesthood and sacrifice with the gold, frankincense and myrrh to the Chosen One, son of Mary. In the older feast, it is the time when the magical child, growing a year in a day, received his name, his arms and his destiny from his mother, and set off in the path of the Sun. Born in a midwinter cave, the Star Child can reach back to the dawn of time, and far forward into our future, for the awaited one is always immanent, and his return is promised.

The second feast after Yuletide is that of the Goddess, who is again virgin, and is the gift-giver of her people. In Celtic tradition 'the Bride's Bed' is prepared with rich cloths and the first flowers, and many candles are blessed. Small gifts of food or drink are made ready as offerings to the Lady of Spring who once again is drawing forth her green skirts from under the pale mantle of winter snow. It is a woman's mystery, and the place is decked out by the women alone, the men being held back until they can make their dedication to the Goddess, and ask from her a wish in return for the thanks they offer for favours granted. Libations are poured and finally the many candles are lit, while her story is told again in verse and song. The Church has borrowed some aspects of this ancient rite and so call their celebration at the beginning of February, Candlemas.

At the spring equinox the Lord of Earth is asked to bless the land that the newly sown seed may be fertile and grow tall. The people used to go out into the fields with poles and broomsticks and leap high to show the corn how to grow, and with bells and ribbons to drive away the evil spirits and bad weather. Now you may see Morris Dancers carrying out these rites in their dances, though some have forgotten the meaning of their mime and gestures. The Sun God is growing in power and he now balances the hours held sway by his Dark Twin.

At May Eve, which can really only be celebrated when the first white blossoms of this sweet-scented tree are to be seen, and the taboo of bringing them into the house may be broken, there is the forest wedding of the Goddess to her Son/Lover, over the Beltane fire. This was the time when many local weddings of young folk took place, too, for the lads and lassies were going off into the hills with the flocks and herds and the older folk would not be around their summer bothies to keep an eve on them. The Goddess, like many an ancient bride, already bears the child she will carry until Yule, and so she and her Lover have proved their fertility to the people. In times past the King was married to his land or the

Matriarch held her power until her fertility waned. In some cultures the King reigned until he was defeated in a fight by a younger and stronger man, just as the stags and stallions and wild bulls fight for supremacy and control of their females. He who is strongest gets the best children, and more of them. When the King became weak or impotent then it was believed his land would die, and the fertility of beast and field diminish too. It was the maimed king who ruled the Wasteland in Arthur's day, and the Grail Knights had to restore him to restore the entire land by asking the Grail question. Few succeeded at that task, for the King was maimed before his time and no hero had arrived to take over his fertilising role, and so his land was barren. The King might serve his term, ended by combat, or a spell of seven years, when he went willingly to the Gods, as a messenger or offering from the people, but in older times the Queen never died. From being the Fertile Mother of the tribe she becomes the Old Wise Woman, the Sacred Crone, halfway to the Realms of the Underworld, from which comes the skill of far-seeing and prophecy. She was once the beautiful and cherished Maiden, who having chosen a husband, became the Mother and often ruler in the oldest clans who could always tell their descent through their Mother and Grandmother, even if they didn't know their own father. It was the Queen who held the power over the land, and her daughters who inherited it. Their husbands might be called King, but the blood of the Mother was the greater, and the power of the priestess more potent than that of the King. The Old Crone was not cast out but respected and her words were heard for she had gained wisdom and spoke for the Goddess.

At midsummer there may well have been a contest so that those who strove to be king might fight, or the enactment of the battle between Dark and Light Twins, the Kings of Oak and Holly, was fought. Now the Winter King succeeds and the Summer Lord begins his dark banishment in the Underworld of inner or withdrawn power. Again, in many cultures there is an important part of the religious life catered for by the Lord and Lady of Death/The Underworld/ Fairyland. We have almost forgotten this place of initiation and ancient source of wisdom. The barrows and tumuli stand silent witness to the forgotten rituals in places where natural caves are not to be found. All who seek the light must enter into the darkness, within themselves or in the secret places. They may fight their other selves in the summer noon, but they will still have to take their turn and go down into the dark regions of subterranean night to be taught the arcane knowledge and gain the inner strength to make their kingship work. Being a priest requires the candidate to undergo these things, either by choice within a true ritual, or by the vicissitudes of ordinary life. Each will be tested to his breaking point, for it is the strongest who is the best, and it is only the best, in any field, who is the Hero.

The year starts to wane, and harvests from field and orchard, from hill and copse are gathered in. The Sun King dies as Lord of the Corn, is gathered into the arms of his Mother/Wife, and his spirit, bound with ribbons the colour of life, is taken to the home altar and kept throughout the winter days. John Barleycorn, Kern King, Harvest Lord, by whatever name you know him, he is cut down and his grain made into the first loaf for the Wake of the Sun God, Lugh, who gives his name to Lammas - Lugh mass, the Mourning for Lugh. His death is the people's life, but the hot August days allow the people rest from their labours, and many Holydays are spent celebrating the harvest.

Day and night become equal once more as the September mists swathe the heavy fruit trees. The Lord of Light now wanes, taking up his abode in the Hidden Land, the place of the Goddess of Inner Earth. The harvest of the land is completed, and the people rejoice if they have done well, and prepare themselves for a long and hard winter if the crops have given poor yields and the animals have been barren.

Finally the end that is also the beginning, Hallowe'en, arrives, when all are gathered again to the household, and the Goddess as Crone and Wise One rules the dark feast. In her guise as Prophetess she will instruct those daring enough to look into her moon-dark glass, or to drink of the sacred wine made of her holy elderberries, red as dried blood. She will allow the brave ones to snatch the apple from the bough, or grasp it within the pool of water, or she will spell out the magic sign of cast apple peel which tells of events and partnerships that are to be. Now is the traditional time of ghost stories, hauntings and apparitions, for the veils between the worlds are thin, and the shades can sneak out, back into the firelit glow of our world. The Ancestors come too, to be consulted, as Wise Ones, about the clan's prospects, and they come to hear the news of the births and deaths, the marriages and partings.

Many modern groups have their own version of these nine sacred feasts. Some they attribute to the Sun God, and some to the Earth/ Moon Goddess, in her changing faces. In some cases the stories are acted out, but those who take the parts or the names of the Great Ones should be careful. With the names and actions also goes the responsibility, the power to change good or ill, and the key to the doors of past and future. These are heavy burdens and many who take them up do so without due thought or consideration. It may be fun to act out the death of the Corn King, but you take on a little of his sacrifice, and you may well find this working out in your own life. If you pretend to be the Goddess, without her wisdom, you may harm those you are close to because you cannot control her infinite power. She, who sees everything, may have no pity, when the future or the true past rushes before your eyes, and you can find no way to shut it out, nor control your frantic dreams. If you always act with respect to the Great Ones, ask their blessing and their guidance, they will certainly help you to learn something of their natures and powers, well within your ability to control, but if you just take on their guise they may not feel so kindly towards you, or they might just share their burden of running our universe with you!

Never, ever, take the Gods, Goddesses, angels, powers or any of these invisible forces for granted, *THEY ARE REAL,* and though the forms we perceive them in may not be their own true shape (for we are no longer trained to see them as they are), the powers of life and death, change and decay they wield are enormous. We cannot stand against them, any more than we can command the Sun to stand still or the seasons change to suit our whim. If you are sensible you will learn to recognise the power of the God of the Sun and the Goddess of the Earth as their works show them in nature, and by working in harmony with these tides and energies you will learn to benefit from the great inner resources.

The number of celebrations you are able to fit in to any one year will depend on your own aims and facilities. You could simply choose Mid-Summer and Mid-Winter, or your birthday and one of the New Year's Days, or you could celebrate the Nine Great Days of the Solar/Earth year together with one phase of the Moon's cycle, like the New Moon or Full Moon. Of course, some of these would fall quite close together and could thus be combined. It isn't simply a matter of taking a new diary each year and selecting dates, because every growing season is different, every area has local magical plants or trees around which some ancient festival may already have been entwined. A little research in the local library or newspaper archives might turn up just the sort of gathering you wish to take part in, revive or rededicate. Do watch the phases of nature. They are far more powerful than any artificial rites you might choose to perform because you feel like it. Learn to sense the tides of the Sun and the Moon and gradually you will see that those acts you perform in harmony with their waxing and waning energies are far more successful, or that your Moon-led inner awareness is made sharper and more accurate, just by choosing the day on which you perform a divination, or some other form of magical work.

One other skill of the Gentle Arts that is associated with the power of the Sun is that of healing. Magical methods may certainly be used successfully to help all kinds of conditions and sickness, but you do have to be aware that if you interfere in the lives of other people, you may be altering their destiny on Earth, and you have a very heavy responsibility. Never, under any circumstance, interfere in the lives of people without their *specific* request. That is the path of destructive magic. Even though performing a healing ritual might seem to be good there are many factors in any person's life which are intended to teach them lessons, make them aware of their needs, and balance the law of karma, that inner cause and effect which operates in all our lives, and of which any occult student should be well aware. If someone is very ill and then miraculously gets better because you have performed some healing spell, you are then responsible for them for the rest of their life. If you change the pattern you may possibly rob them of some important experience by not allowing normal healing processes to take effect. Your best way of going about any form of curative magic is always to put your request into the hands of the Sun God or the Lady of Healing, and ask that they guide you to do what is right for the individual concerned. Healing may take many forms, and often, though in our culture death is still taboo, a gentle release from suffering is the real cure. The old priests knew about sending forth the soul of a sick or dying person or animal, and many of the herbs used in healing have sleep-inducing properties as well. This is one of the reasons that Cunning Men and Wise Women were feared, for the potions that could bring healing and release from pain could also bring death and the hope of rebirth.

We fear death for it seems to be the end of life as we know it, yet anyone who has lived with the power of the Gentle Arts for any length of time must face the inevitability of death, and come to terms with it. Just as the light of the Sun fades at evening and a new vista of the world, silvered by moonlight, appears, so, after the withdrawal at death a new worldscape is shown. If you learn that through meditation, pathworking and directed awareness you can transcend and escape time, then after death, there is a similar journey to the Timeless Lands, where peace, paradise or any form of afterlife has its location. The Wise Ones knew how to set people free from time, just as they would often help women in labour bring forth children into independent life. In their hands were the keys to life and death, just as these same keys can be received into our hands today, if we are willing to take on the responsibility.

The simplest way of healing with the Sun is to get the sick person to sit in sunshine and allow the warmth and golden glow of his rays to penetrate their being to reach the damaged tissue or seat of disease. Indoors, you can use a single gold or yellow candle, and by focusing on the healing power of light build up a spiral of healing energy and enwrap the patient in it. If they are too ill to be present, you can use a link made from a letter, a lock of hair or a photograph. Walk sunwise around the candle seeing the light forming a great vortex of power and then with a gesture which the Sun God or the Lady of Healing will teach you, direct the force into the sick person. They may then make a rapid recovery, or if their time is ended, sink into a peaceful sleep. There are ancient rituals of sending forth but you will have to relearn these from source as the responsibility of this Gentle Art is between the Great Ones and the individual.

You may wish to use the ever-growing, upwelling Earth power which supports trees, and all green life, and this can be done by standing barefoot on the earth, be it wood or park or garden, and sensing with your whole being the slow, thick green-gold upsurge of healing and sustaining Earth-life. When that flow of life-energy is with you, you can imagine the down-pouring, sparkling and shining Sun energy, which fizzes and twinkles with a darting energy. Combine these two within you, one upsurging and steady, the other down-pouring and sparkling, and allow them to build up so that again they can be directed to the sick person. You are acting in this form of healing, as in all true forms of healing, as a channel only. The power to heal comes from the life-force which created the universe which is infinite, endless and continuously available for use by anyone who has bothered to learn to recognise and direct it. In this way, as it is channelled through you, you, too, are filled with health and vitality. If you are unwell or rundown or depressed, please don't try healing others for not only do you then lay yourself open to attracting their complaint, but they could pick up your low feelings to add to their own burden of distress. Use the energy of the Earth and the Sun/Sky to recharge your own stores and then, a little later when you feel better, gather in more of this cosmic energy to pass on in healing. Another point about the ceremonial use of these energies which is important to bear in mind is that they are life-giving. Many people who perform rituals out of books, or derived from the fragments of an ancient tradition encapsulated in modern writings, say that working makes them tired, weary or run down. If you are genuinely in touch with these infinite, creative energies you will end up feeling full of life and zest. As you channel the force through you to heal the sick person or animal, you will end up refilled from the eternal source.

It is very important that you don't use your own imperfect energy source to try to heal someone or you may end up worn out, and if there is any weakness in your own health at that time, both they and you may be affected by it. Learn to sense these healing and energising flows and from below and above, learn to sense the subtle energies in moonlight which can bring peaceful dreams and gentle sleep to restore frazzled nerves and calm anxieties. This, too, can be called down on a bright moonlit night, reflected into water or wine which may be used as a healing medicine, or used to bathe inflamed bruises or aching heads etc. The moon power needs to be balanced by the stabilising Earth force, too, and both energies should always be used together to ensure the control stays with the healer and doesn't allow any forces to leak in or out. If you get into the habit of talking to the Sun and the Moon you will find them to be friends, you will find that you are seldom ill, and that as soon as you start to feel a fever or other complaint coming on, you can ask for their direct healing, and usually within twenty-four hours the cold or 'flu will retreat. These methods are useful to charge you up with energy if you are tired, or before any kind of working or concentration exercise which needs you to be at your best - almost any magical work, in fact.

9.
MASTERING THE CRAFTS

... this would mean that the craftsmen must now also get involved in
lifes 'elemental processes': work on the land, cooking, baking,
husbandry and housework. . .

The Simple Life, F. MacCarthy

Ritual magic, on the whole, consists of a number of intellectual arts
whereas Low Magic, Natural Magic or Folk Magic consists of a
large number of skills of hand and mind. Many of these in themselves
are trivial and basically simple. This is the main reason that they
are seldom found in 'grimoires', the old magical grammars, or in
textbooks written more recently. The vast majority of these extremely
antique techniques rely on intuition and spontaneity rather than
learned formulae, and as such are very hard to teach, even by
example. The spell which will cure a sick animal will not work,
necessarily, on a human being, and *vice versa.* The charm for Fred's
warts may be different for those of Mary, and the charm or talisman
(the first being a natural object or spoken spell, the latter a made-up
design), which you might decide to use in a particular case will
have to be made especially to suit that purpose and no other. It will
depend on the phase of the moon, the time of year and the hour of
the day, for all these will offer unseen advantages and disadvantages
to the success of the working.

Different practitioners of the Gentle Arts will prefer different
methods, each of which will be perfectly efficacious in the particular
circumstances. If, for example, you enjoy and have the facilities for
practising ritual, then there is no reason why that should not be the
way you will apply your art. If, on the other hand, you work alone,
and using symbols or mental patterns, spoken spells rather than

written or talismanic ones, and feel happier working in that manner, then you are just as likely to succeed. For example, if you wished to perform a divination about the future of some plan you had made, and wanted to use the Tarot as a medium of receiving information, you could either set out a circle with the four elements and call upon the Angels of Far Seeing to attend you, burn incense by candlelight, while wearing a particular robe, and await guidance as you laid out the cards; or, more simply, you could focus your attention inwards, think out the problem and just lay out an appropriate spread. In each case you would be shown an answer related to the way you had gone about seeking it, so suit yourself.

Performing rituals requires a certain dramatic way of thinking and though there are a number of books which set out seasonal festivals, rites of the moon's phases, ways of going about common activities like divination, healing and so on, they have lost a lot of their power by being detailed in print. It is far better to decide upon a ground plan, suited directly to your own circumstances and things you feel you need to do to come up with a solution to a problem, or work a specific kind of magic. It will depend on whether or not you work alone. If you have a companion or two you will need to consult them to find out their views and suggestions if you are counting on their co-operation in the work. In magic a little friendly co-operation goes a very long way, for any sort of magical partnership is a special and deep relationship, based on affection and trust, and is of enormous help, especially to novices. You will always have to decide if it is right for you to act magically and apply your crafts to matters other than those of your own life.

One thing which it is important to understand is that of responsibility. It is all very well being extremely psychic, skilled in the healing arts and filled with good intentions, but you should not start applying these things to the lives of other people without their specific request that you help them. Even if they do ask for your aid, you should think long and hard before launching into a complex ritual, making an elaborate talisman or applying healing power to their illness. If you act on anyone else's behalf you are still responsible for the outcome, good or bad! You are taking on some of their karma, some part of their life has been altered by you, and you need to be certain that you are ready and willing to accept that burden.

Often a session or two of quiet meditation, asking that you be guided to do the best thing (which is sometimes nothing, in their case) will usually lead to a much clearer understanding of the situation so that when you do act you will do no harm. There is an old saying 'The Road to Hell is paved with good intentions' and this is particularly true of novice magicians who like to show off their new-found skills without thinking for a moment of the consequences, not only to the recipient of their unwanted gift, but to their own karma. It is far better to be safe than sorry!

Some of the ancient arts have already been discussed, like dowsing and meditation, pathworking and celebrating festivals in a magical way. There are several arts of divination which are worth studying, as well as some of the more basic skills which involve preparing ritual food or wine, becoming aware of the power of nature and making use of it, and developing practical crafts so that you can make talismans, carve pendants, employ the energies of charms, or chant spells as your ancestor did, in her simple hut or cave, thousands of years ago. Again, most of these things are basically simple arts, which require practice and effort, concentration and commonsense, all patiently applied to achieve the desired result. You will learn to look out for useful items on your travels in the country, or on the beach, or in the woods, so that you gather samples of different woods, seashells and beach pebbles, and 'holey stones' which have been used as charms against evil for thousands of years.

Before going into details it is important to understand what divination actually *is*. It implies communication from the Divinity, received by some means and used to determine what is the likely outcome of some event, decision or future activity. Most of the systems we use today are very old, the most common being divination by the Tarot, or the Chinese Oracle called the I Ching, or perhaps by use of Norse Runes on stones or blocks of wood. In each case there is a procedure to follow so that the symbols shown on the cards, runes or the hexagrams (six-line patterns) of the I Ching are randomised, and in practice, allowing the Divinity, the Angel of the Future, the Spirit of the Tarot or whatever you like to call it, to make contact with you or the person who is shuffling the cards etc. In this way the chosen symbols will relate directly to the problem which the enquirer has held in mind during this process. In some cases this can be further ritualised by casting a circle and invoking the spirit of clear vision to help you see exactly what the oracle is trying to say.

Each system has a language. The more possible symbols or combinations of runes the larger the vocabulary of the oracle. If, for example, you toss a coin there can only be two answers, heads or tails, so this gives a language of only two words, basically 'yes' and 'no'. If you select another system, there are usually twenty-four Runes which can be combined in thousands of different ways, and with the Tarot's seventy-eight cards the ultimate number of possible combinations is enormous. You need to bear this language in mind when you ask a question. Always try to make it one which can actually be answered by 'yes' and 'no', but, if the system has sufficient symbols, which can be expanded upon, giving a time, indication of people who will be helpful/difficult in relation to the problem, and so on. Each system needs to be thoroughly studied so that you have a complete understanding of what it is capable of, and which is the best way to consult it. For example, you might be trying to discover if a cafe will give you good value and tossing a coin for 'yes' or 'no' would be sufficient. On the other hand, you might want to enquire if the house you were trying to buy would meet your family's needs, or if there would be a delay in completing the purchase. In these instances the answer can be a simple one, but the Tarot or I Ching can add details about what you will find good about the place, or how long the delay in completion might be.

You will need to learn at least something about the Gentle Arts of Tarot reading, consulting the I Ching, and being able to put up and interpret a horoscope, as well as the practical skills of dowsing which is particularly useful in healing and finding mislaid items. Here is a very simple system which you should be able to make for yourself from small pebbles or discs of wood, each carved or painted with a symbol for divination, which you won't find in the shops.

THE SUN: This stands for the positive energy for healing or men involved in the question, outgoing activities, daytime, the solar year, life and self-determination.

THE MOON: This is the female aspect, one month, inner awareness, receptivity, dreams and visions, night-time, slow change, intuition.

TIME: Restriction, getting old or old people, boundaries, stability, coldness, limitation to plans, persistence, very slow changes or stasis.

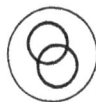

THE RINGS: Partnerships, love, harmony, unity and sharing, working with others rather than for the self, openness, benefits from a partner, freedom of action.

THE TREE: Growth, expansion, help from authority, business success, agriculture or farming, law suits and conveyancing etc., flowering of plans.

THE ARROWS: Quarrels, discussions, delays due to authority, misplaced energy, wasted time, arguments, mechanical breakdowns, transport difficulties.

THE BIRDS: Travel, short journeys, correspondence, phone calls, confusion of information, matters to do with cars, planes, trains or other forms of transport, fast changes, news of friends.

THE WAVE: Long journeys or news from afar, distant relatives, long-term plans, change of life's pattern, the sea, boats, changing tides of events, inheritance.

THE EYE: How events will affect you, your position and aims, your relationships with others, where you will need to take care or advice. (These depend on its relative position within a throw.)

THE EARTH: Home, world affairs, safety and foundation, Goddess worship, plan-making, birth, beginning, New Year, presents, things relating to the home.

WHIRLING WHEEL: Sudden changes in situations, relationships and prospects for better or worse. Things begin to happen which have long-term effects. Movement, progress and advances.

LIGHTNING: This means even more violent changes, but short-term ones. Gambles come off, good/bad luck, hunches should work, prizes be won, plans suddenly work out.

BLANK: This is the intervention of forces of the unseen, magic, unlikely situations resolve. Fate, destiny, karma, and the paying of old debts, contact with the Gods/Goddesses.

You can expand this list to include as many symbols as you like, but you will need to be able to hold them in your hand before casting them on a mat or table before you. As they relate loosely to the planets, you will be able to colour them, if you wish, as follows: Sun, white and gold; Moon, black and silver; Time, black and white; Rings, green and gold; Tree, brown and green; Arrows, red and silver; Birds, black and blue; Wave, sea-green and blue; Eye, natural brown or blue; Earth, brown, green, gold and blue; Wheel, gold and red; Lightning, gold and black. The blank symbol and the backs of all the discs should just be varnished. A very simple way of making these is to cut slices from a thick wooden dowel or a broomstick with a fine saw. Rub them smooth with sandpaper and then paint them exactly the same colour on the backs so that if they are laid face down and shuffled you can't tell which is which. It may take a while to find suitable round slate pebbles in a river bed or by the sea, or to make from a dowelling rod a set of thirteen or so symbols, but this is a practical application of one of the skills you need to master. The colours may be readily available model-makers' enamels, or poster paints, as these are very bright colours, but they will need a coat of varnish to stop them chipping, especially if you choose stones, as they bang together in their box or bag. Paint the backgrounds first and allow them to dry overnight before painting in the symbols with the contrasting colour, each of which relates to the planet with which the symbol is associated, although, of course, you can use any designs or colours you prefer. If you invent your own system from scratch, or combine other sources of information in an original way, that will be even better, from a magical point of view, for it will be totally your own.

To use the completed set of Divining Stones or Discs, grasp the whole lot in both hands and raise them to your forehead. Think about the question you intend them to answer, being well aware of the language which they may use to reply. Stay still and become calm for a few moments, focussed completely upon your query, then gently throw them from you, along the carpet, or onto the surface of a table covered with a soft cloth, or even a special mat, embroidered with magical signs, the layout of a horoscope or what have you. Take note of the positions and relationships between the various symbols which have fallen face up. Those which are face down don't count. Work from those which are closest to you (or the person who has thrown them down, if you are reading for someone else) as these represent immediate effects, and go on to those furthest away, which will occur later in time. Allow inner perception, intuition or the aspect of divinity which can instruct you about the meaning of each individual cast to speak before rushing into an unconsidered interpretation. Muse over the spread, examine it for underlying patterns or relationships of the displayed symbols. Once you have absorbed all that you can, then write down the oracle's answer, or speak it to the person who sought your guidance. Treat both the stones and the answers they give gently, allowing subtle information, not necessarily obviously related to what you imagine the symbols to mean, to seep through so that an in-depth interpretation can be given. Even a simple system can come up with extremely accurate and complex answers, if you allow it to.

Meditate upon each of the symbols, the colours, the underlying correspondences with the planet of the astrological attributions until each one of the pebbles or discs immediately awakens in your mind a series of related images, ideas and concepts. It doesn't matter how long this familiarisation process takes, be it with the few symbols of this basic divination system, or the larger list of the Tarot cards, or even the underlying meanings of the sixty-four hexagrams of the I Ching, together with the six changes possible for each. Meditate by using the image of the pebble or card as a door to a wider understanding. Make it a milestone on an inner journey so that each may gradually instil into you its inner meaning, its ongoing interpretation, so that you recognise each one immediately for what it implies, but can see how all are also causes of change.

Gentleness should be applied to the more intellectual forms of divination, like the Tarot or the I Ching, for each of them can give much more diverse or in-depth answers if you are willing to allow them to speak beyond the dead book meaning of each card or hexagram. Every single part of the pattern is important, every element in the spread has a story to tell if you give yourself permission to listen to that quiet inner voice. No single book of authority can possibly interpret the symbols for *you,* for your life pattern is totally original and individual, as is the path of anyone for whom you might be seeking information from the divining system.

If you really want to become accurate at any of these arts you will need a lot of patience and persistence. There is nothing less reassuring than a diviner struggling through the pages of a book in search of an interpretation of cards or runes. Although it takes dedication and continued effort to learn a 'key word' for each symbol, and its reversed or inner meaning, it is a much more valid way of going about any sort of reading, and is safer too. If you begin to rely on your intuition, which, if you have tried out some of the earlier exercises and techniques in this book, ought to be coming into focus by now, you will quickly realise how it can explain the strange relationships within any divination spread.

One point to take into account is that each Tarot card in particular, relates to an event, a situation or a character within the life-journey of every individual. It is almost as if at someone's birth the whole pack was shuffled and then laid out in a line, so that as the person grows and experiences things, he discovers the true and inner meaning of each symbol. The line may not be a straight one; it is most likely to curve round, and cross its own path, or split and rejoin so that the person returns to a starting point. Look at the symbols with this in mind. It is often explained that the Major Arcana, the twenty-two picture cards, represent the Journey of the Fool, the untaught soul of the neophyte. Through interacting with the forces represented by each of the Trumps, he learns lessons and so progresses. In fact the entire deck is a long and winding road, mapped out in seventy-eight stages, each one individual and in each case, timed to the life span of the person in question. If you study these, and the Rune symbols, with this concept in mind you will begin to see how the cards plot progress and change, adventure and trouble, good relationships and difficult ones, opportunities accepted and those which have been missed, never to come again. You can see the lessons that have had to be learned, and the objects overcome, the mistakes and the sudden gains and prizes. All these are there to be discovered, if you can open the inner sight to look for them. In every spread there will be patterns which relate to a shorter time span, and so you are, in effect, looking through a microscope at a particular phase of the enquirer's life path. This means that the symbols are concentrated and their meanings made more definite and clear, if you can read them correctly.

All forms of divination require responsibility. They need you to be very honest, even with your own questions. You must have the courage to say, now and again, when it happens, 'The symbols are not speaking to me today', or 'The Gods of Divination will not hear my request', or you just don't actually feel like asking. Not only will you sometimes have to admit that you are not getting an answer, but you will need to permit yourself to realise your interpretation could be, or is, wrong. You need the commitment to the art to be able to say 'I don't understand the answer', but to carefully write down the pattern of cards, or the run of runes or hexagrams in your notebook just the same, because as time passes even the most obscure divination may begin to make sense. Another aspect of responsibility is to be thoroughly aware how your words may affect the person you are supposedly trying to help. It is not a good idea to blurt out, if the cards look dodgy, 'Oh, I see death and disaster within the next couple of months. Do you know anyone who is likely to die?' Always remember that people *do act* on the information they get from diviners, so if you see trouble ahead, be tactful and weigh your words with care. Explain that there may be difficulties, that there is the indication that careless actions could lead to accidents or ill health, or that relationships may become a very sensitive area of life soon.

Even if you see only a rosy future or a very successful outcome to some plans, please speak carefully, for things can go wrong, or factors which haven't shown up in the divination can occur and overturn the smoothest path, or events outside the control of the individuals concerned might have an adverse effect on their lives. Take your time over every reading, allowing inner perceptions to advise you, to explain within your mind the subtle interactions of the forces displayed before you in terms of the symbols. Be prepared to discover totally unlikely aspects of any symbol, for even the ancient Tarot, Runes and I Ching are living, and so growing, systems. As our consciousness expands to take in new concepts, so do the oracles grow in their own subtle ways. The I Ching, which is extremely ancient, speaks of ox carts and wells, but will still give accurate answers about space travel and the petro-chemical industry, if you have the wisdom to allow its innate information to expand into the new terminology. In the same way the Tarot can answer queries about computers and plane travel, although magicians and horses are shown on the picture cards.

You will certainly find getting yourself into a relaxed and calm frame of mind is extremely helpful, and to invoke the aid of the Goddess of the Moon, or the power of Mercury, by covering the table for the divination with appropriate coloured cloths, or by burning a candle of the right colour, or some pleasing incense, which is usually available from the specialist suppliers, can assist your perceptions. Try to tune in to the person for whom you are reading and sense what lies beneath the question they may actually ask you, or is hidden in an unseen written request, or unspoken cry for help. If you wish to purify the room ritually, or cast a circle of protection or invocation, you might find this also helps you arrive at the right frame of mind to get good and clear results. All this will depend on your own attitude and feelings about the necessity of such procedures. Of course, if you are doing work for other people, if they are your magical companions, they can help laying out symbols, lighting charcoal and incense and so on. If, on the other hand, you are trying to advise a non-occult friend, the paraphernalia and ceremony mentioned above might upset them and make them feel uncomfortable, so this will prove counter-productive.

Another ancient and gentle art is that of scrying. Most people are aware of crystal or glass globes, in which it is possible to induce visions of the future or of distant events. All sorts of things have been used as 'speculums' or scrying glasses. Dr Dee, Queen Elizabeth I's astrologer/magician used both a crystal globe and a beautiful black mirror, made of the volcanic glass called obsidian. These, and several of his other pieces of magical equipment are to be seen in the British Museum, and if there aren't too many visitors to the gallery, you can still actually scry in these glasses which were used by Dr Dee's assistant and colleague, Edward Kelley. In them, so his writings tell us, they were able to communicate with angels who dictated information to them in a language which John Dee called 'Enochian', after the Book of Enoch, one of the Apocryphal Books of the Bible. It was thought to be the language which the angels used, and it was spelled out, letter by letter, to Kelley as he gazed into one of the specula.

There is no simple way of explaining exactly how you learn to scry. On one hand it might be considered that the pictures actually form within the glass and that you see them there. On the other hand, it is just as likely that what happens is that the surface of the glass distracts you so that you enter a relaxed, altered state of consciousness and see the images or words, symbols or on-going events within the mind's eye, rather than within the crystal ball or dark mirror. It doesn't seem to matter which is the case, and it may be that it is different for different people, but it does take a certain knack, and like all the Gentle Arts requires patience and persistence to allow the right frame of mind to occur, and so start the stream of pictures flowing. Again a very quiet atmosphere is an advantage, and a few minutes' meditation on the purpose of your attempt will help clear the mental channels. It is also a great help at the beginning to have a reliable companion with you, for as you drift into the distracted state in which your awareness focuses within the glass, you will find it hard to think of questions as well as seeking answers, and a quiet voice asking what you can see, or sense, will assist you.

You can buy a glass, or if you are rich, a real rock crystal ball, but it is often easier to learn to scry with something more humble, cheap, and home-made as it will already have the subtle link with you which is such an important part of practical and effective magic. You can always go to one of the ever-increasing number of suppliers of occult equipment, books and regalia, but it is part of the traditional Crafts of magic that you make as much of your own gear as you can. Developing the practical skills to paint some divining discs is just as important as being able to decorate an elaborate talisman. Making some ritual cakes and the wine you drink at a seasonal festival is a far more satisfying activity than strolling down to the local supermarket. Two ways of making suitable instruments for scrying are as follows. The first is a black mirror, used by magicians long before they discovered the use of crystal globes. Get hold of the glass face from an old fashioned alarm clock, or a petrie dish or a circle of thick plate glass and paint the back with several smooth coats of black paint, allowing it to dry thoroughly between layers. You must ensure that the glass is totally clean beforehand or the paint will be streaky and distracting. Wrap the finished item in velvet or silk and keep it in the dark. If you dedicate it in moonlight to the Goddess of Far Seeing and consecrate it with a ritual so that it is cleared of any previous associations, it will become a true mirror of what is to come.

Another simple way of making a speculum is either to paint the outside of a large goblet-shaped wine glass with plenty of black paint, or to coat the inside of a shallow, smooth pottery dish with black paint. Again several layers should be used to ensure that the inner or outer surface is totally covered. Each of these receptacles should be filled with spring water, which is the actual scrying medium. The water and the container should both be cleansed, blessed and dedicated to the Goddesses who instil wisdom through vision, or to the Moon as awakener of psychic powers. The water may even be used to draw down the light of the moon into, or you might discover, as many people do, that allowing moonlight to fall onto the speculum as you are scrying will help you.

When you are ready, become calm and inwardly and outwardly still, clear your mind of any doubts and questions and inhale gently and deeply a few times. Ask a silent blessing on your work, and ask for help or guidance from whomever you imagine to be most helpful, be it Goddess or angel or spirit, and then wait. You may have to wait quite a while, you may even have to go through this process many times before anything starts to happen. Eventually, when you reach the balanced frame of mind and relaxed consciousness the speculum will wake up and your own inner vision start to clear. You may see a misty glow at first, before actual pictures begin to form. You are more likely to be so surprised that you lose concentration at this point and have to start again. After sufficient practice you will see more clearly, and by having your companion ask questions and write them and your answers down, you will expand your skill by mastering this particular ancient art. Exactly what *you* see, and how you interpret the images is up to you. There is no agreed pattern of symbolism, any more than everyone's dreams can mean the same. The things which you perceive will have to be interpreted within the context of the question you may be trying to answer, or within the aspect of your own psyche which uses symbols. Like dream images, these can be very personal.

You will need to experiment, with the sorts of scrying glasses you use, the conditions under which you use them, and any ritual or other special acts you prefer to perform before you begin. If you are wise, at the completion of any work, whether successful or not, it is always worth saying 'Thank you', to the unseen forces which guide and inspire you, even if you aren't too sure if they have done anything. Politeness, not only to the Gods and Goddesses, angels, spirits, powers and elementals, but to anyone who you encounter on your journey through the Gentle Arts, will smooth the way and help to build up those vital but subtle relationships which turn magical study into a calm and effective practical skill.

Companions and friends, whether a loose collection of individuals, or a closely knit coven or lodge, are all special people. To become part of any sort of working group is a considerable honour, and working in harmony and co-operation with others can be a most joyous part of the long and sometimes very lonely road of the Mysteries. Good groups take decades to develop and each member will bring to it a new aspect of human nature, new skills and new questions. Joining any group will change you, just as in a lesser way, your admittance will change the group. If you are able to share your ability as a successful scryer or diviner you will be making a valuable contribution. If you are not very good at these arts, then you will be able to help them in some other way, for all ongoing associations must function by give-and-take from each individual member. It is in that way that the whole is greater by far than the separate parts.

You may still have to walk these winding and strange paths on your own, or with just one or two friends, at present, but it shouldn't stop you trying to master all the arts, crafts and skills which you will need should you eventually seek out and join some established group, or perhaps, in time, feel ready to launch into the formation of one of your own. Most of the magical crafts are those found in any list of handicrafts: being able to draw and paint, to carve and model, to embroider and stitch, to search for useful things in nature and in the shops, and to be able to work with raw materials and turn them into talismans, ritual wine or a special robe for a particular festival. You may need to work with words, to write ceremonial speeches, and poetry, to make up prayers and to be inspired to speak directly with the Goddess and the Gods of your chosen tradition. Look around any handicrafts shop you encounter, visit displays of painting or sculpture, examine anyone else's creative art form and see what you might learn yourself, or better still, share with other people. Teaching is an important craft, for the conveying of ideas by word, gesture and direct explanation is the way that most of the old crafts survived. Apprentices spent years making the tea and sweeping up after the master craftsman, whether he was a mason or carpenter, wheelwright or blacksmith, but in those long years the lad or lass would watch and study the arts, learn unconsciously the use of tools, patterns and equipment, long before they were allowed to touch them.

Few modern students have this sort of opportunity. Adepts have always been pretty thin on the ground, and most of the modern ones already have a home and family, a job and commitments as well as a training group or school to organise. These people work very hard but do nearly all their magic secretly and discreetly. Their colleagues at the office, or their next-door neighbours will probably know nothing of what goes on in the spare room of their home, or during the gatherings when lots of other people turn up at the house. If you ever join such a group, you must consider yourself extremely lucky, and should you be one of the really fortunate few who have a personal tutor in magic, then you have a prize beyond rubies, and I hope you work very hard to deserve such an honour.

Most of you will have to carry on from books, trying on your own to make sense of what is written and to turn advice and instructions into a number of practical skills. It isn't easy. Nothing in magic ever was, or is. The more you learn the tougher it becomes, for the pressure from the inner worlds increases as each student's strength and ability grows. The better you are the harder it gets, just as in running marathons or being a pop star. As your worth becomes more to the inner realms so they push you harder, give you greater tasks to perform, expect *you* to save the world! But it is fun! You discover that every new skill learned, each new art mastered, each piece of work completed and made to fit its purpose gives you a great deal of satisfaction. By trying to discover what your value to the Gods and Goddesses you serve might be, and then following that weird and wonderful path as closely as you can, life will never be dull, and every day becomes an adventure. Certainly there are times when nothing seems to work and the magic has fled, but it is a passing phase, usually clearly shown in your horoscope, and it allows you to rest and recap on what you have learned.

Some other simple arts which are parts of the Old Ways are those of making ritual wine and cakes or biscuits. Britain is a wonderful place to search for the bounty of Mother Nature at almost all times of the year, for she will grant you, for the effort of picking them, flowers, fruits and berries, each in their season, which will provide a hobby which you can share with non-magical friends, and outdoor exercise which your children can also join in. In spring there are dandelions, hawthorn flowers and later, elder flowers from which excellent wines maybe made. In autumn there are many wild fruits, blackberries and wild raspberries, whortles and elderberries as well as anything growing in the garden or orchard, like plums or apples, pears or grapes, all of which can easily be converted into fine wines. The equipment is not expensive and most big towns have a 'Brew-it-yourself shop' these days. So long as you make sure your equipment is kept sterile and no vinegar forming bacteria get into the fermentation you can turn almost anything into wine. Pea pods, parsnips, rosehips, parsley, honey which makes excellent mead with the addition of some wine yeast, even tinned fruit, if you are desperate, will all turn into acceptable wines, given time to mature. You may well be able to do a deal with a local fruitterer, if you are an urban soul, and buy cheaply the bruised apples or pears, overripe grapes, damaged oranges or bananas, at the end of the day. All of these make excellent wines, so long as you don't overdo the sugar (and it is possible to make wine without any sugar at all) and allow them to ferment to a finish, so that the final wine is not sickly sweet. You will find plenty of instruction books on wine making in the library or the local shops as this is a very popular hobby, and if you like wine or beer, mead, cider or liqueurs there is no reason why you can't add this Craft to any others you may learn. It takes about a year for most wines to really mature, and in that time you are likely to gain many other practical skills, so that when the wine is ready to drink, you will be ready to use it in a ritual of thanksgiving.

Ceremonial cakes, biscuits or bread are worth discovering how to make as well. Cooking is very much like magic in that you start off with a selection of unrelated objects, yet within the ritual of mixing and blending, baking and serving you are changing them alchemically into something of greater use and delight. The best cooks, like the best mages, have the recipes and methods in their heads, and only look at books to enlarge their menu or repertoire. There is as much magic in turning out a light and delicious sponge cake as there is in preparing a ritual to communicate with the Angel Gabriel. Many traditional biscuits for rite use are cut into moon shapes. They often contain barley meal, honey and hazelnuts - all are sacred to the Goddess, as is mead.

You will know that traditional kinds of cakes and bread are eaten at different times of the year. Everyone knows about Christmas cake and Christmas pudding, originally a savoury, as were mince pies made with minced meat, often in the shape of a cradle or manger, but there are lots of other ancient seasonal foods which a little research will reveal. At Easter Simnel cake is eaten, flavoured with rare and expensive saffron; often this is decorated with eggs and chicks, not Christian symbols at all. Every region of the world has special foods so you could take yourself on a magical cookery tour, and most of the oldest recipes were specially cooked on the feast day of a local God or Goddess, or to celebrate the coming of one of the seasons or harvests. Perhaps you could develop a ritual cake book to share with your friends and neighbours.

Offerings have always been made of wine, milk, honey, water, oil, or cream poured as a libation to the Goddess, and slices of cake, biscuits or bread, too, are usually shared at meetings and some is left for the birds. When workings are done indoors, the crumbs, wine dregs and incense ash are all poured on to the Earth at the end of a ritual, as a small thank offering. Interesting combinations of the drinks are still made and shared by followers of the Old Religion, and special foods, from the honey roast pork, served with barley cakes, to the all vegetable stew simmered in a representation of the Cauldron of Inspiration are just as important a way of linking together the individuals of a group. A communion is an important part of most rituals and its different aspects should also form food for thought and meditation, as well as a useful way of bringing all concerned down to earth at the end of a powerful rite.

10.
THE MAGIC OF TREES

Of all the trees that grow so fair, Old England to adorn, Greater are
none, Beneath the Sun, Than Oak and Ash and Thorn . . .

A Tree Song R. Kipling

In earlier times peoples' relationship with all the aspects of nature
was so much closer. We may have a great deal more book learning
than our grandparents but we have lost much of the practical, rule-
of-thumb wisdom from which most of the homely folk magic was
derived. One whole aspect which many people, especially those
who have grown up in towns and cities, have lost is our link with
trees. We may recognise the fruit trees in the garden, or perhaps
some of the common park and avenue-side trees in the streets around
our home, during the summer, but to be able to wander through a
winter wood and recognise not only the species of each tree but its
manifold uses have been lost by us. Certainly we don't need to
know the calorific value of the wood, or its durability or lightness,
because we don't have to seek out, fell and season wood for specific
uses, but we ought to know something about the magical value and
associations with each of the most common sorts of trees. Lots of
them are used in medicine, in both the homoeopathic and
naturopathic repertoires, and over thirty are the basis of the gentle
and effective Bach Remedies, which work on the mind and its
anxieties, rather than direct physical ills. Each of the thirty-eight
remedies is designed to help alleviate a sort of worry, fear, depression,
gloom, apprehension or feelings of failure, guilt and the like. They
work slowly and gently, like many natural products, but where it is
the mind which is upsetting the body, as occurs all too often these
days, then these simple medicines, can nearly always help. They

are available from many good pharmacist or health food shops. You can learn to make your own.

Not only are tree barks, leaves, flowers and roots, and decoctions and tinctures made from these used in herbal medicine, but most of the woods have particular uses, so that, for example, tool handles in Britain used to be made of ash, dowsing rods of hazel and porridge bowls of elm, also used for coffins. You will find that there are many excellent books on trees, how to recognise them, their fruits, leaves and flowers, what use the timber should be put to, and the kind of soils they will grow in. Many country towns have rural museums which show the uses of local timbers in furniture (often beech and elm, as well as ash, birch, sycamore and walnut, and as fruit woods for veneers). Whereas Farm implements would be made of hornbeam, Britain's hardest wood, rulers of boxwood, bridge timbers of indestructible alder, hurdles of hazel, and unpainted fences of split sweet chestnut. Not only did most sorts of wood have a mundane and practical use, but often they were associated with either a God or Goddess, or a specific magical purpose.

Magical wands were traditionally made of one of the nut trees; in the Holy Land, where the qabalah came from, wands were made of almond branches which had never borne nuts, whereas here they would often be made of hazel. Oak was used for staffs and cudgels, and it was originally a root of oak which was burned over the Twelve Days of Christmas as a Yule Log, except in Kent where it was a great bundle of the green burning ash, bound up as the Ashen Faggot. Apple wood was used in furniture making, but its dry wood smells exquisite burned on an open fire. Birch twigs were made into the cleansing besom, perhaps a descendant of the Persian Magi's bundle of thirteen sacred twigs, *the Barshan,* or the Roman *Fasces,* carried by the Lictors. Willow wands were used to 'Beat the Bounds', an ancient festival which is now usually carried out at each of the boundary stones of a parish. Now the 'sacrificial victim' is a volunteer choirboy, who is gently dropped head downwards into a shallow hole, or has his head tapped upon the boundary stone. They still use a different lad or lass for each stone, indicating that the previous one was left as an offering! The stones are also beaten with wands of willow, a Goddess tree of healing (aspirin is derived from willow bark) and sadness (weeping willows.)

The lore about trees is endless and absolutely fascinating and varies a great deal from place to place, depending on the soil type and geology which influences the growth and success of different species of trees. Beech, for example, will grow on chalk, whereas hazel thickets are found on heavy, wet clay; birch and scrub willow grow up into the Arctic and stone pines and cedars originate in the warm Mediterranean lands. Most trees are very choosy about their preferred habitat which means that the different regions of even as small a country as England have a very varied and interesting distribution of the species. You will discover, if you begin to build up a collection of information about our native, and long-term introduced trees, that some are very common in your area while others do not grow there at all. Many trees and magical shrubs have local names. Some individual ones have legends attached to them, like the Robin Hood Oak in Sherwood Forest, or the Herne Oak in Windsor Great Park. There is a tree associated with Merlin in Wales, and there is St Joseph of Arimathea's Thorn at Glastonbury. Many ancient yews have tales about their immortality, and some are older than the church whose foundations they are no doubt undermining with their deep root systems.

On another level each of us has a Family Tree and each of us is the single fruit on the end of a branch, descended from our parents and grandparents, back to distant and shared ancestors. Many people are interested in this and collect data on the various branches and descendants, especially if they have a royal or interesting predecessor. It is worth knowing a little about your physical descent, for you may well accept the idea of reincarnation, and therefore who you are now is a result not only of your physical parentage, but of your earlier lives. Certain family trends, occupations and inner skills may be in the blood as well. Studying family history from photographs and letters, old deeds and documents, and later on parish registers of Births, Marriages and Deaths can uncover all sorts of fascinating information which may well have gone to make you the individual you are. Magically, too, it is worth trying to locate those who went before you, whether they were people who bequeathed you certain abilities along with their genes, or the teachers, who in turn were taught by other, earlier magicians or witches. Unravelling some of those intricate threads can reveal all sorts of fascinating information. Many recent books explain the connections between the founders of many of the magical schools which flourish to this day.

As well as having a Family Tree you also have a family Tree, a totem tree which is special to you, and which may help with your occult aspirations by providing wood for magical equipment, like wands and platters, or other uses, for divinations, for example. There are a number of ways of using some of the methods suggested earlier in this book, particularly 'path-working' and creative imagination. A first step would be to discover how many actual trees you can recognise by walking round your home vicinity and seeing how you get on. The reason for this is fairly obvious for if you find yourself wandering in a trackless forest or wild wood, surrounded by trees and eventually find one which is 'your tree' then it would help a lot to know immediately what species it is! You could make such an inner journey and discover that it is winter and there are no helpful leaves to assist you in identification. Also, unless your path is well protected, it isn't likely that you will be wandering in an arboretum in which each species is neatly labelled for you!

Do learn your tree lore; it is an important link with the origins of our shamanistic heritage, for much of Britain was once a wild and tangled jungle of deciduous trees and shrubs, and paths were cut only by water and high land. In this dense forest there were small communities, and farming was much more a matter of hunting wild animals and harvesting the fruits and nuts, the roots, herbs and leaves within the woodland, rather than reaping corn and planting cabbages in the clear fields we find abound today. Certainly this changed long ago but there is much we now have to learn from other forest dwellers who have been able to preserve something of their arcane wisdom and ancient knowledge. We read about the Mexican sorcerers who use magical mushrooms and cacti, of the Native American shamans and their uses of sacred trees and plants for healing, magic and far vision, and the Laplanders' weird collection of magic and mystery which is being researched and revealed these days.

A way to discover your own tree is to settle down for a longish meditation, with a friend or two, if possible, and describe a journey which not only takes you back in time to when forests were wild and covered much of the land, but to a place where no human hand had felled any timber. Here you should begin to make a path for yourself, scrambling over the fallen logs, sliding between closely packed tree trunks, pushing through clinging ivy, vines and honeysuckle in a deep pungent green world, so alien from the tidy streets, the man-made landscape. As you wander through this verdant maze you will hear the rustle of wild creatures in the undergrowth, the roar and thrash of the wind in the upper branches, the trickle of cool water in deep channels among the roots and scrub and brambles. You will smell the summer-sweet scent of honeysuckle, feel the scratch of thorns, and squelch of soggy marsh under foot, the roughness of tree bark and the lash of small twigs across your face. To discover your own tree is not easy. It has been hidden for many a long year, unless you have already made the effort to clear a path through the wilderness, cut back those things which would encroach upon you and hide in the midst of the green forest the special tree which is your own totem.

Imagine each part of this scene clearly. Sense with all your being the ancient forest, the untamed greenwood, the wild kingdom of deer and boar, of wolf and raven, of mighty tree and entangling thicket shrub. Somewhere in that wilderness is your own family tree, and you must seek it out and know it for your own. When you discover it the recognition will be immediate, real and undeniable. You will *know* when you see it that it is what you have come to look for. Sit at its feet, feel its bark, rough or smooth, sense its size, its importance to you, its power. Draw on its ancient strength and its innate, calm wisdom. Allow its green blood to begin to flow upwards through you with the slowness and ooze of treacle, feel its steady life-force being drawn from its deep roots in the heart of Mother Earth to the tips of its swaying branches above your head. Allow this same slow seep of life to fill and change you, bonding with your inner strength, gently opening eyes to green sight which will show you the great Guardians of Trees, many legged and vast in human terms. Wait until you can perceive this second inner vision.

Be very still and learn from the art of stability of a firm and unbending stem, which unlike our flexible skeletons, can only sway. Feel your feet taking root, growing back into the Earth from which your substance was born. Sense the seasons as the trees feel them: expanding, urgent spring; glowing, warming summer; rustling, restless autumn which strips the leaves and bares the soul of the trees. Cold, still winters when everything rests and the brightness of the stars shines with a special light promising change.

When you can sense the slow Earth-upsurge try to feel the sparkling sunlight, the pattering raindrops on the tree's green canopy. Feel the light breezes touching every leaf with the breath of the Goddess, and blessing that tree and the one who has found shelter under its branches. Look closely at the patterns of light and shade the leaves make, notice the way the branches spread and the twigs' long slender fingers brush the air. Seek out the many shades of green, of brown to gold where the sun touches the structure within the green bower. Draw down this darting source of inner light to your own being, allow it to merge with the upwelling Earth power so that Sky and Earth are made one within you. Let all these sensations, of outward touch, of sight and of hearing drink in their fill under your family tree, and then gently and gradually let these images fade, let the sensations of your ordinary environment slowly re-emerge so that you can open your eyes to the familiar scene.

This is the first part of a multi-layered path journey or meditation and it is important to get results from each stage before going on to the next. When you have sensed the wild-wood and wandered there until you have found your own tree, and then allowed it to share some of its sensations with you a number of times, you can go on to the next part of this very powerful exercise. In fact, if you have found out what sort of tree is special to you can go and look for it in the world. Most sorts of trees are planted singly as well as in dense woodland, so you may be able to try out the same exercise with a real tree to lean on, and this will help you, especially if you feel world-weary and depressed. Allow both energies to flow through you and sense them altogether. (Details of this exercise are to be found in my book *"A Modern Magician's Companion"*, *Thoth Publications*.)

Once you are certain you have made a link with your tree you can seek it out again. On each visit it will be easier to find and the path through the wilderness will become smoother and more direct. When you have reached the place and made some sort of salutation, sit down at its foot and allow your senses to merge. On this occasion, not only will you be seeking help from the tree but you will request the presence of a guide and helper. This will be a small animal or bird which you will find in the branches of the tree. If you look about you it will soon make itself known to you. Allow it to approach so that you can see it clearly and it might even come and allow you to touch it. This is a link between the world you know and the world of nature. The tree can only strengthen you and awaken inner energies and calmness but the guiding creature can lead you through the wilderness and help you on your quest for knowledge and understanding of the Gentle Arts. It is possible to think about this animal or bird in the way the old village witches looked upon their 'familiars'. These were never pets in the way we own a cat or dog or canary; they were helpers and it was their magical power, their guidance within the inner worlds of the mind and through the gates of Time and Space which were appreciated. By befriending this creature from another level of existence and getting to appreciate what it can do for and with you, you will enter into an even closer relationship with the realms of nature, the sphere of the Earth Mother herself, for these familars are her children and bring her messages to those who dare to seek them in the wilderness of the inner mind.

Allow the animal to guide you through the trees, perhaps to a glade, or a spring on the bank of a stream, to a cave, even, buried deep within the wild greenery. You might discover healing plants, sweet, wild music, the scents of bright flowers and fruits and berries which will nourish not the body, but the spirit. Drink deep from the clear wells, watched over by the Goddess many call Bride; discover, half-hidden in the foliage, the Green Man, Robin Hood or even Pan. You will recognise his face from the leafy faces the pagan masons carved into old churches, just as you will know the Goddess of Change who can become a hare or a deer, a nuthatch or woodpecker. Ask quietly for the kind of help you need, for the wilderness represents a part of your own being. It is the untamed spirit which may frighten you, it is the unexplored region of your consciousness in which the seeds of dreams grow and prosper, it is the Wasteland of uncompleted tasks and failures, which, unless it is explored, cleared and healed, will never allow you to grow to your full dimensions and spread the wings of your imagination for magical good and wisdom. Gradually, through a number of visits, you will be guided through the thickets, you will explore the streambeds, shelter from showers in the caves and become familiar and safe among the jungle of the wild forest.

When you have made this journey of discovery and found your guide and developed a real friendship and trust in its instructions and help, you will be able to take this quest a little further. The next stage is to discover your personal symbol. This can be something natural, like a special sort of leaf, a flower, a pattern of twigs, a stone or a completely artificial sign, displayed for you to recognise. You will find this if you have already made friends with the small, familiar animal. That has to be done first or it will not be able to lead you to the place, or if it is a bird, fly up into the branches of a tree and indicate the symbol hidden there. The reason this symbol is so important is that it will act as a key to the inner worlds which will take you to deeper levels of personal awareness and magic. Although this exercise in many steps is a modern one, it is based on a number of ancient shamanic traditions through which the warrior, or trainee shaman or shamanka (lady shaman), would travel into unknown lands to discover the totem tree, and the guiding animal or bird, then the symbol which would in turn give the seeker a name to be used only in magic. He or she would be able to walk the narrow path between the worlds where time and space as we know them have no meaning. Ancient people were able to follow this path in the world, but we are cut off from the original physical wilderness and so have to seek these magical items within the inner worlds of the mind.

If you have recognised the symbol which your guiding familiar has pointed out, it will start to turn up in your dreams, showing that one of the secret doors at least is willing to open at that symbol. As times goes by you will find it opens many ways where knowledge, magic and healing are to be found, but as in most of these exercises, it takes time to master each step and to prepare for the next one.

The last exercise in this shamanic tradition concerning the Old Ways is the search for your totem animal. This always helps you with any solo magic if you are willing to make it your ally. You will have to go through many adventures, guided first by your familiar, and you may become aware that you need to use your symbol on a physical object, a magical instrument or embroider it on your meditation robe. This is a way of dedicating yourself to working with the inner forces which have been shown to you. The symbol will act both as a key to open the unseen doors in your path, and as a shield to defend you from distractions and any harmful influences which may be encountered within the forests of the mind. You should always take up a shield or work a spell of protection *only for the time you need it.* If you always set wards about yourself or working space you will cut yourself off from the many friends and helpers which are available to the awakened perception. If you perform banishing rituals every day, guard yourself from unfelt harm, you will become totally isolated, alone and eventually defenceless because your banishing will have no beneficial effect.

When you have really worked hard at discovering a great deal about your tree, made friends with your familiar, found your symbol and made it real by carving, painting, embroidering or otherwise making some practical use of it, this in turn will help you to encounter the totem animal, mythological creature or bird which is your magical family's protector and teacher. You may face a number of challenges on the journey to find the totem animal, you may be tested for your strength of will, your courage or determination, your knowledge or practical skill as you struggle through the inner world. Every part of that test is to find out if you are worthy to be accepted into the Old Family, whose first parents are Gods and Goddesses, or Heroes and Heroines, if you prefer. Admittance by modern people into these ancient and sacred clans has to be worked for, sought through doubt and darkness, and finally won by real and continuous effort. There is no simple entry to this honoured company, you can't buy your way in except by hard work, you can't be given admission by anyone else, nor can you pass on what you have experienced and learned as a gift to another person. If you are allowed to become part of this hallowed association, which has vast and ancient roots in all nations of the world, you will have joined a company of wisdom and power which has no equal. There are no recognition signs you can demonstrate, there is no shared badge, no certificate of initiation, no physical brand or tattoo which shows you are one of that rare companionship, but those who have trodden the same path will recognise you, and you will no longer walk alone.

If that is too hard or you do not feel ready for the long-term commitment and dedication to the Old Ways, then you can seek out other Gentle Arts which still use the trees as symbols and may, in time, still lead through the secret door to the Sacred Clan's inner sanctum, which is not of this world. As discussed earlier on in this book, there are a number of seasonal festivals which have symbolic happenings or stories attached to them. In Britain we also have the tradition of the importance of trees whose names were used as the letters of an ancient alphabet. Various writers have tried to attribute particular trees to each letter and then to associate the tree and letter with a particular time of year, month or what have you. The earliest of these was Edward Davies who published a book called *Celtic Researches* in 1804, and more recently the poet Robert Graves continued along a slightly different tack with *The White Goddess*. Each has some parts of the puzzle and each contains much valuable material for meditation, study and consideration, but most people who wish to work with this set of correspondences would like something simpler and more direct. There is no known source for this original work with trees and letters although the Druids, those ancient Oak priests who flourished until the Romans suppressed them, throughout Britain and Ireland, Gaul and parts of Europe, used this symbolic alphabet in some of their records. To the Druids knowledge was something passed on from mouth to ear, and they spent up to twenty years studying, just as people who become doctors or architects spend the twenty years between the ages of five and twenty-five in qualifying for their chosen profession.

It is known that there were about a dozen schools or universities run by the Druids in Britain, many of which are still seats of academic learning today. Students came from all over the known world to study and share their arts of healing, magic, astronomy and astrology, ritual celebration and sacrifice, law and justice, poetry, history and many other aspects of education. Although they didn't build any of the mighty stone circles or earthworks which the scholars of the eighteenth century attributed to them, for these sites were ancient even in their day, they may well have recognised them as places of power, magic and astronomical alignment, and so made use of them, adding truth to the tales which linked them with the monuments. Each college of Druids was also responsible for maintaining the sacred groves, deep in the heart of the densely wooded land. It is likely that they selected saplings of the special trees of their sacred alphabet and planted them as each novice was initiated, so that at the end of his long training a new grove would be ready for him (or her) to dedicate and use. They had no temple buildings nor did they have statues of the Deities they worshipped, but there are plenty of holy wells, standing stones and wild places which are linked with the Druids, and it is likely that they saw many natural objects as sacred, and dedicated their offerings to them. Only true "far memory" will uncover all their works, but anyone who chooses to work with those symbols can open again these lost and overgrown paths of wisdom and power.

You will find that any decent bookshop or public library will have a selection of books showing the details of all the common trees and it is well worth the effort of learning the recognition signs for each species, both in summer and winter, so that you can collect a twig from each of the main magical ones and from these make a set of 'Talking Twigs', an ancient divination system used by the Druids and other tree-priests in other parts of the world. For this you will need not only the knowledge to recognise each species, but a good sharp pair of secateurs to cut a single, finger-thick branch from each of the twenty or so trees of the magical alphabet.

Although Graves and others have attributed the trees to different festivals, there can be no definitive way of associating these as we aren't certain exactly what each implied to the Druids or their magical forebears, but the following list was taught intuitively and might form the basis from which you can build or develop your own list of feasts and trees, symbols and energies as they pass through the phases of the year. Some of these ceremonial dates are very old, some are linked to nature and not the calendar, others are more recent correspondences, but it is just one of the many ways of associating trees and time.

BIRCH   This is the Birth tree, both as a Norse rune, and in many northern traditions, so it is associated with the birth of the Sun God at the winter solstice. Its white bark is used for starting fires and its stripped bark was made into canoes by the American Indians. As a letter it was called BETH, and it is a Goddess tree.

MISTLETOE   The God tree of the winter solstice, green when most trees are dead, and its green and gold leaves indicate life and the Sun, and its virility-restoring berries are symbols of the seed of the Sun. Grows on apple and lime trees, but rarely on a specific kind of oak, which was especially sacred to the Druids, who cut it with a polished bronze sickle and used it for healing (still called 'All-Heal') and magic.

IVY   A Goddess tree, green in midwinter and in this context, linked with modern Christmas, as an evergreen decoration. The Celtic letter GORT. Ivy was used as a magical wand, when twined around a suitable host, and its leaves were used to make people ecstatic.

HOLLY   Another Christmas evergreen, in modern times as associated with the symbols of Jesus, but long before that its sharp thorns and bright red berries made it sacred to the God of Winter. Again wands were sometimes made of holly, and used in the ritual battle between the Winter and Summer tree kings (Holly and Oak). The Celtic letter TINNE.

FIR

This Goddess tree is linked with the often forgotten festival of Twelfth Night, Epiphany, when the Three Wise Men came to visit Mary and Joseph and Jesus, bringing the magical gifts of gold for royalty, frankincense for priesthood, and myrrh for sacrifice. In the pagan year this was when the young God, now aged twelve, was armed with his weapons and sent forth by the Goddess. Fir cones are a masculine symbol carried by priestesses in many ancient religious rites, endowing the young God with virility and protective power.

ASH

This is the tree of the Hero, the King and the Warrior for its strong, straight limbs were made into spear shafts. The Ashen Faggot of thick branches is burned at New Year, for its wood will burn green and wet as well as dry. It is the Celtic letter NION.

HAZEL

Not quite a tree, but sacred to the Goddess of Spring, when in early February, at the feast of Candelmas, its yellow catkins and tiny scarlet flowers are to be seen. It is dedicated to Bride, whose festival this is, for she is the guardian of the holy and magical well surrounded by nine hazels, in which the oracular Salmon of Wisdom swim, feeding on her autumn nuts. Often used as a magical wand, for divining rods, for hurdles and in its purple leafed form, Witch-Hazel, for healing. Celtic name COLL.

ELM

A God tree; at the time when the God is withdrawn from view, this is a slightly sinister tree, which can drop a branch on the unwary even on a still day. Elm wood was used for coffins and wine barrels, the coffin of the vine. Letter AILM.

WILLOW

This Goddess tree is used for healing, for purification, for the handle of the besom with its hazel shaft was bound to the birch twigs with willow withies. The Pussy-Willow already bears its fluffy buds at the time of the spring equinox and so indicates the return of the Goddess of Spring, as well as its disguised hint at sexuality, for this is the mating time of the God and Goddess, whose Star Child is born at Yule, although, like many a country wedding, it is not celebrated until the Goddess is known to be with child, in May. The letter is called SAILLE.

ALDER

This is the tree sacred to Bran, the Raven and Sun God, Giant, Hero, King and eventually oracular head. The alder's imperishable wood, when immersed in water, was used for piles and bridge timbers, and roads of its branches 4,000 years old have been excavated in the Somerset marshes. Dyes of red and black and green were extracted from the twigs, leaves and roots of this water-loving tree, and at the spring equinox when day and night are equal it is right to recall the words of the ritual about Bran, which says 'Span for me the waters of Life, Bridge for me the river of Death...' Called by the Druids FEARN.

HAWTHORN

Whitethorn or May is the Goddess tree whose white flowers indicate the time of Beltane, the Good Fires, which burn away the evils of winter and announce the arrival of summer. The land has many sacred Holy Thorn trees on which prayers for help or healing were pinned, and at whose foot offerings were left. Thorns were protective trees and Whitethorn, Quickthorn and Hawthorn are all sacred to the Goddess. The Celtic letter name was UATH.

SYCAMORE   This is a God tree, and though it is not as old as many of the others in this list, it has a long magical association, for its leaves are often those shown on foliate heads of the God of Nature, Jack-in-the-Green, found as a pub sign and in old churches. The wood is used green for carving, and is often used for Welsh 'Love-Spoons' given as tokens of betrothal at around May Day, when the phallic May Poles were put up on many a village green and the folks celebrated the marriage of the White Goddess to the Green Man, or Robin Hood. Its branches are used to deck the houses in Cornwall in the places where the ancient, pagan 'Obby 'Oss whirls his way through the streets and a week later, the Helston Furry Dance spirals in the power of green growth to the Earth, in a garden full of sycamores. It doesn't have a letter name, but no one has attributed the Druidic PETHBOC to any particular tree, so that would do.

ELDER   This is another magical shrub long attributed to the Lady, for it produces, at about midsummer, a great mass of foaming, fragrant white flowers which make excellent Elderflower champagne. Later on its dark berries may be used in many a healing draught, and its dried pith used to relight the Midsummer bonfires, still to be seen on Cornish hilltops. It is unlucky to burn this wood, except on ritual fires, and to destroy a bush is asking for trouble, for this is a plant beloved of witches. Its Celtic name was RUIS.

OAK   Mate of the White Goddess at Midsummer, when Lord, the Druids' tree, under which they met for ceremonies, to give judgement, for it was always he fights and wins over the Holly King is the Oak sacred to Jupiter or Jove, father of the Gods. Oak is a preserver, and to this day its strong wood is used to impart a special flavour to whiskey, sherry and oak-smoked kippers and trout. As his wife the Elder tree is associated with Ceridwen, the White Sow goddess, the Oak is linked with pigs which feed on its acorns later in the year, and the Flying King, Bladud of Bath, who was healed of leprosy when he followed pigs to their wallow in the sacred groves around the hot springs. The Celtic name for oak is DUIR, and the Welsh is DERWEN, which is still used to signify 'magician'.

CHERRY   This white-flowered tree is the first to provide a harvest of edible fruits, about the time of Lammas, the start of the wheat harvest. It also provides hard wood to be carved, sweet-smelling resin which is used in incense, and bark which is used in medicine. Together with the other stone fruits, like plum, damson, sloe, greengage and peach, it is sacred to the Goddess as she nourishes her earthly children.

GORSE   This prickly plant is easy to recognise by its shrill yellow flowers which are always to be seen, right throughout the year, but particularly at Lammas, the Loaf-mass, and 'Mourning for Lugh', the Sun God who is symbolically slain with the corn, which is harvested in August. Again, this isn't a tree in the way that a birch is, but the ancient people recognised its magical power, its symbolism of the Summer Sun and even made wine from its sweet-scented flowers. The Druids called it ONN, and a local name is Frey, the Norse God.

ROWAN   Mountain Ash, Quicken or Rowan is a small, delicate Goddess tree found in mountainous areas as well as many suburban gardens. Like Elder, it is a Witch tree, and is often planted as a guardian. With creamy-white flowers in the spring and brilliant scarlet berries in the autumn, it is easy to see. A traditional way of protecting a house or barn was to cut two twigs from a rowan you had never seen before, tie them into a cross with red wool, and weave it into a diamond shape between the four arms. Rowan wands are used, not only in magic, but to drive horses and cattle and ward off evil influences. In the autumn, around Michaelmas, this elegant tree looks most colourful with red and gold leaves. The ancient people called it LUIS.

VINE   This plant, best known in Europe for the lush grapes it produces, was grown in the warmer parts of Britain too. It is a God tree, and its wood was used as the symbol of office in the Roman army. The Christians adopted it as a symbol of Jesus, but before that the pagan Bacchus was associated with it and wine made from its fruit. As the grapes ripen in the late September sun a harvest and thus a sacrifice is taken from it. In England brambles and even wild clematis, Grandfather's Beard, filled a similar twining place in folklore, with many tales. To the Celts the Vine was known as MUIN.

YEW   This is the tree of the Dark Aspect of the Goddess, the Old Crone, steeped in wisdom as Lady of Knowledge. At Hallowe'en when traditionally ghosts walk abroad, this fateful tree, which is the symbol of immortality as some yews may be thousands of years old, offers a gateway into the otherworld. Samhain, 'summer's end', was the Celtic New Year, and was a time when not only the spirits of the dead were abroad, but also those of the unborn children. A branch of yew was nearly always included in the ceremonies at this time of year. The letter name for Yew is IDHO.

APPLE This fruit tree is a very sacred one to the Celtic world, for the Apple is the symbol of eternal life, and it was to the Isle of Apples, in Avalon, that the dying Hero/King Arthur was taken to be healed and made ready for his next great task. A 'Silver Branch' of apple wood could be carried by anyone who wished to enter the Otherworld and then return safely to the world of the living. At Hallowe'en, games are played with apples which predict the future, or competitions when the magical fruit was snatched in the teeth from a string or from a bowl of water. The Celtic name for this tree is disputed, but may well have been QUERT, the questioning letter which we have as 'WH' as in WHat, WHere, WHen, WHo and How?

Yew and Apple promise entry into the world of the Ever Living and a safe return to the world of men, and both symbolise the end of one era and the start of another. Hallowe'en brings you round to the dark evenings and cold and misty nights of autumn, leading in turn to the start of winter, when in the darkest of nights, the Star Child is born of the Goddess in a cave, surrounded by animals, as totems of the realm of lowly creatures. By working with the twinned traditions of the trees and their magical interpretations and the symbolism of each of the many ancient festivals it becomes possible to construct for yourself a completely new system of celebrations, based on antique foundations.

A further complete set of occasional rituals or magical workings can be set upon the Celtic division of time which worked with Lunar Months, beginning on the sixth day after the New Moon, what we would recognise as the first quarter, when a half moon rides like a letter 'D' in the night sky. There are thirteen lunar months and so it is possible to attribute the trees and their collection of tradition, symbolism and magic to each of these, if you work upon what is happening in the realm of nature. The Earth Mother and the Sun Lord will demonstrate clearly the rising or falling energy of each month, if you open your eyes to the gentle perception of these green and white tides. Watch for the various harvests, observe the garden plants, the wild creatures and the birds, for they will instruct you.

A way in which the trees were used by the Druids, which has been almost totally overlooked since, is a form of divination in its own right. Writing at the end of the eighteenth century, Edward Davies quotes Tacitus's *De Moribus Germonicus* anicus on the subject of divining by lot or twig:

> They cut a rod or twig, taken from a fruit-bearing tree, into little short sticks or tallies, and having distinguished them one from another by certain marks, lay them, without any order, or as they chance to fall, upon a white garment, then comes the priest... and having prayed to the Gods, looking up at heaven, he takes up each stick, three times, and determines his interpretation from the marks ... .

It is possible to try out this method of divination by setting out, preferably in winter when the trees are resting, with a sharp pair of secateurs, to take a single branch about as thick as your little finger, from the twenty or so magical trees. If you cut thicker twigs you will not be able to hold the entire bundle in your hand at the start of a divination. Because this is a magical ritual you should take only one piece from your chosen tree, being prepared to spend a lot of time studying the branches in easy reach to select a straight twig of the right size. The length of the twigs when finally cut from the longer section should be about your own handspan long, 8 or 9 inches (20 cm). If you don't recognise the trees in winter you ought not to be trying this form of divination, for basic knowledge is important on which to build the divinatory meanings of each twig. Certainly, if you recognise the tree when you cut the branch, you might still not recognise the twig when it is dried and has been cut down to the correct length. (It is useful to stick a band with its species around each twig as you cut it to identify it.)

The Druid's twigs were marked, probably with an Ogham letter. Ogham is an ancient Celtic alphabet, supposed to have been explained to humankind by the God Ogmios (Og is a Celtic Sun God.) It consists of a number of straight or diagonal cuts either on the corner of a squared stone, or a tally stick. The easiest way to mark a set of divining twigs is to cut a flat surface at the bottom end of each stick and write or paint a letter or sigil on this when the twig has dried and seasoned. If you select a part of the branch which has a clearly defined feature, a small side branch, a twist in the bark or something, you will find it isn't as difficult to recognise the bare twigs when you come to read their messages. You will need to leave the bark on, again to help identify each sample, but the ends of the wood should be carefully rounded and smoothed with sandpaper. You can varnish the wood, but it is not really necessary. You will need either a cylindrical box or a bag of velvet or silk to keep the finished twigs in, and a white cloth to shake them on to. It is possible that the Druid's 'white garment' was in some way embroidered to indicate a zodiac, for example, as a way of determining each area to be investigated. The simplest way to divine with the twigs is to shake the whole bundle until several sticks have been cast out, and do this three times. By seeing which twigs are nearest the questioner and which furthest away you get a sense of time: by seeing which are touching or crossing, you see inter-related prognostications, and by noticing whether the twigs fall with their marked ends nearer or further away you can determine good or less good fortune, or events or material gains moving towards or away from you.

It will help if you have a fair knowledge of the uses and magical and folk traditions associated with each tree, its virtues or implied warnings and so on. It would take a whole book to go into the matter fully, but if you combine the search for the right woods, the discovery of their meanings together with a bit of applied meditation and other forms of the Gentle Arts, you are certain to be shown exactly how *you* should use this ancient British form of forgotten divination. You may not receive the same instructions as anyone else, but that is the way of magic, and especially the Old Folk Magics, which were nearly always more or less spontaneous and worked by 'rule of thumb' rather than rule books. Treat each tree you cut from with reverence, and ask the Goddess of Nature or the God of the Wildwood to help you find a tree which will spare you a tally stick, and no doubt they will hearken to your request.

When the sticks are fully dry you will find that when they are shaken together they have a soft musical chattering noise and it is possible that it was for this reason they were sometimes referred to as 'Talking Twigs' or 'Singing Sticks' in some of the more poetic Druidic references, and that *'Cad Goddeu'*, the poem about the Battle of the Trees, discussed at length by Robert Graves, takes on a new and more magical light. Even the scorned idea of 'talking to trees' may have a different meaning if you are willing to reawaken this ancient and gentle art.

11.
THE MAGIC OF THE UNDERWORLD

The UnderWorld Initiation fulfils the mediating role of humankind.
Only when the individual has been through the UnderWorld can he
or she mediate solar energies into the land, or bring the Light and
Dark together . . .

The Underworld Initiation, R. J. Stewart

The Gentle Arts have brought us on a long and sometimes extremely
convoluted journey. This journey has led us through the elements of
Earth and Water, Fire and Air, and has taken us to the stars, yet the
most important part of this winding trail is yet to be explored. That
is the short and immanent journey within. The idea of seeking for
wisdom, for the Holy Grail, for the Hidden Masters and many
another secret or sacred goal has been with us since the earliest
people sought a safe dry cave in which to make their picture magic.
Always there has been someone with better luck, keener eyesight or
more awareness of the patterns of nature from which the sources of
water or food could be located. Always there has been the shaman,
the One-set-apart, whose knowledge was of benefit to his or her
tribe. Usually this was an individual, whose natural talent, inherited
knowledge or magical training made him an asset to his community,
yet his presence might be feared and his company shunned. Not a
lot has changed. Today, those who walk the Hidden Path, master
the Old Lores and practise the Gentle Arts are still, to a certain
degree, likely to be suspect, and their motives and activities
questioned by those they may casually come into contact with.

If you have read this far, no doubt you will have thought about some of the more seemingly anti-social or 'supernatural' ideas discussed here. Perhaps, if your studies have turned to practical work, you will have met with the sideways glances, the cold-shouldering and the non-acceptance of statements about your studies that you have made. It is a lonely path, it always has been, and to gain the greatest sources of wisdom and power these ancient arts have made people walk alone, in the dark and deserted places, in the wilderness, and even, using Bob Stewart's concept, into the UnderWorld. It is a place which has many entrances, and although it generally seems to be necessary to 'go down' this may only be a relaxation of consciousness, a sinking into a meditative state, rather than a descent into a cave or tunnel.

Looking back through the history of ways in which people grappled with acquiring the impossible, or sought initiation, or enlightenment, or any of the other objectives of the inner quest, certain concepts emerge time and time again. The initiate has to be alone, he has to be set apart, in a cave, a sanctuary, inside a pyramid or temple, and in Britain, most of southern Europe, Malta, Greece, and probably originally, Atlantis, special places were created for this purpose. Inside an earth structure is a stone chamber, or sometimes several, wherein the Initiate lay to be reborn of the Earth Mother when a revelation of enlightenment was received when a certain length of time had passed. Not only was there the inward journey within an actual cave or specially constructed underground chamber, but there was the vital aspect which was the journey within the self, to the deeper level of perception which reaches far beyond normal awareness. In every tradition there is this kind of ritual separation, incubation and then illumined rebirth from the deep places. It may take various forms, some involving physical pain, ceremonial tattooing or marking in some way, fasting or any other method which changes not only the consciousness at the time of the ritual, but does something to the Initiate, so that he is actually changed thereafter. Not only do the ritual scars or ceremonial attire indicate he has survived his ordeal, but some attitude of mind, or awakened awareness, show that he is no longer one who went down into the dark.

Of course, lots of modern initiatory groups enact some sort of death and rebirth scenario. Sometimes the candidate is naked and deprived of the things within which he normally hides his persona, in other cases he is robed in new garments and perhaps expected to keep a long and lonely vigil in some sacred or magical place. In some ceremonies, especially those based on Craft Masonry, there are ritual bindings, oaths and symbolic movements which are shown only to initiates. In the older rites the Initiate would swear on his Mother's grave, an indication that by touching the Earth, he was touching the resting place of the Earth Goddess. In some traditions those who perform the initiation represent the candidate's magical parents, or his Ancestors. Or, where the rite is enacted by the candidate alone, he has to enter the sacred chamber and there seek out his forefathers, to be instructed or guided. Going under the earth is a way of re-entering the world of the Spirits of both the Dead and of the Unborn to become, for the time being, a newly awakened soul, to be reborn of his ceremonial parents, or of the Earth herself. Shamans go up into a tree to receive this kind of rebirth, so it would seem that it is always the Earth Mother who offers initiation and instruction.

Merely going through some rite, however, will not necessarily awaken that subtle level of perception. It isn't something which can be offered as a gift from someone who has been through a similar rite either. True Initiation is a real waking of the inner senses and occurs far more rarely than those who administer the rites imagine. Sometimes the candidate is properly prepared, has had some indication of what is to happen to him, what to expect fully explained to him. In other cases the individual is simply cast into the ritual, frightened as to what he might be expected to do or experience. Sometimes the ritual is all too familiar for it has been taken from a well-read book and the only surprise is in the actual experience of becoming a part of the group. In any of these cases it is possible for the candidate to be genuinely awakened, but the well prepared and informed novice will probably get more out of the working than the one who is scared out of his wits and has no idea of what is going on. Certainly there is a reason for magical secrecy, but a simple explanation of what is going to take place, what is expected of the candidate and his total agreement to it will help all concerned.

For many people this whole concept of being initiated into a group of some sort is just 'pie in the sky', either because they have no desire to be a part of any organisation, or because of the pattern of their life makes it impossible to join the stability of group work. These are the ones who will need to make the individual, and just as valid (and in many cases even more effective), solo assay into the Underworld to seek the wisdom and power they wish to possess. Ultimately it is a matter of finding a way to make a new start, to be reborn into a new life or to go in to a path of personal development which is at a tangent from the earlier trail through life. Initiation means 'I go in' so it is merely an entry point, a beginning, rather than a completion or change of its self. Symbolically there may be a casting off of the former self, the taking of a different name, title or motto, and after due consideration, setting out upon a new quest through life. This can be a part of a group ritual or it can equally well be achieved by the individual seeking these things for himself, on his own.

Originally, initiations were one of the many 'Rites of Passage' performed on young people as they grew up within the structure of the tribe or clan. Often, at birth, they had no name and it was only later, when they had reached a certain age and developed the characteristics which determined their position within their society that they were formally given a real rather than a 'nick' name. There used to be rituals at birth, similar in some ways to the Christian ceremony of Baptism, at the age of puberty, which in many parts of the world symbolised the transition between childhood and adulthood. There might be later stages on a long ladder of initiations, to mark the acquiring of a skill, a partner in marriage, a first child, and so on, to the final rites of passage performed after death, when the individual's spirit was set free to return to the spirit land, or to be reborn, or whatever far distant place it might travel to, according to local tradition. In most modern societies none of these ceremonies exist. At a certain age a young person may drink in a pub, may drive a car, may marry, may vote in General Elections, and so on, but at no point is the child helped to 'become an adult' with all the responsibilities, commitments and respect due to an adult, from that moment on. Young people wander in a kind of living limbo, between childhood and adulthood, often unguided, unhelped and feeling very lost. Leaving school, seeking a job or further education is a time of great stress, for in many cases it can be the first time a youngster has had to stand on his own feet, make his own decisions, leave his childhood home, and there is no 'village elder', or prophesying shaman to point out his path, offer advice or recognise the transition to adulthood. Our society has cast away many valuable psychological milestones when it left behind the seemingly 'primitive' concepts of 'rites of passage', and reduced them to a mere party at the age of eighteen.

Not only is there the entry into the world of adulthood, but for the individual who is following the secret path, mastering the Gentle Arts or living out the way of the quest, there is need for a distinct division, a mental marking stone which acknowledges this transition. Each one will have to decide what is the ideal, whether it is the acceptance into a group, lodge or coven, or the solo path through the woods, and then go about bringing that desire into reality. In each case, it is not as easy as it might appear. To join a group implies that you have first found one, which follows the tradition into which you are seeking entry. It suggests that you know what you want from your magical work and the kind of people you wish to share it with. But most students cannot see that far ahead. Many vaguely think it would be fun to be part of a coven or lodge but have never really thought about what it involves in terms of time, commitment, personal choice of action and direction. Every well-established group has its own 'Group Soul', often developed over a long period of time, and this will have a profound effect upon anyone who is brought under its influence. It will cause changes in you over which you will have no control. You may also be expected to swear an oath of secrecy, with unpleasant consequences if you should break your given word. You may be expected to behave, dress and act in accordance with the will of the High Priestess or Magus, and have little say in the way the group progresses or in what it does. There is little real democracy in magic, those who know how to raise and wield the power tell the others what to do! In some groups you will be carefully instructed in the mythology, symbolism and rituals of the group, in others you may well be left alone to blunder along as best you can. There are no rules and no way of telling before you join, so always be prepared to ask questions, seek explanations, and explore your feelings about the people you have met. Only go forward if you are certain it is right.

Only in the secret societies, in the magical lodges and the witch covens do some of these ancient marking ceremonies reappear, and then only in a dramatic and ritual sense, rather than one which is done openly, before the whole community, at a specific moment in the life of the candidate. Certainly the Old Wisewomen and the Cunning Men had no sense of grade or status or hierarchy, nor did the series of degrees play any part in their practices. What mattered within their community was how effective they were when the people called upon them. No one would have much trust in the local healer if she never cured anyone, nor would they visit an ineffective diviner for news of distant friends. Within a village community, information about the success or lack of it would soon be common knowledge. This would work in both directions. The shaman or healer would be well aware of any troubles among the people of the village, their loves and hates, their illnesses and those of their livestock, so that when the Wise One was consulted she would already know something about the question. This is equally true today, and again, it is your success as a Tarot reader, or healer or maker of talismans which will show how well you have mastered these ancient crafts, not the 'degree' you have passed in some ceremony, or the number of notches on your wand.

The same applies from a point of view of religion. You are either dedicated to the varied pantheon of Gods and Goddesses, which has become real to you because you have had personal experience, or you have a more orthodox faith. That is up to you. You cannot be a second degree child of your earthly parents, so how can you become a second degree worshipper of the Old Gods? You either are dedicated to their service and work with their power, because you have dared to make that inner contact, alone, in some desolate place in the wild, or simply sought it, deep within your own being, by a personal act of dedication and self-initiation. There is no ladder of commitment you can climb, in real terms, anymore than you can be a second degree Christian or a third degree Jew etc. You either accept the tenets of a specific or unorthodox faith and consider yourself an adherent, or you don't. The choice of belief or practice is entirely up to you, but to follow the Old Ways totally will involve some sort of religious commitment, which can equally be orthodox or nonconformist. It has to be a real experience and personal way of communicating with the Deity you feel most drawn to, after thought and meditation. When you have made up your own mind it doesn't give you the right to try to force your opinion or religious views on anyone else, though, so try not to persuade others.

Much of the working of the Gentle Arts is an individual and lonely process. It has always been so. Many of those who tried to understand the ancient powers in Earth and Air, Fire and Water, and the natural methods of healing with time and lunar tide, were shunned because of their different views of life by the superstitious majority. This still seems to be true. Magic, witchcraft and the psychic arts are not well understood by those who practise them, let alone the world at large, and if you are serious in your studies and take them beyond book-learning, you are certain to meet with distrust, with misinterpretation, or with fear by some of the people you meet in your ordinary life, if they ever get to hear about your interests. It is up to you to maintain discretion and secrecy, especially if you share your work with others. Don't brag about your magical skills, or any successes you may have had, for you will either be inundated with requests for help, many of which it would be unwise or unethical to deal with, or you may find yourself shunned by those around you, for they are frightened of the idea of magical power. There is an old adage, 'To Know, To Will, To Dare and To Keep Silent' which should be thought about very thoroughly.

If you choose to become an initiate, whether by your own efforts and the agreement of the Gods and Goddesses you have chosen to serve, or at the hands of some group which offers, hopefully, practical training as well as initiation, you will have made a life-long commitment. You will have promised or sworn an oath to act with discretion, to obey the rules or to conform to the system. This is not a joke. Joining a magical group, should one invite you to, is as serious and long-term an activity as getting married, and it should only be entered into with as much forethought and love. You must trust, respect and feel kinship with the people whose company you are agreeing to join. If you have any doubts, or fears, or questions which they will not answer, then wait. No one *has* to join a group, no one has to be initiated by someone else, and if you have the slightest hesitation, then give it a miss. A better opportunity is certain to turn up in due course.

Real magical orders are very few and far between. Most of the good ones run training groups or schools to give seekers the basic knowledge and practical skills which they will need if they are found worthy to be initiated. You may encounter one of these schools or 'Outer Courts' if you search for them, and if you desire above all things to be a part of a lodge or coven, but you are just as likely to be disappointed and have to struggle on alone. You will have to seek that other road, that of the Hermit, the Grail Questor, the Village Witch or the Shaman. It is a hard and winding road, but most of the fears and difficulties come from within. They are just as likely to be encountered in a group-situation, but there, at least, you have someone to hold your hand, or pat you on the back, and say 'There, there, it will soon be over'. But inside a group you will also encounter 'personality conflicts', 'power-play' and the in-fighting which can happen in even the best sorts of magical associations. There may be a structured hierarchy and people can struggle for position or preferment which you won't be faced with if you tread the paths alone, or with an equal companion. The old ways and the new ways work best with balanced pairs of men and women, for polarity, of the inner and the outer, is the balance point which makes magic work. If you are alone you will have to come to terms with your inner self, your Holy Guardian Angel or Anima/Animus (to use Jung's terms for the inner self which is of the opposite sex to your physical body). There is a guide and guardian within all of us, and by working with it, in double harness, as it were, you will find a reliable and constant companion.

To become an initiate, to discover and have conversation with your Holy Guardian Angel, or to make a personal dedication are all similar processes. They involve initially the decision to go through with such an act, of your own free will, after a good deal of care and thought. You will also need to plan exactly what form this act might take. Of course, you may already have the option of joining a group, or already be a member of one, renewing your vows or making them for the first time. You may well be an initiate from a previous life, and your ventures on the paths through time may have brought back such memories to you. In any case, it is a good idea to plan a renewal of your dedication once in a while so that you don't forget what you are about.

Ideally you should be willing to spend twenty-four hours making the real dedication, which is a very different matter to a quick initiation rite at the hands of some group. You will need to meditate about the step you are about to take, being absolutely certain that you want to become a shaman, witch or magician, a practitioner of the Old Arts or whatever. This is the Vigil, and must be carried out when you are alone, preferably in some lonely and undisturbed place, ideally out of doors. You might choose to fast, or at least drink only pure fruit juices instead of your usual meals. In tribal societies this exile from company could last weeks and involve fasting, ceremonial tattooing or other forms of painful ordeals which tested the candidate's courage and determination. Sometimes the novice had to catch his totem animal and prepare the skin or flesh in some ritual manner, or make a shield, or build a hut or in some other way demonstrate he was ready to be accepted into his society. You might choose to make a piece of equipment, or a ceremonial robe during this Vigil, as well as spending a good deal of time actually meditating and thinking in more ordinary ways of what you are doing.

The next stage of the process was the ritual death or burial of the candidate, when ordinary consciousness is put aside, and the individual goes to meet the teacher or the Ancestors or the Gods and Goddesses of the tribe. Here it is possible to receive a new name or the details of a tribal secret, taboo or totem animal etc. You will have to write or record a suitable pathworking which takes you from the place to that of your ancestors, Gods or whatever source of power you wish to dedicate yourself to. It is safer, at this point, to put up the wards and make a magical 'place between the worlds' wherein you can retire to seek this inner knowledge or the keys to your future. You may wish to chant or dance, drum or play a simple whistle or other instrument, much as the shamans do. You can pour out offerings of corn or flour, honey or wine, milk or oil, even, making your circle with them, if you are out of doors. You could trace patterns with bread crumbs, seeds or flowers as an offering to the wild creatures and birds. Take your time, and eventually become very still and receptive, for now is your chance to walk the inner paths and discover your magical roots, be taught your 'magical' and very secret name, your totem animal and family tree.

Be patient. Allow lots of time for knowledge to come to you. You should be willing to devote hours to discovering the correct road through the Mysteries which may be opening up before you. You may wish to sing or write poetry, chant or follow a pattern of rhythmic breathing. You might ring a bell, or strike a cymbal or hit two hard pieces of wood in a particular hypnotic beat, or play a drum until that subtle change of awareness steals over you and you perceive for real the forces of nature or your ancestors or teachers. Allow yourself to 'feel dead' and rest and prepare for rebirth with a new name and a new purpose. Be prepared for surprises, for even if you know the pattern and structure of the rites you are taking yourself through, the inner worlds will have their say, too.

Next you will have to make a personal dedication, swear an oath or make a promise about what you intend to do. It should imply you will treat your knowledge and magical power with discretion and respect, and always act responsibly when using the Gentle Arts, not interfering with the lives and affairs of other people unless specifically requested. Ask for the sort of help, powers, abilities and strengths that you feel you will need, but also offer your own life to the process of evolution and growth. To make this promise formally you should touch bare earth and swear upon the body of your Mother Earth, and then reach up and promise by the spirit of your Father Sky (or any similar deities), vowing that from the soles of your feet which bring you balance on Earth to the top of your head in which are your thoughts of Heaven, you are totally dedicated henceforth to your magical path. Obviously you should have thought this all out beforehand and perhaps written some sort of promise on paper, which you can symbolically burn to indicate that it has passed into the inner records and cannot be wiped out on

Earth.

After you have been silent to allow any kind of reply to be received, and waited until you are ready to go on, you might feel the next part of this dedication process should be a kind of renaming ritual. You can find a way to cast off your previous name, or even a 'nick-name' and take on the new one, which should have been taught to you earlier in the day. You could rebaptise yourself by pouring water which has been blessed in the name of the Goddess over your head as if you were being reborn as her child and gaining a name in the process. Think about this for you are sure to be given help as to what to do if you are really serious about your intention.

Another part of the ceremony is the communion. This can be of bread, cakes or biscuits, preferably which you have prepared yourself, and wine, mead, fruit juice or even spring water from a sacred well. Although you will be alone when you come to this traditional part of most rituals, you will be sharing the sacred meal with all other initiates, all other people the world over who are dedicated in some way to the Old Faith, or the continuance of the magical ideal. Also, the God and Goddess, or elemental beings will be with you, even if you are not yet able to perceive them. These are your family and they will share the bread and wine once these are blessed and offered to them. Do remember to pour a libation to all beings and sprinkle a few crumbs to the Earth. Think about 'absent friends', the kind of people, who, though you might not have met them yet, you would like to be sharing this feast with, and how you might come across them in the days to come. It is correct to empty the cup and turn it down on the platter on which your ceremonial bread was placed. Of course, you can turn this into an elaborate meal, if you wish, especially as you may have been fasting since your evening meal the previous day, if you are doing this in the old-fashioned way.

The last part of the dedication is for you to offer to help the world, as a whole. It is no good being all excited about becoming a 'real pagan' or whatever, if you scatter tins and rubbish about the place, and take far more from the natural resources than you are willing to repay. You will possibly have to change your whole way of living, your diet, your hobbies and activities once you learn what is greed and how it is possible now to regain something of the harmony between mankind and Mother Nature. You will no longer have the excuse of 'not knowing', for if you make your dedication even half-seriously you will be taken at your word, which in magic is always your bond. If you promise to live in a different way and then break your word, the Lords of Karma will soon bring things back into balance, no matter at what cost to you. If you strive always to do good, to take only as much as you need, and wherever possible, pay back into the universal bank through your life, things will always go well for you. If you encounter difficulties, bad luck, ill health and uncomfortable relations with others in your life, these are all your own fault! It isn't a gang of black magicians doing evil things to you, it is just all the unresolved greed, selfishness and unthinking acts which you have left behind you, suddenly being resolved by the power of the Gods and Goddesses.

You can help them by making 'the Wasteland blossom' as the Finder of the Grail was supposed to do. This can be by planting a new garden, or helping restore woodland or riverbanks to pleasant places, full of wildlife and safe for children to play. You can work on an allotment, grow food and flowers, plant fruit trees, and bushes which have berries for wild birds to feed on in winter. You can take a little of Mother Nature's bounty and make wines to share in friendship, and nuts for cakes to eat at ritual meals. This is not the same as belonging to a coven and being a spectator at some indoor rituals, it is living in the wild world of the Earth Goddess and the Sky Lord, sharing with them your desires and joys, your failures and your successes, asking for help and giving thanks, as naturally as you would talk to one of your family or a close friend. Some of this work can be mixed into your Day of Dedication or whatever you choose to call it. Conservation cleanses and heals the Wasteland, both on the face of the planet, and within the souls of the people. Gardening is a much safer therapy for depression than modern drugs, and if it is also addictive, it will do the gardener a great deal of good. As you will see, this commitment to the Old Ways is a very long-term project. Once you have sought to become one of those who have 'gone in' to initiation, there is no turning back.

Your one-person save the world campaign may be carried on in a variety of ways, but always try to find methods which are not violent or destructive. Preventing wild animals from being captured or killed must be done in a way that does no harm to any person or trees either, for all are parts of nature. You might find you can do far more to preserve the natural world by changing your diet and way of living so that you grow much of your own food and know it to be free of chemicals and that your home-made shampoo has never been tested on animals in a laboratory. Part of rebuilding these subtle, inner links requires you to become very aware, not only of your own acts and motivations, but of those about you in all fields of life. Becoming dedicated makes you more involved with the rest of the world, not less so. If you wish to put aside your responsibilities as an aware individual, then you had better seek a place in a monastery or nunnery, for the pagan path is one which insists that you not only care about the world and all its children, but that you do all you can to help them.

'As you sow, so shall you reap . . .' it is written, and this means you will remain responsible for any seeds you sow, even in later lives, when they have grown into mighty oak trees. You may find that by going down the dark path which leads to the eternal Otherworld which is within you that you also transcend time, and can relive, with as much feeling, as much pain or love, any of your many previous lives. You can learn to create a path journey which deliberately takes you backwards across the flow of time's spiral, so that in a few brief moments you can become as you were a hundred or a thousand years ago. You *do* become yourself, with all the sensations, thoughts, memories and knowledge, and it can be a hard and difficult experience, not to be contemplated without a really good friend at your side. You may be frightened, sick, injured or in danger, and you will feel these as if they were a part of your life now. You will also find the memories remain, even when you have been called gently back across the bridge of lives to the present time. Once you have recalled the fragments of who you once were, it is as much a part of your memory as events last week. You may discover, in such trips to the Otherworld, the reasons for fears or dislikes, loves and hates in this present incarnation. Again, this is a door you should only open with due thought and attention to the possible consequences, or, if you are sitting in with one of your magical companions, what effect it might have on him. Will you be able to cope with the thought of death and rebirth?

Again, when you have made your dedication you may wish to find a simple way of marking the passing festivals in your home and life. One of the oldest ways of doing this is to create a shrine. This need not be very elaborate; in fact, if you live in a house with other people who do not share your interests or practices, it is a wise move to make it fairly inconspicuous. Perhaps there is the top of a cupboard or bookshelf where you can display a potted plant (better than cut flowers), some pine cones, sea shells, souvenir statues of aspects of the Gods or Goddesses you work with, or symbols of the elements. This need not be a large display, but should others of your kind visit you, they will recognise the symbolism, whereas other folk would see just flowers.

There is a lot of research you can do, if you wish, for as I mentioned at the beginning, most of the Old Ways were simple arts and crafts, kept fresh in the memories of the people who used their magics, or kept the festivals, or practised the crafts. Few of these really ancient, yet until recently, still continued skills, were written about or recorded in a way that makes it easy for students to follow them. We do have a vast store of knowledge, but it isn't neatly set out in books or on tape or film. It is in older folks' memories, in simple customs set in a particular village, and carried out come rain or shine. It is in the real folksongs, the carols and dances, the seasonal feasts and celebrations, in poetry and story, tale and legend. These we may still find set out for us to read, to hear or to watch, but we will need the inspired eye of the artist, the awakened ear of the songster, the bright mind of the poet and the living spirit of the true follower of the Old Ways to make sense of these scattered crumbs of wisdom.

This knowledge is in the Otherworld too, the Akashic Record, the Collective Unconscious, the Book of All Time, and those who diligently follow the Gentle Arts may seek it out there. None of this store will be lost, it might become much harder to find, just as a single book in a large and strange library is harder to locate than in a small one, but it is all there for us. Most of it can only be of use if it is practised, if it becomes personal experience rather than seen only as second-hand. The more effort you put in to mastering these essentially simple yet none the less powerful skills the greater wisdom you will gain. This, in turn, can be applied to help those around you, to revitalise the Wasteland and make it blossom and fruit for the benefit of the many. You will learn to heal, if you so wish, and with that, gain the wisdom of knowing when healing will work, and when it won't. You will become well and always healthy so that people will remark about your complexion, and you will join the company of folk who never seem to age, although the years pass them by. You will open doors deep within you so that your own store of kindness, compassion and love will be released and shared, and so multiply, bringing you true happiness, especially if you are accomplishing great works.

Such knowledge and power costs, but you should find as the years of study and practice pass speedily and are filled with joy, with friendship and a sense of wonder that is hard to explain. If you are really willing to put yourself wholeheartedly into the service of the Old Ones you will gain such treasures into the store of experience and reality that will make you wonder what life was about before you stepped upon the Hidden Road. Not only is there much to regain from the past, there is much to build for those who are to come.

We are living at the transition point between two Ages, that of Pisces the Fish and Aquarius the Water Bearer. In the last age the pattern of people's lives has been a communal one, with the whole concept of mass-employment, mass-education and other material and industrial conditions whereby individualism was repressed. We have grown up in the last generation of a world dedicated to conformity and collectivism. When the world finally reaches the Aquarian Age, a great deal more personal freedom, self-reliance and self-determination will be the rule. Now we are between two traditions, seeing the way things are dying out and great changes taking place, not only in the industrial west, but in the Third World. What is most hopeful, in these black-seeming years, is that attention is finally being drawn to the root causes of starvation, of mass-unemployment, or internal revolution. Not only are the causes being seen and understood, they are out in the open so that all the world can see where greed, misuse of natural resources, bad housing, incorrect diets and many other local and world-wide troubles have grown from, so this can be altered for the better.

Many diseases have been wiped from the face of the world in the last few decades, but many new ones have been identified. The way of medicine and healing has begun to be scrutinised, so that ancient methods and simple arts can take their place beside the super drugs and operating theatres. In education and in science what has gone wrong is being examined openly and so nuclear power and the education of children are each being held under the microscope to see what better ways can be found to serve the people's needs. A lot is happening, even in the political world, with change of direction happening in even the most unreasonable regime, often brought about by peaceful demonstration and inner revolution. This is only the start of the many changes the next couple of hundred years will bring. We could be on the verge of a true Golden Age, for the Water Bearer is the Grail Carrier who has found the vessel of rebirth and brought it into the world that its redeeming waters may be poured out for all in need. Also, the magical and supernatural arts will surely be allowed to take their place among the technologies of the future, and the inherent wisdom, power and dedication which their use implies will be available to any who seek to learn and use them.

We are the bridging generations, who can still draw on the recalled memories from the past and yet who will surely be able to see the way the new age is dawning. If we are strong enough to be able to accept change and therefore the magic it brings, and to act with that change, in harmony with the Old Gods and Goddesses, whose being has always been immanent in some form, a wonderful future lies ahead for us. It may be hard to see, looking at the state of the world, feeling the fears, the regrets, the losses of patterns in the past, but mankind is an evolving species. It is because we have been able to adapt through the Ice Ages, the changes in climate, in foodstuffs, in locations on our long and wandering path across the face of the Earth that we are still here. We have not lost that ability to adapt, and the level on which the most changes are due to occur is that in the field of the mind. Our technologies have explored the face of the

Earth, the depths of the sea, the highest reaches of mountains, but that inner world, the vast expanse of human consciousness has hardly been looked at. That is the material from which all magical reality is built. Within the trained consciousness of the practitioner of the Gentle Arts lies the seed of the future developments, in such widely diverse fields as those of healing, invention, psychology, art, poetry, music, creativity and the practical applications of true will.

When you have learned to enter the Underworld of the inner mind, and safely return to everyday life, you will have opened an ancient channel so that others may also make that journey to the seat of wisdom and the source of creativity. Everyone who is willing to seek within will come forth rewarded in greater or less measure, depending on their needs. The path lies at your feet, the methods are ancient, simple, readily available to all who have the courage, dedication and common sense to seek them. If you walk in those hidden roads alone now, you may well encounter others who desire to share your company and journeys, and you will in time meet them in the outer world, and become friends. As you learn and master these arts you will become a greater person, of more value to the world, and all your efforts on behalf of others will bring you rewards which will not necessarily increase your bank balance, nor grant you a newer car or a bigger house, but they will enhance your life, bring you peace and love, and success in things you desire. Many have trodden that way, and though they do not appear on television every night, and they are not known in the papers for their good works, for many years they have striven to change the world for the better so that the keys of freedom and personal expansion are available to all who want them. You never know, one of them may live next door to you, and the kind of group or teacher you secretly wish to encounter may be found at the end of your road. These Gentle Arts may show you to their door.

12.
FINDING YOUR OWN MAGIC

By now you will have decided if the ideas in this book are sensible. You will know that you have been drawn to renew your links with Mother Nature and the Old Gods of the Land, or that this is not the path for you. Choice is a very important concept in magic. All the time you have to choose which course of action to take, just as in the real world you have to decide which brand of breakfast cereal to buy, or how you will spend your leisure time. Perhaps the choice you have to make now will be whether to carry on your studies alone with books, or to seek others with the same interests. At the end of the millennium there are many thousands of people from all walks of life actively pursuing these ancient ways. You are not alone. You may be quite happy that way, but there are other options.

Another important thing to note is that whatever you decide today, or sooner or later, is that you can change your mind. If today you settle for the solo path, guided by books and personal exploration, tomorrow or at least when you have gone as far as you can, you may choose again. This same thing applies if you join some sort of study group or are admitted to a coven. No one can make you continue along a route that you no longer wish to follow. The magic arts are like any other course of study. You will recall that you attended various schools for several years as you progressed from the Infants to the Juniors to Senior School and perhaps University. These subjects are similar in that you may need to spend a few years on each one, mastering the techniques of hand or mind, but eventually you will move on, grow up, walk a different path. Of course, you may well discover some byway in the realms of Natural

Magic which so intrigues you that you continue on it for many years, even lifetimes, but you can change, it is allowed no matter what anyone may say.

Nothing you decide today need be forever. However, the reverse side of that coin says that each art or technique needs time to learn and to get to work. It is easy to turn to the last exercises in any book and try them and fail to get results, because like any other subject, there is a graded set of techniques which need to be mastered in order to give you the skills needed for later ones. If you can't or won't meditate then many of the forms of divination will be closed to you, because to see clearly in a crystal ball or read a spread of Tarot Cards you need that clear inner vision which only arrives after some practice. It is far easier to realise that now, and work on the basic arts than keep trying different things from various books and waste time and effort. Most magical skills take a matter of weeks or months to learn. The same is true of anything else that is worth doing. Regular work helps, too, rather than concentrated work at long intervals. Imagine you were learning a new language or a different sport, would you be fluent in days, or a world class player in weeks?

Magic is the same. It requires the mastery of the language of symbols by which we talk to the Gods and Goddesses, and they communicate with us. It requires regular effort at repetitive exercises, just as the sports player has to perform these. Not every day is the Olympics. Of course it may take up time that you would rather spend on something else, and that is your choice. Some of life's necessities do have to be dealt with first. Getting to know Mother Nature is no excuse for abandoning your children and family when they need you and meditation must give way to the needs of your job, especially if others rely on you. Certainly you can use your occult knowledge to ease the burdens of everyday life. It is usually best to try out your newfound esoteric arts on yourself first in any case. As you learn the ways of divination you can attempt to discover what is going to happen in your own life and use it as a blueprint of the future. If you are practising your skills at making talismans, try one to assist you in your job or your health.

This may sound rather selfish, and selfishness is not to be

encouraged. However, you are actually using yourself as a guinea pig to try out techniques which later on you may use for others. It is far better to try out healing methods where you can feel and see the results than apply them to other people, untested. If you really need something, and you have tried all ordinary methods without success, then you may turn to the Great Ones for help. Magic really does work in the case of need rather than greed. For example, at one time I found myself homeless. The lease on the flat I had been living in had run out and the landlord needed the place for his own growing family. Trying all the local renting agencies was taking a long time, (an author's income is so unreliable that a mortgage was out of the question,) and the friend whose house I was looking after in her absence was about to return, and I really did not fancy having to camp out in a cardboard box under a railway bridge. Also I had a huge library of books stored in a rather unsuitable warehouse and needed them for a new book project. I was really very desperate. So I resorted to performing a magical ritual.

I set out clearly what sort of dwelling place I needed to continue my work as a teacher and writer, defining as sharply as I could the sorts of space, facilities and transport which were important, and I asked the Great Goddess to help. This was in March, just before the Equinox, not necessarily the most auspicious time to be house hunting. Despite regular visits to letting agencies, phone calls to prospective landlords, nothing was on offer. Then I spotted a small advert in a local paper. The owner was offering a furnished house in a village near a big city. I went as quickly as I could to inspect it, expecting to find it cluttered with furniture and fittings, (I already had a good sized dwelling's worth of contents,) but it was in fact empty and partly decorated. The landlord sounded a bit off-putting that wet Tuesday, but said he would take up references and so on. By Thursday I was on tenterhooks when I phoned for his verdict, but he said if a cheque could be in his hand and the papers his solicitor offered could be signed, the place was mine the next day. I moved in just in time to celebrate the Equinox, and am still here. The garden that was a wilderness is in full blossom and there is almost too much soft fruit to eat, but some of the half decorated rooms still aren't finished. The Goddess heard my plea and answered.

I was desperate and really needed a home, so did my thousands of books and my electric typewriter so that I could meet the book deadline - it wasn't greed or desire for a large house, I feel, which made my plea acceptable to the Gods. Exactly the same sort of result has been achieved by many other people, using simple, old-fashioned methods. They have found worthwhile and fulfilling jobs, met up with new friends with similar if peculiar interests, (like witchcraft and occult philosophy,) they have developed new skills brought about by divinely inspired career changes and so can serve their families and the Old Ones better. Many have discovered that it is safe to quit the rat-race and take up different paths in healing and divining, leaving the office and factory for an alternative therapy practice or job as a travelling Tarot consultant. Others have become professional Graphologists, checking the handwriting in letters to big companies to see if newcomers will fit in, or discovering whether applicant's Natal Horoscopes make them suitable for the company's employ.

Although magic can help solve many of those problems in life that nothing else will touch, the pagan path is also a spiritual one. Most people who set out to become witches soon learn that it is a religion as well as a philosophy. It is often hard, to discover that the orthodox religion, or none, which you were brought up in no longer satisfies. Many seekers feel a longing for a female deity, or for the balance of a Divine Mother as well as a Divine Father. These yearnings are met by modern pagan beliefs. What has happened in the very recent past, (since about 1940 AD,) is that a new pagan current has arisen, combined with the fascination with magic, that is reaching ever growing numbers of people all over the world. This new spiritual energy is very different from that of the pre-Christian or Classical pagans, however, and though many modern wiccans claim an antique origin for their faith, there is a large gap.

The Classical pagans of Egypt, of Greece and the Roman Empire all worshipped many gods and goddesses in many forms. They had elaborate Temples dedicated to their deities and large priesthoods to serve them. They operated, as do the priests of other modern religions, conducting public ceremonies at certain festivals, leading processions and offering sacrifices. Some contemporary writers would have us believe that these offerings were of fruits and flowers but in fact most gods and goddesses demanded certain kinds of animal sacrifices. From a bull or horse down to the doves and sparrows, each ancient deity, some of those still worshipped in today's pagan recension had a favoured victim. It was these blood offerings which among many other things upset the early Christians, who believed that Jesus had died once and for all as a sacrifice for humanity. Go to any museum and look at the ancient altars displayed there and you will see the images of lines of animals and flowers and oil jars and so on to be offered to the deities of the past. That is a real part of the pagan heritage. Of course, we do not know if the ancient gods actually wanted or requested such offerings, but if you take up the pagan ways you cannot ignore history.

Today we still make offerings during rituals and celebrations, usually of sweet incense, wine and bread, and of course the burning of candles, which in its own small way will undoubtedly add to global warming! The pagan religion should be one of living in harmony with Mother Nature, the Earth and the Universe, acknowledging divinity in male and female beings, and seeking to be at peace with the rest of humanity. If this were accomplished it would be a great thing indeed, but like followers of other faiths, pagans can be careless and short-sighted. What the Earth needs is understanding and for people to live by Her tides and energies. She does not ask anyone to blast bits of pretty rock (crystals,) out of one part of her structure to be buried in another. She does not ask those who choose to hold rituals at places they consider ancient and sacred to leave offerings of candle wax on stones set up by our distant ancestors, nor other less pleasant debris distributed around these holy places. It is said that visitors to other wilder and distant countries should take nothing but photographs and leave nothing but footprints. Pagans should bear this in mind when they visit some special and delicate place. Even the photographs may be held in the memory rather than a camera, to return to in meditation and inner journeying.

The religion of the modern pagan presents all kinds of problems, not least for its new adherents. Most other major religions have some kind of agreed mythology/history which forms the basis of religious practice and the patterns of festivals. Nearly all the major faiths have a Book to be guided by. Most major religions also have only one god. Pagans, on the other hand, worship a wide variety of classical deities, folk heroes, mythological characters and personal goddesses. No two pagans would agree that they honour the same gods in exactly the same way, with precisely the same festivals and rituals as each other, let alone all pagans worldwide. There are certain concepts which the vast majority of pagans would accept as factors in their beliefs which include both a Goddess (or many Goddesses,) and a God (or many Gods). Some also believe in a Creative Spirit which transcends gender, though not all. It has been said that where three pagans gather to discuss their religious beliefs there will be at least five opinions!

Many accept the idea of reincarnation, though the way that the human spirit returns to Earth or another planet, and how often, and so on remain matters for discussion and experiments in Past Life Recall. Some followers of Northern paganism seem to worship Odin above other deities of that pantheon. There is no book of rules to follow, and though there are several popular currents in modern paganism which do unify and share many tenets of belief these are not gospel. Again, in some quarters moves to rationalise and standardise things like the dates of major festivals and so on have been tried. In practice most people gather on the nearest weekend, which to my mind defeats the whole idea of working with the seasons of the Earth Mother and gets back to the rigid structure of the orthodox faiths modern pagans have abandoned.

What most thinking pagans do accept is that the Goddess and the God or Gods are immanent, that is within reach. They may be seen or felt during rituals, they may, under certain conditions, be consulted or called into the worshippers, to speak or advise. Their power is accessible for healing, to enlighten through divination, to bless and to empower. Their life story may be enacted during the passing festivals of the year, their presence may be sought in the wild places, and in the silence of midnight, or on the seashore when the moon is full. The patterns of Nature offer signposts as to the doings of the Great Ones and symbols through which they may be communicated with. The Goddess in her varying form of Maiden,

Mother and Matriarch is real, She is close, She is approachable. So is the God, as Lord of the Wildwood, Harvest King and Divine Infant, and the interwoven pattern of the Goddess and the God's lives gives a secret structure to the turning year. No one is made to believe these things, there are no pagan missionaries, but more and more people in their own ways are finding a home in the pagan paths, and comfort and strength from the Old Ones.

Because pagan beliefs are so varied, it means there are lots of different sorts of pagans. In fact, these days you can be pagan and be a witch, or a modern wiccan, a Druid, a Shaman, an Odinist or Norse pagan, a Celtic pagan, a Classical pagan, or follower of any of the vast number of Native religions of America, or Africa or elsewhere, or a ceremonial magician of various traditions. Not all magicians are necessarily pagans though, for example, those who work with the Qabalah. There are Jewish Kabbalists, Christian Cabalists and those who study the arts of the Mystical or magical Qabalah. Each spelling represents a different branch of this ancient tradition, some of which have always been aligned to orthodox faiths. I am sure there are lots of people today who simply consider themselves pagans because they worship the Sun or the Old Gods or Mother Nature, but who have not really considered the possible ramifications of their beliefs and practices.

One thing that all pagan traditions do have in common is that they offer initiation to their adherents. Paganism is a Mystery Tradition, in that there are things which can only be gained from personal experience. They cannot be taught, or sold, or given except by each individual undergoing some personal spiritual experience. In some cases this is in the form of an initiation ritual into a particular group. Some traditions insist that every witch has to be initiated by another witch, although who performed the first in this chain of ceremonies is debatable. Others seek to receive their initiation directly from the hands of the Great Ones, either alone, or within a group. In each case, something will happen to confirm that the new initiate has been received into the body of the Craft. It may happen during the ritual, or it may be a more gradual process which allows hidden depths of the psyche to gently awaken. In the end, that initiate will have been changed forever. Many groups are completely separate, and may not accept the initiation of a person into other groups, and in England it is not common for people to visit lots of different groups. Meetings are private and secret, and there are few public celebrations which outsiders can join in. The situation in the USA is rather different, with huge rituals shared by many different covens at major festivals.

If you do decide to explore any of these occult ways you should consider exactly what you personally believe. Many different users of Natural Magic do not believe at all, they have had a number of direct experiences which put them in touch with their chosen deities. First hand experience and considered thought are far more valuable ways of dealing with these ever changing philosophies, because now, at the edge of a new millennium, (at least for the Christians,) and a new Zodiacal sign of Aquarius for those who favour astrology, there are new currents of spirituality abroad. In fact, it is almost certainly the effect of the dawning of the Age of Aquarius which has led people's new religious movements. The last sign, Pisces, the Fishes, represents group activities, thinking and acting like a school of fish, turning with the tides and staying with the shoal. Aquarius gives a new and far more individual impulse, for its symbol, the Water Carrier represents a person who is bringing fresh water to others. The Water Jar is another symbol of the Holy Grail which will heal and refresh all who discover it and drink from it. This was originally a cauldron in pre-Christian days, which offered inspiration and wisdom from the Mother Goddess.

You will no doubt come across references to different traditions of witchcraft and wicca, and may wonder what is correct when some writers imply, (like leaders of orthodox faiths,) that theirs is the one true path. Simply put in witchcraft there are a number of basic divisions. One is Hereditary Witchcraft, which like its title means the powers and rituals are inherited within a group of families, and the only way to join is to be accepted into the family as the wife or husband of an existing member or by a kind of adoption. There certainly are a small number of families in Britain who have maintained the Hereditary line.

A second stream of this ancient knowledge is that of the Traditional Witch. These men and women have always existed in rural areas, and for the most part, do not call themselves witches. These are the archetypal Wise Women who work alone to solve the problems of their immediate community. Women witches were involved in everything to do with people, helping at childbirth, laying out the dead, dealing with the ills of mind and body of their village, offering charms to protect the frightened, and advice and spells to assist the love-lorn find their beloved. These old witches acted as the doctor, the psychiatrist, the counsellor, the pharmacist and the nursemaid to those around them. Their male counter part, sometimes called a Cunning Man or Wise Man, would normally deal with the animals of the community. He might be a 'Horse Whisperer' who could control wild and untamed horses, a farrier who shod them and a vet for all the other creatures in the neighbourhood. Either might be able to dowse for water, or see the future in water or a shiny black stone, or tell what was going on at a distance. They would use the local plants in their healing potions, and know from the sun and moon the best moment for conception, or sowing crops, or beginning a new venture. The store of traditional wisdom about the weather and all aspects of Nature was phenomenal, and their work continues silently and secretly in the less travelled places in the countryside. They do not advertise, but their arts show them up, if you know where to look. Some Traditional witches admit newcomers as apprentices, and gradually teach them their herb and nature lore, their animal skills and the particular rites for the seasons.

The largest group of those who explore aspects of witchcraft today are the wiccans. This term, supposedly derived from Anglo-Saxon, (actually wicca is pronounced witcha, or witche if female,) was adopted at first by followers of Gerald Gardner, particularly in America, because people felt that 'witch' was too emotive a word. Gerald Gardner had a considerable effect on the new witchcraft movement because he wrote several books which popularised his own version of the rites and practices. He had spent much of his life abroad, ending up as a customs officer in Malaysia, and on his retirement he returned to England in about 1938. He had become fascinated by the magic and rituals performed by the peoples of Malaya, and he collected their ceremonial knives, called Krisses.Later on knives called athames were to become important wiccan working tools. Gerald made friends among the members of the Folklore Society, and because he was a Freemason he had other contacts with ritual fellowships. At some point he met up with members of a witch coven from the New Forest, in the south of England, and was admitted to some of their ceremonies.

During the late 1940 and 50s Gardner met a number of magical people, including Aleister Crowley, whose poetry forms part of the rituals used by Wiccans. Some commentators allege that when Gerald rewrote the rituals for the covens he paid Crowley to do this for him, but it seems that Crowley's Gnostic Mass and 'The Book of the Law', from which the words are taken were originally published in the 1920s and because the text seemed appropriate it was included. There were a number of ceremonial magical groups, particularly the Hermetic Order of the Golden Dawn, founded in 1887, and its later offshoots, which offered rituals and techniques which have found their way into modern wicca. The use of pentagrams drawn in the air at the quarters of the magical circle derive directly from Golden Dawn documents, as do the summoning and bidding depart of guardians of the Elements. Gardner's system of witchcraft draws to a small extent on earlier published material, including the Key of Solomon and Barratt's book 'The Magus' from the 19th century. It also includes three degrees or levels of initiation just as Craft Freemasonry does, with rituals enacting death and rebirth.

When Gerald Gardner wrote his two most important books, 'Witchcraft Today' in 1954 and 'The Meaning of Witchcraft' in 1959 he provided those who were seeking an alternative religious current and a new spiritual direction something to get their teeth into. I don't suppose that he thought for a moment that he had launched an entire new religion. Certainly what has been published by and about Gerald does contain small fragments of magical wisdom which is quite old, but the vast majority of the rituals, arts and festivals were rewritten by Gerald and his friends. One of the unsung heroines of this tradition is Doreen Valiente, at one time Gerald's High Priestess and a poet of some note. The Charge of the Goddess, one of the most evocative prayers of the wiccans came from her pen, and much that is beautiful and powerful was written or influenced by several minds other than Gerald's.

Because Gerald was a nudist he introduced the idea of working skyclad in the ceremonies, which then meant that most rituals in England, famous for its varied climate, have to take place indoors. Followers of other branches of the tradition have always preferred to dress in their ceremonial best, as is suitable for the prevailing weather, and meet or work alone out of doors, close to the skin of Mother Nature. There are advantages to both methods. Gardner and those who came after him have provided books of instructions, words of rituals, lists of equipment, and details of how to go about things which are a great help to those looking for the comfort of such basic material. Other traditions, which by their nature were very secretive and didn't write anything down, provide less structured material, only the barest concept of going to a place where you can see the sun or moon, where there is some water be it a stream, river, pool or the sea, and making direct, informal contact with the Great Ones of the land.

He popularised the idea of witches gatherings in covens of up to thirteen members, ruled by a High Priestess and High Priest. In the past witches worked alone on the whole, and so didn't have either covens or priestesses, and may have celebrated many times each year. He published set dates for festivals, (just as the Church had before him,) constructed rituals with various techniques of bondage and scourging in them, and produced a whole framework which newcomers today can read and work with. He described a system of three degrees of initiation, just as Freemasons have, and devised esbat full moon rituals and sabbat rituals for eight festivals. Others have come after him, notably Alex Sanders, who despite claims of receiving information from his family, used variations of the ceremonies that Gardner and his friends had compiled. Sanders was also interested in the Qabalah, and explored more formal kinds of rituals. His ideas have been presented in books by Janet and Stewart Farrar.

Although these initial resurgences of witchcraft took place in Britain, the ideas very swiftly crossed the Atlantic into America, and High Priestesses and High Priests initiated many new people. This spawned its own variations of wicca including Dianic covens which don't admit men, and a wide selection of covens and groups like Circle Network and the Covenant of the Goddess. This expansion on both sides of the Atlantic led to an increasing list of pagan and witchcraft magazines. Some of these are small, simply produced publications while others are large circulation glossy productions. Each in its own way will have contributed to the numbers of people being admitted or initiated into the Craft.

Today there are hundreds of published works on these revised forms of witchcraft and many covens and Outer Court Training groups all over the world. Many of the people who knew Gerald and the others in the 1950s are still going strong, continuing the coven tradition which he saw spreading like wildfire, from the small beginnings in a wooden hut in the pre-war years. It is a popular approach, but it is not the only one. If you do want to go further there are many valuable books to read, some describing the patterns of festivals and rituals for all seasons, other discuss the history and recent developments of the Gentle Arts, others again deal with the magical arts and mind skills which need to be mastered, and there are biographies of the main protagonists, historical works by Classical Pagans and historians who examine the true story of past pagans, mythology, poetry and pseudo-history rewritten to suit the newcomers who can't face the truth. It is not an easy path, because there is still a lot of misinformation about the beliefs and practices of witches, but it is rewarding, magical and fulfilling.

Perhaps, in the end, it comes down to a personal choice. Some people really enjoy being out of doors, in the starlight, breathing the same air and their Gods, unfettered by books or words, unless they come direct from your heart, at that moment. Others prefer the companionship and hierarchy of having a High Priestess and High Priest to guide and share the rituals with. These are not the only options, and if you choose this path you will encounter many friends and companions as you go along. Today's freedoms mean that there are a great number of possibilities.

CONCLUSION

It was more than ten years ago when I first wrote 'The Gentle Arts' and a lot has happened in the pagan world in that time. One of the most important in Britain, at least, is the growing size of the Pagan Federation. This was set up over twenty-five years ago, initially as blanket organisation for all the Wiccans in the UK, and it published a magazine, 'The Wiccan'. Once the upsurge in interest in all things pagan began, the Pagan Federation needed to expand to cater for them. Because it aims to represent all branches of the pagan tree the name of the magazine was changed to 'Pagan Dawn' and it is becoming more and more widely available. The Pagan Federation itself welcomes everyone who accepts a few basic principles, whatever their individual beliefs happen to be. It holds an annual conference in the London area, and there are all kinds of local gatherings, moots, regional conferences and other events. Although based in England its members come from all over the world, and like the pagan movement, it is expanding rapidly. In order to offer information to those who are new to the Gentle Arts a number of information packs have been prepared and may be purchased for a small fee.

A great many books have been written in the UK, Europe and in America to assist anyone who has an interest in the ancient ways, so much so that it may be hard for the beginner to discover which will be most helpful. For that reason a list is included at the end of this book. Many of these authors have written other titles, or will be doing so in the near future. It is always worth encouraging your local bookshop to get copies of the most popular titles for their shelves. They will certainly order any that are in print if you ask them. Not only are booklists continuing to grow, but also there are many small magazines, shops and mail order suppliers who specialise in magical equipment and information. There are tapes and videos, numerous kinds of Tarot packs and other divination systems, especially as these seem to be growth industries, and magical developments designed for the computer-literate with pages on the World Wide Web.

Although it may be possible to keep your magical diary on a disc, instead of in a book written in your own handwriting, and to participate in rituals with others via the internet, in the end it is the personal relationship between you and the Earth, you and the Old Gods of which ever pantheon you feel drawn to, and you and your friends and partners in the Gentle Arts which matter. Unless you are able to explore your personal beliefs, expand your own abilities and strengths all the words in the world will not help you at all. Now, more than ever, are there opportunities to learn through practical short courses, and even if you set out as a lone and tentative student, you will quickly meet others who share your feelings. One day courses, those weekend workshops and longer summer schools all provide those first, vital experiences, and perhaps lay down the threads of enduring friendships, with those around you and the unseen Gods of the Land. Magic and the Gentle Arts are not things to be merely thought about, discussed or considered, they are experiments to try, hidden paths to walk, and above all keys to a wider experience of life. They may seem ancient and archaic, but those antique arts which heal, inspire, and assist with human evolution are just as relevant today as they were when Stonehenge was just a green field. You can use the ancient skills and crafts to be at the forefront of human experience through the Gentle Arts. Why not try them now?

USEFUL INFORMATION

THE PAGAN FEDERATION, BM Box 7097, London WC IN 3XX, UK. Offers basic information for a stamped addressed envelope, and packages of information on the activities of different branches of modern paganism for a small fee. They publish a magazine called 'Pagan Dawn' which is available at some occult bookshops, but generally by subscription from the above address. It contains articles, information on local meetings, contact addresses for other organisations and lots more.

THE INVISIBLE COLLEGE is run by Marian Green and offers a variety of short courses on different aspects of natural and ceremonial magic. These vary from One Day gatherings, sometimes in people's homes, to week long intensives in Europe. There are frequent Weekend residential and non-residential courses with Marian Green and other tutors, covering a wide range of practical subjects.

Through the Invisible College, Marian Green also runs correspondence courses on both Natural Magic and the Arts of Ritual Magic, using her books as study texts. If you would like further information write to the Invisible College, BCM-SCL Quest, London WC IN 3XX, enclosing an s.a.e.

QUEST magazine has been produced four times each year since 1970, and is edited by Marian Green. It covers all aspects of the Western Mystery tradition, with articles by well known magicians, witches and other practitioners, as well as listing events, reviewing new books, and providing safe and practical material for the new comer and old hand alike. There are also lists of other publications. QUEST has held an annual Conference since 1968, allowing readers to meet the authors and others at the forefront of occult thought. QUEST also produces booklets on Witchcraft, Ritual, Incense and other related topics.

Marian Green has also issued a number of Inner Journey and talk cassettes. Send a s.a.e. for further information, or £1.00 for a sample copy of QUEST, to BCM – SCL Quest, London WC IN 3XX.

MAGIS BOOKS hold a large stock of second hand and out-of print books on the Western Mystery Tradition for their Mail Order customers. See **www.magisbooks.com**

THOTH PUBLICATIONS publish many classic works covering the Western Mystery Tradition by some of the most respected authors within their own fields. A list of these titles can be found at **www.thothpublications.com**

BOOK LIST

Marian Green usually has copies of all of her books which are in print, available from the QUEST address.

BETH, Rae *Hedgewitch* Hale 1990

BOURNE, Lois *A Witch Amongst Us* Satellite Books 1979

CARR-GOMM, Philip *The Druid Way* Thoth Publications 2006

CROWTHER, Patricia *Lid Off the Cauldron* Muller

CROWLEY, Vivienne *Wicca, The Old Religion* Aquarian Press 1989

CROWLEY, Vivienne *Living as a Pagan in the 21st Century* Thorsons

FARRAR, Janet & Stewart *Life and Times of a Modern Witch* Piatkus 1987

FARRAR, Janet & Stewart *The Witches' Way* Hale 1984

FARRAR, Stewart *What Witches Do* Hale 1971

FORTUNE, Dion *An Introduction to Ritual Magic* Thoth Publications 1997

FORTUNE, Dion *The Circuit of Force* Thoth Publications 1998

FORTUNE, Dion *Moon Magic* Inner Light Publications

FORTUNE, Dion *The Sea Priestess* Aquarian

GARDNER, Gerald *Witchcraft Today* 1954

GARDNER, Gerald *The Meaning of Witchcraft* 1959

GLASS, Justine *Witchcraft: The Sixth Sense* Neville Spearman 1965

GODDARD, David *Sacred Magic of the Angels* Weiser 1996

GREEN, Marian *The Elements of Natural Magic* Element 1989

Green, Marian *Everyday Magic* Thoth Publications 2021

Green, Marian *Wild Witchcraft* Thoth Publications 2021

Green, Marian *Natural Witchcraft* Thoth Publications 2021

GREEN, Marian *The Path Through the Labyrinth* Thoth Publications 2021

GREEN, Marian *A Witch Alone* Thorsons 1991

GREEN, Marian *Practical Techniques of Modern Magic* Thoth Publications 1990

GREEN, Marian *A Calendar of Festivals* Element 1989

Heselton, Philip *Witchfather A Life of Gerald Gardner* Vol.1. *Into the Witch Cult* Thoth Publications

Heselton, Philip Witchfather *A Life of Gerald Gardner* Vol.2. *From Witch Cult to Wicca* Thoth Publications

HOFFMAN, David *The Holistic Herbal* Element

HUTTON, Ronald *Pagan Religions of the Ancient British Isles* Blackwell 1991

HUTTON, Ronald *Stations of the Sun* Blackwell 1996

JONES, Evan John *Witchcraft* Hale 1990

Kelly, Aiden *Inventing Witchcraft* Thoth Publications 2007

LUHRMANN, Tanya *Persuasions of the Witch's Craft* Blackwell 1989

PENNICK, Nigel *Practical Magic in the Northern Tradition* Thoth Publications 1994

MATTHEWS, John *The Celtic Shaman* Element 1991

Stewart, R.J *Living Magical Arts* Thoth Publications 2020

Stewart, R.J. *Advanced Magical Arts* Thoth Publications 2020

Stewart R.J. *Power Within the Land* Element 1992

VALIENTE, Doreen *Natural Magic* Hale 1975

VALIENTE, Doreen *The A B C of Witchcraft* Hale 1973

VALIENTE, Doreen *Witchcraft for Tomorrow* Hale 1978

VALIENTE, Doreen *The Rebirth of Witchcraft* Hale 1989

INDEX

Other titles from Thoth Publications

AN INTRODUCTION TO RITUAL MAGIC
Dion Fortune & Gareth Knight

At the time this was something of a unique event in esoteric publishing – a new book by the legendary Dion Fortune. Especially with its teachings on the theory and practice of ritual or ceremonial magic, by one who, like the heroine of two of her other novels, was undoubtedly "a mistress of that art".

In this work Dion Fortune deals in successive chapters with Types of Mind Working; Mind Training; The Use of Ritual; Psychic Perception; Ritual Initiation; The Reality of the Subtle Planes; Focusing the Magic Mirror; Channelling the Forces; The Form of the Ceremony; and The Purpose of Magic – with appendices on Talisman Magic and Astral Forms.

Each chapter is supplemented and expanded by a companion chapter on the same subject by Gareth Knight. In Dion Fortune's day the conventions of occult secrecy prevented her from being too explicit on the practical details of magic, except in works of fiction. These veils of secrecy having now been drawn back, Gareth Knight has taken the opportunity to fill in much practical information that Dion Fortune might well have included had she been writing today.

In short, in this unique collaboration of two magical practitioners and teachers, we are presented with a valuable and up-to-date text on the practice of ritual or ceremonial magic "as it is". That is to say, as a practical, spiritual, and psychic discipline, far removed from the lurid superstition and speculation that are the hall mark of its treatment in sensational journalism and channels of popular entertainment.

ISBN 978-1-870450-26-3

PRACTICAL MAGIC IN THE NORTHERN TRADITION
Nigel Pennick

The Northern Tradition is the indigenous spiritual and magical system of European peoples north of the Alps. With its origin in archaic shamanic nature-veneration, it embodies the observances, practices and tradition of the people of the Celtic, Germanic, Scandinavian and Baltic realms. Practical Magic in the Northern Tradition cuts through the meaningless barriers between people, for these traditions and practices are linked with one another at the deepest level through common themes. The underlying magical principles are identical, being relevant to the same set of environmental conditions.

Many Northern Tradition observances have continued unbroken to the present day as folk customs, rural practices, household magic and the veneration of saints. Now, the Northern Tradition has emerged again in its own right, in a form appropriate for these times. This book is the definitive work of the tradition.

When we view the world in this way, Nature, personified as goddesses, gods and spirits becomes approachable. It is all too apparent that the materialist ways of modernity can lead only to the destruction of Nature. The Northern Tradition provides another way, one of harmony with the natural world. Northern Tradition magic gives us the tools to bring ourselves into a dynamic interaction with the cyclic workings of Nature., By following the age-old festival customs described in this book, we can become attuned to the natural cycle of the seasons and harmonise ourselves with Nature and our fellow human beings.

ISBN 978-1-870450-16-4

PRACTICAL TECHNIQUES OF MODERN MAGIC
Marian Green

What is the essence of ritual magic?

How are the symbols used to create change?

Can I safely take steps in ritual on my own?

How does magic fit into the pattern of life in the modern world?

Will I be able to master the basic arts?

All these questions and many more are answered within the pages

of this book.

ISBN 978-1-870450-14-0

THE PATH THROUGH THE LABYRINTH
Marian Green

The Quest for Initiation into the Western Mystery Tradition.

Underlying the evolving culture of the West there hides a complete strata of folk-lore, of traditional skills and wisdom and of ancient arts and festivals.

These are still emerging in myth and legend, in song and celebrations, each retaining aspects of a very great initiatory system rooted in the land and its magic.

Most available sources tell the reader about the how to of magic, but for the first time this book explores the way of magic and what happens when... of modern magical techniques.

In *The Path Through The Labyrinth*, Marian Green, a highly respected practitioner and teacher of the Western Tradition, examines these questions and guides the reader safely to the heart of the magical maze and then out again.

ISBN 978-1-870450-15-7

THE WESTERN MYSTERY TRADITION
Christine Hartley

A reissue of a classic work, by a pupil of Dion Fortune, on the mythical and historical roots of Western occultism.

Christine Hartley's aim was to demonstrate that we in the West, far from being dependent upon Eastern esoteric teachings, possess a rich and potent mystery tradition of our own, evoked and defined in myth, legend, folklore and song, and embodied in the legacy of Druidic culture.

More importantly, she provides practical guidelines for modern students of the ancient mysteries, 'The Western Mystery Tradition,' in Christine Hartley's view, 'is the basis of the Western religious feeling, the foundation of our spiritual life, the matrix of our religious formulae, whither we are aware of it or not. To it we owe the life and force of our spiritual life.'

ISBN 978-1-870450-24-9

A MODERN MAGICIAN'S HANDBOOK
Marian Green

This book presents the ancient arts of magic, ritual and practical occult arts as used by modern ceremonial magicians and witches in a way that everyone can master, bringing them into the Age of Aquarius. Drawing on over three decades of practical experience, Marian Green offers a simple approach to the various skills and techniques that are needed to turn an interest into a working knowledge of magic.

Each section offers explanations, guidance and practical exercises in meditation, inner journeying, preparation for ritual, the arts of divination and many more of today's esoteric practices. No student is too young or too old to benefit from the material set out for them in this book, and its simple language may help even experienced magicians and witches understand their arts in greater depth.

ISBN 978-1-870450-43-0

THE CIRCUIT OF FORCE

Dion Fortune *with commentaries by* Gareth Knight.

In *The Circuit of Force*, Dion Fortune describes techniques for raising the personal magnetic forces within the human aura and their control and direction in magic and in life, which she regards as 'the Lost Secrets of the Western Esoteric Tradition'.

To recover these secrets she turns to three sources.

a) the Eastern Tradition of Hatha Yoga and Tantra and their teaching on raising the "sleeping serpent power" or kundalini;

b) the circle working by means of which spiritualist seances concentrate power for the manifestation of some of their results;

c) the linking up of cosmic and earth energies by means of the structured symbol patterns of the Qabalistic Tree of Life.

Originally produced for the instruction of members of her group, this is the first time that this material has been published for the general public in volume form.

Gareth Knight provides subject commentaries on various aspects of the etheric vehicle, filling in some of the practical details and implications that she left unsaid in the more secretive esoteric climate of the times in which she wrote.

Some quotes from Dion Fortune's text:

"When, in order to concentrate exclusively on God, we cut ourselves off from nature, we destroy our own roots. There must be in us a circuit between heaven and earth, not a one-way flow, draining us of all vitality. It is not enough that we draw up the Kundalini from the base of the spine; we must also draw down the divine light through the Thousand-Petalled Lotus. Equally, it is not enough for our mental health and spiritual development that we draw down the Divine Light, we must also draw up the earth forces. Only too often mental health is sacrificed to spiritual development through ignorance of, or denial of, this fact."

"....the clue to all these Mysteries is to be sought in the Tree of Life. Understand the significance of the Tree; arrange the symbols you are working with in the correct manner upon it, and all is clear and you can work out your sum. Equate the Danda with the Central Pillar, and the Lotuses with the Sephiroth and the bi-sections of the Paths thereon, and you have the necessary bilingual dictionary at your disposal – if you know how to use it."

ISBN 978-1-870450-28-7

THE GRAIL SEEKER'S COMPANION
John Matthews & Marian Green

There have been many books about the Grail, written from many differing standpoints. Some have been practical, some purely historical, others literary, but this is the first Grail book which sets out to help the esoterically inclined seeker through the maze of symbolism, character and myth which surrounds the central point of the Grail.

In today's frantic world when many people have their material needs met some still seek spiritual fulfilment. They are drawn to explore the old philosophies and traditions, particularly that of our Western Celtic Heritage. It is here they encounter the quest for the Holy Grail, that mysterious object which will bring hope and healing to all. Some have come to recognise that they dwell in a spiritual wasteland and now search that symbol of the grail which may be the only remedy. Here is the guide book for the modern seeker, explaining the history and pointing clearly towards the Aquarian grail of the future.

John Matthews and Marian Green have each been involved in the study of the mysteries of Britain and the Grail myth for over thirty-five years. In *THE GRAIL SEEKER'S COMPANION* they have provided a guidebook not just to places, but to people, stories and theories surrounding the Grail. A reference book of Grail-ology, including history, ritual, meditation, advice and instruction. In short, everything you are likely to need before you set out on the most important adventure of your life.

This is the only book which points the way to the Holy Grail Quest in the 21st century.

ISBN 978-1-870450-49-2

www.ingramcontent.com/pod-product-compliance
Lightning Source LLC
Chambersburg PA
CBHW020353100426
42812CB00001B/49